Green Strategy

Green Strategy

The Path to Fundamental Transformation

By Marc Russell Brodine

INTERNATIONAL PUBLISHERS
NEW YORK

Library of Congress Cataloging-in-Publication Data
Names: Brodine, Marc Russell, author.
Title: Green strategy : the path to fundamental transformation / by Marc
    Russell Brodine.
Description: First Edition. | New York : International Publishers, 2018. |
    Includes bibliographical references.
Identifiers: LCCN 2018031208| ISBN 9780717807604 (pbk.) | ISBN 0717807606
    (pbk.)
Subjects: LCSH: Environmental policy. | Environmental protection. | Economic
    development--Environmental aspects. | Global warming--Economic aspects.
Classification: LCC HC79.E5 B7446 2018 | DDC 363.7/0561--dc23
LC record available at https://lccn.loc.gov/2018031208

ISBN-10: 0-7178-0760-6   ISBN–13: 978-0-7178-0760-4
Typeset by AarkMany Media, Chennai, India

Cover Design by Matthew Wenz, Wenz Creative
Back Cover photo by John Olsen

Dedicated to the women in my life: Virginia, Cynthia, Janine, Rosario, Vonetta, Francesca, Jenny, and Maria

Table of Contents

viii   Table of Contents

As I worked on the third draft of this book in the summer of 2017, my home in central Washington State was threatened by the Jolly Mountain Fire, which consumed over 36,000 acres. My wife and I had to pack in a hurry when we woke up one morning under a Level Two Evacuation Warning, meaning that we must be ready to leave at a moment's notice. We had to decide, that Saturday, which papers, photos, clothes, and other essentials we would throw into our car in case we had to leave immediately. Some of our friends hit Level Three, meaning "go right now." I had to leave town for almost a week due to the hazardous air quality making my asthma worse.

Thanks to the heroic efforts of hundreds of firefighters, the fire was stopped at almost three miles from our house. We returned home and started to bring our stuff back, which we had stored at a relative's home near Seattle. We breathed a sigh of relief that it did not get worse for us, that the winds hadn't blown embers closer to our house. It could have been devastating for our whole community in Upper Kittitas County. We were lucky.

Though we never suffered the destruction so many others face from extreme weather events, it made me aware of just how devastating the power of nature can be, how fast the conditions of life can change, and how difficult the decisions forced on millions of people are.

During the same period, millions of people had just lived through Hurricanes Harvey and Irma, which caused devastation in Texas, Florida, parts of other Southern states, and on the U.S. Virgin Islands. After Hurricane Harvey, some of the Texas chemical plants spewed toxic fumes as plants exhausted their limited safety systems.[1] Then Hurricane Maria jumped from a Category 1 to a Category 5 in one day and directly hit Puerto Rico, knocking out power for many months (in comparison to Cuba, which restored power within a week). This hurricane strike resulted in an humanitarian crisis caused in large part by Donald Trump's failure to rush supplies, personnel, and equipment as fast as possible and in part to the incompetent Federal management of the crisis response.

Simultaneously, almost eight million acres of the West were on fire, one million of them in Montana alone. India and Bangladesh suffered the worst monsoon season on record, with flooding in Bangladesh killing over 1,200 people.

These events, widely separated geographically, are not random. They are all natural disasters made worse by global climate change. They are real crises for millions of people, faced with devastation and destruction. Climate change is not an abstract theory, not an academic debate about problems that might or might not affect humanity in some distant future. None of us will escape the impacts—the exact threats are different in different parts of the world, but they are all connected by the results of human activity, by increased greenhouse gas emissions. We are living the climate change future right now, and it will get worse. Our choice is whether or not to act to keep it from becoming catastrophic for billions of people.

At their root, the dangers posed by climate change affect people. Husbands and wives, children, grandparents and grandchildren, aunts and uncles, loved ones of all kinds. Precious mementos, family photos, art, and music. The tools we use to cook every day. The homes filled with memories of family gatherings, dinners with friends, parties, and joyous occasions.

Many discussions and books about climate change are filled with possibilities, probabilities, and projections. They offer important contributions to understanding the challenges the world faces and contribute to public education about the issues. They attempt to explain the research about and scientific details of climate change. You can find some that I recommend listed in the bibliography.

This book does not try to compete with them. Instead, I address several aspects of the issues of the complex, interrelated environmental challenges humanity faces, and the necessary long-range movement and goals to create lasting solutions. My aim is to contribute to the development of an overarching strategy for the environmental movement and its allies.

Climate change and environmental degradation impact the quality of life for people all over the globe already. These changes in the systems of the natural world are challenging all that we hold dear. Our plans and expectations and lives are threatened in one way or another by the harm done to the natural world on which we depend. Over the next few decades, hundreds of millions of our fellow human beings will be faced with terrible and wrenching decisions. They will be forced to respond to disasters that transform their lives in a matter of days, hours, or even minutes. Over the next century, those numbers will become billions of our fellow human beings—their loved ones, their memories, their homes, and their very existence. That is why we need to care—for ourselves, for our children and grandchildren, but also for the billions of other people with whom we share this amazing, beautiful, terrifying planet.

Barry Commoner said it well:

> The environmental crisis arises from a fundamental fault: Our systems of production—in industry, agriculture, energy, and transportation—essential as they are, make people sick and die . . . But that is only the *immediate* problem. Down the line, these same production processes threaten a series of global human catastrophes: higher temperatures; the seas rising to flood many of the world's cities; more frequent severe weather; and dangerous exposure to ultraviolet radiation. The non-human sectors of the living ecosystem are also affected by the crisis: ancient forest reserves are disappearing; wetlands and estuaries are impaired; numerous species are threatened with extinction. Nevertheless, the environmental crisis is a human event; it is caused by what people do, and the ultimate measure of its impact is the health and well-being of people.[2]

Polar bears, for example, have already been significantly harmed by climate change, are already in crisis from having their habitat fundamentally altered with a rapidity which makes it difficult or impossible for them to adjust. Many species are facing extinction, unable to cope with the crises human activity has inflicted upon them. We have to care about all of them.

However, we can't organize the polar bears to create change. Only people have the potential power to fundamentally change the direction of human society and to transform our relationships with the rest of the natural world.

My family was lucky this time to avoid the worst consequences of this particular fire, due to the way the winds blew and to the robust, though overburdened, firefighting infrastructure throughout the Western United States. Compare this to families very similar to ours in Puerto Rico, who had their houses destroyed, their electric grid destroyed, who suffered from public services which were totally inadequate to address their problems, and a pitiful, mismanaged Federal response.

My family faces ongoing threats from increased fire danger, fire frequency, and fire intensity; others are dealing with the consequences of multi-year drought or 100-year floods that now come every three or four years. Our problems are all linked by climate change, and they won't fix themselves.

What is destructive to the natural world is also destructive to all of us, and it is up to all of us to take action. We can't count on our current political system nor on our current economic system to solve climate change for us, we must all join to create fundamental transformation in the many human systems which surround us, in order to protect the natural systems which are essential for humans to survive and thrive.

The strategy I advocate is not some hidden agenda, some left-wing conspiracy theory, as right-wing fabulists claim. It is about preventing the worst changes in the natural world on which humanity depends, and in the process improving life for billions of our fellow human beings.

We need a green strategy to help us organize ourselves into a mighty worldwide movement. Building that movement is the ultimate subject of this book.

Acknowledgements

Thanks to Wadi'h Halabi, Dave Zink, Dave Schmitz, Janine Brodine, Cordy Cooke, and Len Yannielli, who all read and commented on the manuscript, which helped me make it better. Their encouragement and comments are much appreciated. Any remaining errors are mine alone. Thanks to all those who have been in writing groups with me over the years, and to those with whom I worked on political issues over many decades.

Thanks to my parents Virginia & Russell Brodine for setting me on this path of Marxism and environmentalism, among many other things. Thanks to Richard Levins for his scientific use of dialectics and for sharing his knowledge with me. and to Barry Commoner for his groundbreaking environmental writing, activism, and research. All have now sadly passed.

Thanks to the *People's World, Political Affairs,* and *International Critical Thought* for publishing articles on which parts of this book are based. Thanks as well to the Communist Party of the United States (CPUSA), to the Communist Party of Finland and their Arctic Initiative Conference, and to the Third Forum of the World Association for Political Economy on "Marxism and Sustainable Development," for whom I prepared reports on which parts of this book are based.

Finally, thanks to Gary Bono of International Publishers for bringing this book to publication.

It is important to clarify the way some words and phrases are used in this book. My hope is that the language I use is accessible, using common parlance and easily understood descriptions. I've chosen to use *climate change* and *global warming*, without claiming that these phrases are the most comprehensive.

One set of semantic confusions about nomenclature has to do with what phrase we use to describe the impact of greenhouse gas emissions on our climate and weather systems. First, "global warming" became used popularly. Then, some conservatives started using "climate change," thinking it was less threatening to Republican framing. However, it was also more accurate, since the warming is not uniform everywhere in the world and some of the effects are not tied only to the warming aspects of climate change.

Others want to use a phrase that is even more scientifically accurate, such as "rapid, socially-induced climate disruption" or "the rapid, socially-induced poisoning of nature." These may be more accurate, but are not as readily understood.

"Movement" is another term used frequently in this book as a descriptor. This is a bit generic, so let me explain what I mean. A movement is *not* watching an Al Gore film, though that can help in the process of public education. A movement is *not* private investment in renewable energy, though that is a positive or at least necessary step at the present moment.

A movement *is* organized, engaged, and energized millions of people, who petition, lobby, protest in the streets, force elected officials to take a stand, and exert pressure from the local level to the international level. A movement builds alliances with other movements, builds trust and ties across political and ideological lines, engages in actions from writing postcards to civil disobedience to mass protests to community efforts to build resilience such as farmers markets and Community-Supported Agriculture co-ops (CSAs). Boycotts, public relations campaigns, social media campaigns, educational efforts, door-to-door organizing, and enrolling new people to engage in all these efforts—that is what makes a movement. Creating and sustaining permanent organizations and institutions of struggle are a necessary part of a lasting and effective movement.

Green Strategy

Humanity, society, economics, politics, science, the natural world, and the limitations of nature must be seen as an integrated whole. The key to creating fundamental change is to create a movement broad enough, diverse enough, powerful enough, and sophisticated enough to embrace billions of people the world over.

Trying to solve global warming without integrating our knowledge about the many additional looming environmental crises will result in our not being able to solve global warming. Looking at environmental problems separate from the society and economy that created them will prevent us from finding fundamental, lasting solutions. Focusing on the science and the challenge to humanity while ignoring the kind of political movement we need to build will result in frustration and anger but not in fundamental change.

We can confidently predict that the environmental movement will grow—in size, sophistication, importance, political impact, that it will develop alliances with other movements, and that it will grow in strength (a combination of all those factors). We can confidently predict that there will be more innovation and experimentation with improving technology to address climate change and our energy needs.

We have reason for hope, to have optimism in the face of horrifying news. We have hope due to the response to our rapidly changing reality, and in response to our growing knowledge. Billions of people are moving into motion on climate change—in electoral struggles, street actions, mass demonstrations, civil disobedience, changes in personal habits, changes in public opinion, in concern for future generations.

The strongest reason for hope is that billions of people will take action to preserve their own future and the future natural world for their children, grandchildren, and future generations. This movement is the only force capable of creating fundamental economic, political, environmental, and social change on the scale humanity needs. The growing movements are in the process of learning how to fight for that.

We can hope because there is a movement which has moral, political, ethical, economic, personal, technological, practical, and "impractical" dimensions (meaning not currently politically practical) which will transform the world in the coming decades.

This growing movement needs to understand that no one issue, organization, or national part of this movement is enough. Only together can we accumulate enough knowledge, experience, and power.

What This Book Does and Doesn't Try to Do

Much of the discussion about global warming and other ecological crises promotes a valuable goal: educating the public about the gravity of environmental problems and the need for action. However, much of the media attention blames the problem on overly-broad and misdirected concepts and generalizations such as "overpopulation" or "excessive consumption." In the long run this defeats the goal of decreasing the amount of greenhouse gases, the main immediate causes of global warming, and of solving the other symptoms of the imbalanced human relationship with the environment on which we depend. This misdirection, intentional or otherwise, lets the capitalist system off the hook and distracts from finding the basic solutions we need.

People are thus relegated to the role of victims, who are blamed for the problems to which they are subjected. People in advanced capitalist countries are blamed for a profligate lifestyle while corporations advertise endlessly for more consumer spending, more consumer debt, and more consumer behavior that ignores the effects of the increasing burden on the environment.

Approaches that blame people fail to address the underlying causes of global warming. Few people, in any country, have or had much to do with the decisions that cause rapidly-developing environmental crises. Those decisions were private decisions, made by capitalists and their managers. As long as that continues to be the case, efforts to slow global warming and solve other environmental problems will fall far short of the fundamental transformations needed in our economic, political, agricultural, industrial, transportation, and social systems.

We need to understand the depth and reach of the environmental problems we face. We could transform the energy systems of the entire world (and we should) but that wouldn't solve the underlying problem: the wide-ranging imbalances between the ways that humanity impacts nature and the limits of the resources that nature is able to provide.

Most discussions in the mainstream media about global climate change and other serious environmental challenges are limited. The problems are seen only as problems of human interaction with natural systems (which they are) or as problems in need of technological solutions (which they are). But little is done to connect our environmental challenges to our economic and social systems. In a private property system, when we collectively face problems that need collective solutions (and it doesn't get much bigger or more collective than global climate change, both on the problem side and on the required solution side), the system hampers efforts to fix the problems. Any efforts at partial solutions very quickly run into private property rights and private decision-making about production, land use, resources, waste disposal, and investment. We also run into the limits of capitalist-funded political systems and capitalist-oriented legal systems which privilege private property rights.

Partial solutions are often proposed, sometimes with much truth and great emotion. But essential aspects of creating fundamental, permanent solutions are most often missing. Those partial solutions are elements of basic transformation, but by themselves they will be insufficient, especially if we don't transform the economic system which plays the major role in constantly recreating the problems.

All humanity is headed for serious adjustments, both planned and involuntary, which are necessary to recalibrate the balance between people and the natural world on which we depend. Taking steps to lower the human population growth rate on the planet at the same time as we take steps to change our agricultural, industrial, and distribution processes can provide positive synchronicity and reinforce positive benefits. If we wait until nature does it to us, most of the synchronicity will impose negative impacts on human life.

It was striking for me, a few years ago, to read in the introduction to Al Gore's book *Our Choice* his assertion (correct, in my opinion) that the only thing lacking to solve climate change was the political will, but then he spent the whole book discussing technology, never addressing how to develop the political will!

This book attempts to address this issue of how to develop the political will to create essential change. Fundamental transformation requires a movement for fundamental transformation; it requires a strategy that links the science, the technological fixes, the personal changes, the transformation of our basic systems of production and distribution and provides a coherent framework to understand how all of these are linked. We need an overall strategy that acknowledges that progress for all humanity requires a struggle for political and economic power for all people.

This book is also an effort to point out the interconnections between climate change, soil degradation, water stress, many kinds of pollution, and species extinction. It attempts to connect environmental struggles to the struggles of workers, to the need for working-class power, in order to solve environmental challenges. It attempts to place seemingly disparate issues, like technological fixes, energy transition, and social justice, into a linked, integrated framework.

Most discussions of environmental issues, even those critical of capitalism such as Naomi Klein's excellent *This Changes*

Everything, do not speak directly to developing a long-term strategy for the environmental movement. They focus on tactics, on one aspect of the problem or solution, or limit the discussion to scientific or technological fixes. But to accomplish the fundamental transformations we need in all aspects of human life—in agriculture, production, distribution, and in society, politics, culture, and personal habits—requires a movement bigger, broader, deeper, and more worldwide than any we have yet seen.

Even more comprehensive strategies, which encompass the whole range of environmental issues humanity needs to tackle, end up being utopian when they ignore or downplay the importance of building the kind of movement necessary to implement any serious strategy of fundamental transformation. We certainly need to know what kinds of changes are necessary and possible in human systems, but that knowledge by itself will not result in change. That requires a movement of tens and hundreds of millions of organized activists.

Developing ideas and plans about any piece of the whole puzzle of environmental challenge and change are worthwhile but incomplete, such as the plans for a Global Green New Deal.[3] Until we realize that plans without a powerful movement capable of implementing them are not realistic, we will be stuck in frustration.

Building a massive worldwide movement for environmental change must be our prime focus. Without that movement, no amount of passion, anger, or intellectual insight will accomplish the scale of change that humanity needs.

The earth is a series of linked systems, a series of gigantic feedback loops. We must approach it holistically. For example, there are some processes which increase carbon and others which absorb carbon. We have trees which absorb carbon and emit oxygen. We have the permafrost which absorbed carbon that now has been frozen for millions of years. Our oceans play a role, still not fully understood, in absorbing excess carbon dioxide—in the process increasing ocean salinity and acidity in ways that harm fisheries,[4] coral reefs, and the smaller creatures at the bottom of the ocean food chain. We depend on these contradictory systems to keep us in a balance that works for humanity.

We can't look at the systems one at a time, separate from each other, not if we want or need to develop full under-standing. We can't separate humans out of those natural systems. We need to look at problems from many angles, and not only in linear ways; we need to understand that qualita-tive changes happen—leaps to a new state, "tipping points" in environmental jargon. We have to understand the world as a place of constant change, as systems and networks of inter-locked processes which react with and upon each other.

Thinking in that way is different from what science has typ-ically done, which has been to break systems and processes into their component parts and work to understand the details of those processes. Often this has been done by reducing the problem to the level that it can be understood as a linear pro-cess. That is an essential step, but we haven't always taken the next step, which is to put processes back together to under-stand how they work as an integrated whole.

Matching Strategy to Struggles

The size, scale, and scope of the problems we face are so mas-sive, so ingrained, so seemingly intractable, that people often seek to limit the issues to ones we feel we can actually do something about. Too many in the environmental movement focus on one or another immediate problem, one or another urgent crisis, without considering how to combat the deep-seated forces who fight change. This can be as a result of an understandable and natural human reaction to simplify in order to understand a massive issue.

One problem in defining strategy is that the boundary between strategy and tactics shifts with the scale of the issue being addressed. A winning strategy for a particular progres-sive candidate certainly counts as a strategy given the scale of that particular campaign, but when seen through the lens of national progressive election campaigns, it is but one tactic among many utilized across the country for electoral struggle. And the strategic concerns of national election strategy are but a variety of the tactics that must be used by those developing a strategy for the fundamental transformation of society.

Those working on developing strategy for any one aspect of the broader progressive struggle may point out that their considerations are strategic on the scale of the issue or problem they are seeking to address. But this book is about developing a strategy to address the issues and crises that will confront all humankind over the next century and beyond.

Developing strategy has to first of all define the scale of the issue or campaign being addressed. Otherwise, it will be difficult to match the strategy to the size, scale, and importance of what we are trying to change. We need a sense of the scale of the problem, which is the concern of **Part One: The Framework**.

But knowing the framework is just the beginning. We also need to define our philosophical outlook, our way of understanding both the environmental problems we are attempting to address and the problems of the movement we are trying to build. That must be combined with an understanding of the patterns of social, political, and economic change, the subject of **Part Two: The Philosophy**. Without a philosophical outlook to help us proceed in a coherent and unified way, we will get sidetracked by smaller issues or by urgent demands of the moment which are but a piece of the longer-range struggle we must engage in.

A strategy which includes the scope of the issues and has a consistent philosophical outlook lays the basis for seeing the kind of political, social, and cultural movement we need to build, the kinds of political issues we need to wrestle with, the kinds of unity we need to seek and build. These are specific concerns related to movement building. That is what **Part Three: The Movement** is about—how to learn from the struggles of the past, how to build alliances across organizations, movements, and issues, how to link seemingly disparate efforts into a mighty river of power, and how to avoid some of the traps and divisions that arise as we gain strength.

But to build a movement, we also need an idea of the short- and medium-range solutions we are working for, of the efforts around which we will build that movement. This enables partial and smaller victories which offer a pathway to deeper solutions, enables confidence-building campaigns which demonstrate the power of joint action. **Part Four: The Initial Solutions** is a beginning at designing such a program.

But partial solutions and temporary victories, essential though they are, are insufficient by themselves. We also need to understand the way to create permanent solutions. That is what **Part Five: The Vision** is about—why we need fundamental economic, social, and political transformation, why winning smaller victories is a positive step but not enough, why we need environmentally-conscious socialism. It also looks at the limitations of socialism and challenges to socialist theory and practice, how to place environmental concerns as an essential part of socialist transformation, and how environmental issues provide a new path to socialist consciousness.[5]

Part Six: Putting It All Together summarizes the whole book, putting all the pieces of an overarching green strategy together in one place.

A strategy for a single or smaller aspect of this global transformation might not need to delve into all these details, might not need to be so comprehensive, might be able to get away without taking all these considerations into account. But creating a sustainable balance between humanity and nature, involving all aspects of human life, can't be done on a hit-or-miss basis. We are not talking about a strategy for the next few months or about a local campaign that might last a year; we must prepare for a decades-long, maybe even centuries-long series of battles in the campaign to reach a sustainable and humanistic balance between nature and humanity.

Strategy is about measuring the size of the problem, estimating as best as possible the balance of forces between the contending sides and what is needed to change that balance in a positive direction, figuring out what the shorter-range goals and longer-term aims are, and making sure we are creating a strategy that will match the entire scope of the problem.

Some may ask, "why should we spend our time going into all these aspects of developing a strategy when we are faced with immediate worldwide crises?" Aren't there enough imminent threats to move us into action? Aren't there urgent problems demanding immediate attention?

We need to spend the time and effort to develop a comprehensive strategy if we want to create a movement capable of building the political power to implement fundamental change. There is no shortcut around this need. We might defeat a particularly nasty development project or a specific pipeline, but without a massive worldwide movement, the problems we face will keep recreating themselves. This will happen because the economic system will keep creating incentives for particular industries and capitalists to ignore the needs of all humanity in the interests of their short-term profit and power.

The reality is that environmental crises and environmental challenges will occupy a larger and larger share of the public space, will grow to play an ever-larger role in policy disputes, in electoral campaigns, in demonstrations and movements, in education, and in many aspects of our economies. Participating in environmental struggles is an essential part of what must be done. But our whole movement will be stronger, more prepared for the long haul, if we see them in the context of the whole strategic path, if we find ways to connect each piece of the struggle with the broader, overarching movement and change we need.

It is also essential for the climate movement to understand that a comprehensive green strategy cannot be just about the environment, cannot focus on environmental issues alone. Only alliances with other progressive movements can build the political force capable of creating fundamental change. Green strategy has to align itself with the strategies of struggle for peace, justice, equality, health care, immigrant rights, full democracy both political and economic, and many other movements. And those movements need to align their strategies with that of the environmental movement as well.

The goal of this book is to contribute to the ongoing discussion of basic long-term strategy for the environmental movement.

The Impact of Climate Change

Bill McKibben noted, in his book *Eaarth*, that, "global warming is no longer a philosophical threat, no longer a future threat, no longer a threat at all. It's our reality. We've changed the planet, changed it in large and fundamental ways."[6]

Climate change has been a naturally-occurring aspect of the world's atmosphere and other natural systems for millennia, just as fluctuating levels of carbon dioxide have been. We rely on carbon dioxide in the atmosphere to keep the earth warm enough for human life and agriculture. However, when human action adds too much carbon dioxide to the atmosphere, it traps more and more of the sun's heat and holds it in, heating the earth's atmosphere. We end up throwing natural cycles out of whack in ways that can harm humanity—what is known as the greenhouse effect. As well, climate changes that result from natural processes usually take many hundreds or thousands of years to develop, while human-induced climate change is happening at a comparative warp speed, making such change problematic for many natural systems to adjust to.

As global warming raises the temperature, chains of consequences result. Glaciers melt, ice at the poles melts, oceans heat up and acidify. There is more water in the atmosphere. There are more extreme weather events of many kinds. The ocean expands because it is warmer and fresh water is added from melting ice; these result in a rise in the sea level.[7] There are increasingly intense weather patterns and more intense storms. All of these are chains of consequences linked to global warming. Humans have been making global warming worse: we continue to burn fossil fuels like coal, natural gas, and oil, which add carbon dioxide directly to the atmosphere. Methane emissions are also growing—from cattle, fracking, melting permafrost, and untreated waste.[8] The global warming from these increasing emissions is the root cause of these chains of consequences, which ripple throughout the natural systems that humans depend on.

The world is not mechanical; it is not a single, simple, straightforward process. The earth exhibits many contradictory phenomena. As a result of climate change, some areas will get more rainfall, some areas less. Global warming will lead to more droughts *and* more floods, more rainfall *and* more intense hurricanes.

Climate change is in some ways the most basic and most crucial environmental challenge we face. It makes all other environmental crises worse.

The earth will find a new balance; nature will survive. The question is, "What will be the impact on humanity?" If we want to improve life for ourselves, we'd better change how we operate, and change in fundamental ways.

The Sci-Fi Scenario

A dystopian nightmare is headed our way: massive droughts, floods, rising seas, ocean acidification, decreasing agricultural yields, rising food prices, more climate refugees, more extreme weather such as Hurricanes Katrina, Sandy, Harvey, Irma, and Maria, more extreme forest fires, melting permafrost releasing carbon dioxide and methane, and in the process destroying houses, roads, and other infrastructure, and more.

Many sci-fi books and stories have been written exploring what might happen if the world's existence became threatened, if humanity faced an apocalypse from natural disaster, disease, or alien invasion. Would people and nations join together to fight the threat, or would they give up in despair? Would they try to unite, or devolve into warring factions? Would the world revert to pre-industrial times, or all the way back to the Dark Ages?

We no longer need to look to science fiction for the answers. Climate change is just such a crisis. It is worldwide in scope. It involves a series of threats to basic aspects of human life like water availability, agricultural yields, and the homes of billions of people who live near oceans.

The answers must come from ourselves and our actions. Thus far, our actions have fallen very short of the need for fundamental change.

You don't have to look very far to find credible doomsday predictions from scientists, based on detailed and alarming scientific studies and reports. When scientists share their worst fears about where our planet is headed, they come up with a great variety of very scary prospects. Skeptics point out that some of these scenarios are overblown or seemingly improbable. Some critics imply that we should take solace that doomsday might not happen for 50 or 100 years. But that shouldn't give us any confidence in a wait-and-see approach.

For example, several years ago there were dire predictions that humanity was near the point of peak oil, the point at which it would become increasingly difficult and costly to extract oil, much of it of lower quality. This development was predicted to result in imminent industrial collapse.[9] With fracking, shale oil, tar sands, and other technologies, the world is now not anywhere near peak oil. But the reality that this particular crisis hasn't happened yet should not give us confidence that we can wish away the looming environmental catastrophes that have already begun hitting us with fury and force. The reasons why we should work for a huge decrease in the use of oil have to do with climate change, not an oil scarcity crisis.

We can't now predict exactly which of the interlocked environmental problems humanity faces will first lead to major negative tipping points. But when we are faced with only one potential world-shaking crisis, the probability of that one crisis may be small enough to risk. But when we are threatened with a series of different but related potential crises, the chances that one or another of them will happen are much greater. Because we are confronted by so many related environmental problems, we can be pretty sure that if we don't act, one or another of these crises is going to get us.

"Compound extremes" are the likelihood that one extreme weather event or climate catastrophe will trigger another, and that the combined impact will increase exponentially. That's the nature of risk probability: many risks multiplied by many opportunities for system breakdown exacerbated by inaction (or inadequate action) results in inevitable crisis. Because the world is a complex of interlocking processes with dynamic interrelationships, once any one of these crises hits, the chances of the others occurring escalate rapidly.

When we factor in human activity, that can increase the impact. For example, when we build more housing for more people closer to the oceans, then more powerful hurricanes, massive rainfall, floods, mudslides, and storm surges will affect exponentially more people immediately and directly.

Global warming is connected to permafrost melting is connected to more carbon dioxide and methane released. As global warming heats the areas of the earth covered by permafrost, the permafrost will melt, releasing millions of tons of methane and carbon dioxide which have been safely frozen for hundreds of thousands or millions of years. This will put more tons of greenhouse gases into the air. Together, these will cause more global warming, making the crisis worse. There is also the potential reactivation of ancient viruses long extinct in the frozen bodies of long-dead animals.

Similarly, more global warming leads to dryer soil and drought in many areas, leading to more forest fires which, by burning massive amounts of wood, release more carbon dioxide into the atmosphere, causing more global warming.

More forest fires heat the atmosphere, melting more permafrost, releasing more greenhouse gases, melting more glaciers, causing the earth to absorb more of the sun's heat, causing more global warming. Each crisis exacerbates and escalates the others. All these are interlocking path-dependent processes, each affecting all the others, acting as force multipliers.

The risks and costs of waiting until we gain perfect certainty are unacceptable. We can already see glacial melting taking place in Greenland, the Arctic, and in Antarctica[10] at much faster rates than anyone predicted even a few years ago.[11] Huge glaciers in Glacier National Park and at the top of Mt. Kilimanjaro are well on their way to disappearing (as are almost all glacial systems, with a few exceptions). We can measure the increased amounts of carbon dioxide and methane in the atmosphere, and we know how much of this is coming from human activity. We understand some of the potential for seriously negative impacts on human society.

Taking action is part of what will lead to more knowledge. Taking steps gains us more knowledge that we need for our practical purposes. Some political commentators on the right argue that because we don't know everything, that means we don't know anything, or at least not enough to begin taking action. However, not taking action leaves our knowledge in an unformed, abstract state.

Some doomsday scenario predictions have failed to materialize, which tells us that real life is both more complex and more fundamental than our theories. Some use this to claim that therefore all predictions of looming danger are false. However, inaction would leave us more helpless in the face of natural forces unleashed against the needs of humanity, and leave us with less knowledge, less experience, worse problems, and less capacity to create positive change, and make such change much costlier.

If we wait to act, we risk it all.

Current projections of increases in the average yearly world temperature of 5.4 to 9 degrees Fahrenheit by the end of the century are calamitous on their own. But those predictions have not completely factored in greenhouse gas emissions from thawing permafrost—which could drive temperatures much higher.

The permafrost across much of the far north, from Alaska, Russia, Canada, and the Scandinavian countries, is beginning to melt, and this poses an alarming danger. This threatens to be a crucial tipping point in the fight against global warming, since it could start a cascade of greenhouse gases being released, warming the atmosphere, causing more permafrost melting, releasing even more greenhouse gases. Earlier predictions of the effects of climate change did not (and most current predictions still do not) include calculations of emissions from melted permafrost, since few studies had been done that would enable us to make accurate predictions. But now, evidence from many areas of scientific study has accumulated to show we are poised near the start of a runaway train to climate disaster.

Nor have they factored in the potential of a massive upwelling of greenhouse gas emissions from the ocean floor—a suspect in a previous calamitous climate change event which occurred millennia ago. There is increasing evidence that at least one episode of a massive increase in carbon dioxide in the atmosphere resulted from a release of accumulated excess carbon dioxide in the ocean leading to an explosive upwelling. A run-away greenhouse effect called the Paleocene-Eocene Thermal Maximum[12] (PETM)[13] may have warmed the entire planet, 55 million years ago. This nightmare scenario is made more likely since ocean acidification makes it more difficult for oysters, clams, and other shellfish to form shells which store carbon. Shell formation uses carbon and is one way that carbon dioxide is absorbed. As a result of climate change, there is more carbon dioxide in the ocean with no way for it to become sequestered. Eventually it has to go somewhere.

An example of the impact of ocean acidification is that some oyster farmers in the Pacific Northwest have been forced to have their oysters start their lives in Hawaii, since it has become harder for oysters to begin to develop their shells properly in the waters of Washington and Oregon.[14]

A related issue is that of oxygen retention in ocean waters. As the ocean acidifies, it no longer holds as much oxygen in the deep waters, causing crabs off the coast of Oregon to suffo-cate on the ocean floor.[15] The lack of oxygen helps create mas-sive dead zones, not only in the Gulf of Mexico[16] but also on the Oregon coast, with a dead zone periodically reaching from Newport to Florence.[17] Coral reefs are dying off rapidly, in danger of complete death, destroying crucial habitat for mil-lions of creatures who play essential roles in the ocean food chain and in species diversity. Massive icebergs are calving off from Antarctic ice sheets into the ocean, icebergs the size of Connecticut and Manhattan. Glaciers in Greenland are melting faster than previously predicted. The list goes on and on.

To the alarm of scientists studying the ice sheets, Green-land has begun to experience fires, which release more carbon dioxide and also deposit ash on glaciers, decreasing heat reflectivity and increasing melt rates.

A satellite first detected the blaze in Greenland at the end of July in reindeer-grazed tundra 90 miles north-east of the town of Sisimiut, not far from the Arctic Circle. The largest fire ever recorded on the great ice island, it was smaller than most of the 6,400 wildfires that California experienced this year between New Year's and Labor Day. Yet for science it will be more memorable. As the far north warms and permafrost begins to melt, peat is exposed and becomes combustible. Peat fires can be almost inextinguishable; in remote polar regions, they could potentially burn for years. (Los Angeles spent two years futilely fighting an underground peat fire in the La Cienega – Spanish for 'bog' – area in the late 1920s.) Along with the release of methane from thawing tundra and continental shelves, the carbon dioxide emitted by a burning Arctic is the wild card of global warming.[18]

In 2012, Bill McKibben, environmental author and founder of 350.org, wrote a letter to the United Nations Doha Climate Change Conference saying in part:

> 2012 saw the shocking melt of the Arctic, leading our greatest climatologist to declare a 'planetary emergency,' and it saw weather patterns wreck harvests around the world, raising food prices by 40% and causing family emergencies in poor households throughout the world.
>
> That's what happens with 0.8°C of global warming. If we are going to stop this situation from getting worse, an array of institutions have explained this year precisely what we need to do: leave most of the carbon we know about in the ground and stop looking for more.
>
> If we want a 50-50 chance of staying below two degrees, we have to leave 2/3 of the known reserves of coal and oil and gas underground; if we want an 80% chance, we have to leave 80% of those reserves untouched. That's not "environmentalist math" or some radical interpretation—that's from the report of the International Energy Agency last month.[19]

The latest data on carbon dioxide accumulations in the atmosphere shows them continuing to rise. We are already long past the supposedly "safe" point of 350 parts per million (ppm); it now stands at over 400 ppm and is still increasing.

We must meet many challenges on many fronts to address the imbalance between how humans create the energy which enables developed human existence on the one hand, and the needs of nature upon which humanity depends in even more fundamental ways. We need water and air—there are no other "products" which can be substituted if these become dangerously polluted with toxic substances. If we don't want a nightmare sci-fi scenario, the world needs to take drastic action now.

There is hope. If we create ways to transform our relationship to nature by changing our social and economic systems, we may be able to adapt and create a new ecology that will enable our species to continue. Otherwise, we will be acted upon. We will be subjected to the often-brutal workings of climate change and natural selection.

If serious action had been taken when the first major scientific warnings were issued (the famous Congressional testimony of Dr. James Hansen from NASA's Goddard Institute was in 1988; the first major international discussion was at the Rio Environmental Summit in 1992), then we might have gotten by with less drastic and less expensive action, but that time has long passed.

There have been many efforts to address the crisis, from UN negotiations and reports to 350.org demonstrations, from individual efforts to make personal changes to public campaigns to prevent the building of new coal-fired electricity plants, from cities working to meet the goals of the Paris Climate Accord even when Trump has decided to withdraw the U.S.[20] to technological experiments with unique ways to create solar energy, from massive national investments in clean energy (like Obama's Recovery Act which made a $90 billion down-payment on energy transformation) to increasing fuel standards for new cars.

Many cities and states are already making efforts to decrease emissions and increase mitigation and adaptation efforts— from California's efforts to impose higher fuel-efficiency standards[21] to Chicago's green rooftops program.[22] Many cities and states have already adopted greenhouse-gas reduction goals, even as the Trump administration continues to delay and reject any U.S. commitment to international action and enforceable treaties. This little-noticed shift in U.S. political culture is important for many reasons, putting cities and states in advance of the Federal government, not waiting for federal action to initiate positive programs. Since the Trump administration announced that the U.S. would pull out of the Paris Accords, several states and hundreds of U.S. cities responded by reaffirming their commitment to the Paris goals.

There are many steps we need to take to address the linked series of environmental problems facing humanity. Some are changes in individual behavior; others are major changes in how we produce food, energy, and industrial commodities. Both kinds of changes are needed—if we only focus on changing the habits of individuals but keep running our industries in ways that produce pollution, carbon dioxide, and methane, we won't make much of a dent in the environmental problems we face. For example, personal trash constitutes less than 5% of the total waste stream in the U.S., even less if all industrial, mining, agricultural, building waste, and waste water is included. We could recycle 100% of personal waste, yet only make a small dent in the total amount of waste.

Personal recycling is part of the solution to our waste issues, but only a small part. Social, economic, industrial, and agricultural changes are required to solve environmental problems. Capitalism is a big part of the problem, and engaging in struggles to solve ecological crises are part of the path to replacing capitalism.

Environmental change doesn't and won't happen just because it "should," just because humanity needs such change. Environmental change *requires* organized social forces to push for and create such change. Fundamental change requires class and mass struggles, alongside scientific, technological, and educational work. It is not enough to understand environmental problems and their causes, we must change our industrial, agricultural, energy, and transportation systems; we must change our economic, taxation, and financial systems. We must deepen our understanding of political processes and coalition-building in order to create the political force able to make the necessary changes.

The labor theory of value contends that "all value comes from nature altered by human labor." In the past, economists from Adam Smith to Karl Marx have mostly focused on the labor part of that equation, noting that how human labor is organized and how production is organized are the fundamental determinants of the kind of society we have. The basic (though not the only) differences between forms of society are rooted in the different laws and practices that govern who owns and controls the means of production, and in the level of technology embedded in production. For example, the Industrial Revolution resulted in changes in law, education, politics, and culture.

Climate change and other environmental challenges are forcing us to look more closely at the other part of the equation. It is not just labor which is fundamental, so is nature, so are the natural resources and conditions humanity depends upon for survival. If there are insufficient resources to feed, clothe, and house humanity, to provide the natural resources which are acted upon by production and technology, that too will have fundamental impacts on what kind of society we have.

All material value to humanity comes either directly from nature, or from nature altered by human labor. If we compromise nature's ability to regenerate the materials we need for our survival, we compromise our own ability to survive. We face a series of linked environmental problems—from climate change, to water use, to soil depletion—which have the potential to negatively affect sea levels, weather systems, our ability to grow food and drink water, and other essential aspects of human life. We can't endlessly alter the balance of natural systems like the atmosphere or the oceans without suffering the consequences of that alteration.

Environmental struggles are not just another in a long list of struggles, they are fundamental to the future of humankind. If we live in a world that is inhospitable to human life or to the agriculture which feeds us due to heat and water stresses, all the overgrowth of ideology, laws, and philosophy won't matter much. When the four million people who live in and around Cape Town, South Africa run out of water very soon, no pious words will ameliorate the crisis they will face daily, an ongoing crisis that has already begun and is guaranteed to get much worse.

Capitalism

Capitalism exploits labor, that is basic to the operation of the system. But capitalism also exploits nature in ways which are harmful to the future of everyone. The ways in which capitalism exploits nature are determined more by the short-term profit interests of the few rather than the long-term survival needs of all. It is now clear that Exxon and other oil corporations knew many decades ago about the reality of climate change, but that reality was in conflict with their short-term profit interests. Instead of informing the public and changing their business models, they funded climate denialism. This was not because they didn't understand the science but rather because they wanted to continue garnering excess profits.[23] About 70% of the greenhouse gas emissions which have accumulated in the atmosphere over the last 100-plus years were emitted by only 100 corporations.[24] They not only exploited labor and nature, they exploited our common future.

There are also serious indirect costs from the operation of the capitalist system, as capitalist production and agriculture over-exploit the non-renewable resources we depend upon in an ever-speedier race to catastrophe.

The limitations of our finite world must be an essential component of economics, which has focused most often on labor, development, finance, and growth, to the exclusion of the need of nature to be able to regenerate itself. Also, to the exclusion of humanity's need to let nature regenerate itself.

Infinite, endless growth is not possible in a finite world. Yet capitalism depends on endless growth: in markets, in commodities, in profits, and in exploitation of labor and nature. It exploits natural resources at the start of the production process, exploits workers and the waste-absorbing capacity of nature in the process of production, and exploits the waste-absorbing capacity of nature after goods have been consumed. Capitalism also measures growth without reference to values of sustainability and resilience, nor to quality of life.

There are potential ways to alter the supply of natural resources. Nanotechnology, acting on nature at a microscopic level, offers great possibilities to create and produce in new ways. Finding new ways to utilize the resources of the oceans and space are two other potential avenues to tap for expanding the resources humanity can use for production, agriculture, and other aspects of survival. But these resources too are not limitless and at present are mostly theoretical or experimental, not practical. We can't base a strategy on the hope that new technology will magically solve our basic problems for us within the time-frame we need, any more than technology by itself can solve human exploitation.

Solutions require a shift of class power and also a shift in our economic planning. We need socialized decision-making. But when socialist economic planning does not sufficiently take the requirements of nature into account, that can result in disaster—as for example the efforts to create a new cotton-growing region in the Soviet Union by tapping the tributaries of the Aral Sea for irrigation which resulted in the near-destruction of the sea and also of the productive land around it, along with fishing, small-scale agriculture, and many towns.

We have to see environmental issues through a working-class lens, as they relate to basic issues of class power, justice, equality, democracy, and peace. We all must work in coalition with many others for immediate survival needs in the present and for long-term survival needs for the future of all humanity. We fight for living-wage jobs for all, and for jobs that enable humanity to live and thrive as well.

We must struggle against those, right or left, who pit immediate struggles against long-term solutions, for whatever reason. When the environmental movement talks, correctly, about protecting the environment for the future, but doesn't talk about the need for jobs in the present, we must criticize this short-sighted, go-it-alone strategy. When one or another labor union supports environmentally-destructive jobs, we need to understand the real reasons why they do this (unemployment, job loss, falling real wages), but also criticize this approach as short-sighted and not in the long-term interests (including the job interests) of their members and other workers. Our task is to make links between these movements, to build on the real commonality of interests they share, and to fight for programs and policies that make those common interests explicit.

For example, a proposal by the labor movement to rebuild and repair our nation's existing gas pipelines would create many more jobs for construction workers than the Keystone XL pipeline and DAPL projects, would help the environment by fixing leaks and preventing spills, and would avoid the unnecessary "jobs right now" versus "destroying the environment in the long-term" argument. A collaborative approach is necessary to enable a united movement to craft solutions which are a win for workers *and* for the environment, for the short-term *and* the long-term, for people *and* nature.

For another example, in Washington State the labor movement is a key member of the Alliance for Jobs and Clean Energy, which has over 170 member groups ranging from labor to health professionals to religious groups. Their statement of purpose asserts that positive public policy:

1. Will respond to climate change by adopting standards and policies that reduce carbon emissions and hold big emitters accountable.

2. Can grow our economy, business sector, and labor movement by incentivizing homegrown clean energy and technology, which creates good jobs and better choices for consumers, and improves health.

3. Must invest in communities of color and communities with low incomes disproportionately harmed by fossil fuel pollution. [25]

The coalition filed an initiative for a carbon tax, including provisions addressing all three principles: jobs, racial justice, as well as carbon dioxide reduction. They filed after the state legislature failed to act on a similar bill.

The greenhouse gases already emitted will change the climate for centuries to come, and current human activity is continuing to make the problem worse. Social decision-making, based on the long-term needs of humanity rather than on short-term profit interests, is an essential aspect of the necessary changes. Climate change, for example, is worldwide and can't be solved unless shifts are made to stop private interests from making the situation worse for everybody, making us pay in the long-term while sequestering the immediate profits in their own pockets.

A successful long-term strategy calls for uniting the core forces for change: workers, the racially and nationally oppressed, women, and youth. Allies in the peace movement, the LGBTQ movement, the existing environmental movements, and the movement for full democracy, among many others, need to be gathered around these forces to build the massive coalition necessary to create fundamental change. Environmental issues, especially climate change, are basic issues which all progressive movements need to integrate deeply into their programs and work.

For real, lasting, long-range solutions, socialism is a necessary goal. Otherwise, any partial or temporary progress we make in fighting environmental crises will remain under attack by a system focused on short-term profits. But socialism by itself is not sufficient for solving the environmental crises we are already experiencing and the ones that will happen in the next few decades.

Frederick Engels, in his graveside address for Marx, noted that "Marx discovered the law of development of human history: the simple fact, hitherto concealed by an overgrowth of ideology, that mankind must first of all eat, drink, have shelter and clothing, before it can pursue politics, science, art, religion, etc."

This points to the fundamental realities of all human life. We need nature for our survival. Our lives are based on air, food, water, and other resources that come from nature. As well, the ways in which we create and distribute food, drink, clothing, and shelter impact the natural world we depend upon.

If the air becomes too polluted for human health, we can't simply breathe something else. We can't stop eating; we require water. Pollution that is blown away goes somewhere else; it doesn't just disappear. Humans are not separate from their environment, and the environments of different countries are not separate from each other. What we experience in one region of the world is intimately connected to what people experience in other regions; what happens to natural global systems happens to all of us. Climate change, extreme weather, and pollution do not respect borders.

The potential of looming environmental catastrophe isn't a single problem with a simple solution. The climate crisis, excessive garbage and toxic waste, an increasing list of endangered species, pollution and toxic chemicals in the air, water, soil, and in our food, our workplaces, and our homes, are among the myriad problems we face.

The real question is: *Will we continue to force natural systems to work together* **against** *humanity?*

Or put another way: *Will we restructure our personal, social, cultural, economic, agricultural, financial, legal, and industrial systems to work in harmony with natural systems?*

Part One:
The Framework

Chapter 1

Human Society Needs to Change

The crises that threaten us are not just environmental; they are also crises of our social and economic systems. Environmental catastrophe exacerbates social and economic problems and contributes to social instability and conflict. The genocide in Rwanda in the 1990s is one example: while global warming and competition for limited degraded agricultural land were not the only causes, they certainly contributed to the extent and intensity of the genocide.

The adaptability of human social and economic systems is more limited than general human adaptability. The rate of change possible in large-scale social systems is much slower than the adaptability of individuals and small groups.

When a society comes into unresolvable conflict with its environment, there are three basic adaptations that can happen:

1. the society can move elsewhere and continue as before in a new place (the main adaptation in ancient times), or
2. the society and people can die out, or
3. people can stay where they are and transform their society and economy.

There are many examples of the first two adaptations occurring over the course of human history, including the Mesopotamian Fertile Crescent, North Africa, the Mayan Yucatan, the Midwest Dust Bowl, and parts of the Nile Valley.

In Mesopotamia, one of the cradles of civilization and one of the few places in the world where agriculture started, there were successive waves of intensive agriculture followed by collapse due to the salinization and degradation of the soil, followed by abandonment. In some places, repopulation occurred hundreds of years later after some soil recovery.

The world's globalized economy and globalized environmental crises have now left us with nowhere else to go when we face agricultural collapse or environmental catastrophe. We can change our economic practices or else perish, or perhaps survive in a diminished fashion in a more inhospitable world.

In the 10,000 years of agriculture and the four or five centuries of capitalism, humans have transformed our relations with the microbial world, the seas, the vegetation, the animals and insects, the crust of the earth, and now the atmosphere. We have reached a new successional stage in our relations with the rest of nature. The ecological crisis of our species is inextricably entwined with capitalism and its inefficient use of resources for the private profit of a relative handful of individuals.

When oppressive, class-divided societies are stressed by external events, whether war, economic crisis, or impending environmental collapse, the ruling class first transmits the main burdens of that crisis to the oppressed and exploited classes, using money and power to escape the consequences as long as possible.

The world will survive. That is not in question. The earth has been through many more cataclysmic changes than global warming will bring. Nature *will* reach a new equilibrium. The question is whether or not our species will be able to survive that new balance, whether we will thrive or instead face constant crisis and the devolvement of advanced civilization. And if we do survive, will our survival be compatible with developed human existence, with the existence of human sustainability at a level of complex technology, cultural advancement, and agricultural and water sufficiency?

We must create fundamental change; otherwise, we will be subjected to the often-brutal workings of climate change, environmental catastrophe, natural selection, and societal conflict. If we create ways to transform our relationship to nature by changing our social and economic systems, we may be able to adapt by creating a new ecology that enables our species to continue and thrive.

We can either work with nature, or nature will work against us. Nature doesn't "care" about humanity; humanity *must* care about nature. We must work to enable nature to sustain us. We must pick the third option: transform our society and economy.

Recognizing Necessity

Only by recognizing environmental imperatives will we be free to make the right choices for humanity's survival. Only by recognizing the restraints and limits required of us by natural systems can we become truly conscious actors capable of improving the world for ourselves and our descendants.

Global warming is but a symptom, a profound symptom to be sure, of the imbalance in the relationship between human activity and the nature on which we depend. This imbalance is the crisis of our times, of which global warming is one major part. We most certainly must cut carbon dioxide emissions, and fast. Global climate change is an escalating challenge. But it is not the only challenge we have to work on.

Global climate change is throwing other looming crises into sharp relief. As climate change causes shifts in weather patterns, rainfall patterns, and seasons, that also highlights serious problems with the way we conduct agriculture. When we depend on irrigation systems for increasing agricultural production, we base our ability to grow food on the stability of those water systems. Melting glaciers, rampant development in water-stressed regions, over-tapped underground aquifers, and rainforest destruction are all turning water into a threatened resource. When we don't have enough fresh water in the right places to grow the food we need, how will we feed ourselves and our growing population?

When we increase agricultural output by an over-reliance on chemical fertilizers, we place an unsustainable burden on the non-renewable oil which is used to produce fertilizer. What the fertilizer does is enable us to speed up the rate at which we use up the natural ability of the soil to grow food. We turn the soil into an addict, requiring ever-larger doses of fertilizer and pesticides to get the same results.[26] As well, in the process of production, packaging, and use, unnecessary carbon dioxide is released. In the process, we unintentionally, and in some cases ignorantly, harm the microbiome, the teeming mass of invisible animals and bacteria which work to create rich soil in the first place.

Agricultural issues are one example of the problems humanity faces due to our imbalance with nature. Oil and natural gas depletion, industrial pollution, the build-up everywhere in the world of persistent organic pollutants (POPs)—many of which harm human and animal reproductive systems, rapid desertification, increased extreme weather events, and massive amounts of waste can all be linked to and added to global climate change as examples of how humanity is helping to degrade and stress the ability of nature to support us.

Are goods and food distributed justly? Is there sufficient potable water for everyone? It is not good enough for there to be sufficient, food on average, there must be sufficient afford-able, and available food for everyone.

We need more productive agricultural production systems which don't rely on excess water consumption, on chemical fertilizers, on mechanized farm equipment to spread fertilizer, and on fossil-fuel burning airplanes to spray pesticides indis-criminately. We need transportation systems that are much more efficient to move goods including agricultural produce (trains rather than trucks, for example), and that don't sub-stitute for local production and distribution. We need indus-trial production which doesn't waste energy, which doesn't produce massive amounts of waste, and which utilizes solar energy (many forms of renewable energy come from the power of the sun in one form or another—solar, wind, wave, biomass, and others). We need linked series of industrial plants, where the waste products and energy from one factory provide the raw materials and energy for the next.

Justice, peace, environmental sustainability, world health, all require planning, cooperation, and democratic decision-making. We need an economic system that measures all value by human need rather than individual profit for the 1%. Focusing on one problem, no matter how serious, without considering its relationships with related problems wastes time and can lead to self-defeating policies. Waiting for some magical technological or "market-driven" solution wastes time we need to readjust our agricultural, industrial, and distribution systems.

The Illusion of the Way Things Look

Change mostly happens incrementally; the way the world around us looks doesn't change much from one day to the next. This week is pretty much the same as last week, within a fairly narrow range of weather. Our daily experience of life only recognizes major change when it happens in unexpected ways—a hurricane-driven storm surge hitting New York City, the hottest temperatures ever recorded, a five-year drought in California. But for most people, dramatic change is not an everyday occurrence. We go about our normal lives and expect, on the basis of our entire experience, that those lives will continue normally.

Addressing climate change requires an understanding of discontinuous, non-linear change, an understanding that even when things look very much the same, the underlying realities on which our observed and lived experience are based can be undergoing basic transformations. Over time, those underlying changes will result in dramatic shifts in extreme weather, forest fires, droughts, floods, heat waves, water stresses, and other aspects of the natural world on which we depend.

As Mike Davis notes, in a *London Review of Books* blog post, the entire fire ecosystem of the West is changing:

> The big picture, then, is the violent reorganization
> of regional fire regimes across North America, and
> as pyrogeography changes, biogeography soon
> follows. Some forests and 'sky island' ecosystems

will face extinction; most will see dramatic shifts in species composition. Changing land cover, together with shorter rainy seasons, will destabilize the snowpack-based water-storage systems that irrigate the West. The Pacific Northwest, according to most researchers, will become even wetter, yet drought years will be more extreme, making great fires more common. In California, on the other hand, a drier, hotter climate will be punctuated by extreme rainfall events, reproducing the drought-fuel accumulation-firestorm cycle that we have seen over the last year. In the desert Southwest, studies point to the weakening of the North American monsoon that slakes Arizona's thirst in late summer; as Phoenix becomes more like Death Valley, condo sales soar in San Diego.[27]

We have to see shifts in the basics of the natural world and learn how they will affect us in the long run—even when they are not visible on the surface of day-to-day life. We must all learn to look beneath the surface appearance of our daily world, to learn about the changes happening in the natural world which are not visible to the naked eye.

It's Not Only Climate Change

When we focus obsessively on climate change, we can miss other catastrophes headed our way: soil degradation for example. As we use up the nutrients in the soil and degrade the soil through excessive use of pesticides, herbicides, insecticides, fungicides, and fertilizer, we end up destroying part of the soil's potential to continue to feed us. Our agricultural practices predate the Industrial Revolution and the start of the cycle of excess greenhouse gas emissions. Industrial agriculture has made our impact on the soil much worse. The "green revolution" increased agricultural output in the past but tied farmers to a debt-ridden cycle of excess water use, excess fertilizer use, mechanized equipment, and yearly purchase of seeds in many cases.

Agricultural output around the world has been decreasing over the last few decades—at a time when the world population is increasing, and available agriculture land is mostly already in use. We need to work to fix our soil problems in concert with our climate and water problems, or we risk solving one in ways that harm the other linked aspects of the natural world we depend on.

Human survival requires a rebalancing of human activity with natural systems and resources. The list of environmental problems and crises that humanity faces is long and growing:

1. global climate change,
2. decreasing agricultural yields,
3. increasing water stresses,
4. the accumulation of persistent organic pollutants in the water, soil, and air which affect human, animal, and plant reproductive systems,
5. ocean acidification,
6. coral reef destruction,
7. depletion and destruction of fisheries,
8. the depletion of many kinds of non-renewable resources,
9. annihilation of many species of plants and animals,
10. increases in extreme weather events,
11. rapid increases in urbanization without corresponding increases in water and sewage infrastructure,
12. destructive mining practices,
13. deforestation,
14. expanding and changing ranges of diseases, parasites, insects,
15. and more.

We have to find ways to work on all these interlocked problems and issues simultaneously. If we don't, whichever problems we ignore will create their own crisis sooner or later. The answer for now about many aspects of climate change is that we need to know much more, we need to act while finding out more, and we need to act to *enable* us to find out more.

Agriculture accounts for large amounts of particulate matter in our air—those particles come not just from cars, trucks, and industry. As well, emissions from synthetic fertilizers and farm animals combine with industrial and vehicle pollution to create deadly particles in the air of both rural areas and cities. Rural problems exacerbate urban problems and vice versa.

We face some less-understood dangers from the overuse of chemical pesticides and insecticides. There has already been a disastrous drop in the number of flying insects in many parts of the world, and some of these insect species protect us from other bugs while providing a crucial food source for birds.[28] We have seen major outbreaks of bee colony disorder, dangerous because of the niche in many plant reproductive systems filled by bees.

While some who deny the dangers of climate change blithely talk about excess carbon dioxide helping food to grow, research is showing that in some cases, extra growth comes at the cost of nutritional value. As a result, some kinds of animals are becoming obese, needing to eat more carbohydrate-laden food to gain the same amount of sustenance.

Similarly, our over-use of fresh water puts us in a bind, polluting it with pesticides, herbicides, and fertilizer, increasing toxic run-off, and creating dead zones in parts of the world's oceans. This is combined with the reality that billions of our fellow humans do not have adequate access to clean fresh water for drinking. Climate change makes all these worse, but fixing climate change will not, by itself, solve our water, soil, or pollution problems.

Tipping Points and How We Find Them

There are dangerous tipping points in the environment, and we absolutely need to learn about them through more science, not by going over any climate cliffs.

Many studies and writings about climate change discuss the essential tipping points we must avoid to maintain hospitable human life on earth, sometimes referred to as *planetary boundaries*.[29] Some studies propose nine, others break it up a bit differently.[30] These range from the level of greenhouse gases in the atmosphere to ozone levels to ocean acidification.[31]

Many scientists argue that humanity has already forced nature to pass several of these tipping points,[32] some by a wide margin. This is certainly true of the level of greenhouse gases in the atmosphere, now consistently over 400 parts per million (ppm).

Some commentators frame these boundaries as opportunities. They point to spectacular growth in sustainable, renewable energy and to many other technological advances being made. But the ripple effects from crossing one boundary could be devastating and could trigger the crossing of more boundaries.

Three of those potential tipping points, which would be fairly catastrophic quite quickly, are:

1. the already mentioned melting permafrost in the Arctic, which as it melts releases some of the billions of tons of greenhouse gases that have been frozen for millennia;[33]
2. the frozen methane and carbon dioxide lying on the bottom of the ocean, which is rapidly changing due to increasing acidification and warming— another instance where billions of tons of methane and carbon dioxide are just waiting to overwhelm our atmosphere, and
3. potential changes in the ocean's currents, driven in large part by salty water sinking to the bottom of the ocean in the North Atlantic. As fresh water melts from the ice sheets on Greenland, the change in ocean salinity in that part of the world could affect ocean currents[34] all over the world (the phenomenon nicknamed the "conveyor belt"[35]).

We do not know exactly where the last straws of these tipping points are, and we need to know. However, finding out by crossing them into massive environmental catastrophe is the wrong way to find out—we need more science, more research, more data.

These are in addition to recent studies of the health of the world's oceans, which offer dire warnings about the changes already taking place, in ocean acidity, warming, sea level rise, accumulating plastic waste, the growth of dead zones, and fishery health.

The reality is that the world can no longer afford our current energy systems, our current financial system, our current industrial system. All these and more will have to change in order for humanity's balance with nature to readjust to sustainable levels.

Issues of building the capacity to save the planet from environmental devastation are issues of democratic power for the majority. This means power for workers, their families, and poor people, who together make up the vast majority of all societies.

Health Issues

Climate change issues are public health issues. As the planet warms, disease ranges expand outward from the tropics—malaria, for example, as do the ranges of swarms of insects who spread disease. This also includes expanding ranges for the ticks who carry Lyme disease, and for the mosquitos who spread Dengue Fever.

In 2003, a heat wave struck Europe in August, including France, where August is a traditional vacation month for many citizens, including many health care professionals. Several thousand deaths occurred from heat stroke and other health problems related to the heat. With so many health workers gone, hospitals were understaffed for such a crisis, making it even worse than it could have been.[36]

There are more than a few parts of the world, including within the continental United States, which within this century will have summer temperatures that are incompatible with human life. As the world warms, many places are experiencing longer allergy seasons. Combined with the asthma epidemic, we face more life-altering and life-threatening respiratory problems. Particulate matter in the air from the burning of fossil fuels and other industrial pollution is the key suspect in the alarming increase in the incidence of asthma, including among young children. As well, global warming and the resultant changes in seasons is a suspect in the widely-observed increase in pollen and allergy problems.

Increased heat from climate change is not the only crucial environmental health issue. Burning waste in incinerators creates dioxin, one of the most carcinogenic chemicals in existence. It is a hazard to the general public, but even more to people who live near incinerators and even more than that to the workers in the plants.

Mental health is also impacted from living in a much more stressful world. "Doctors in countries with bad heat waves report an upswing in psychosis . . . In the wake of Hurricane Katrina, the incidence of severe mental illness doubled in the affected areas, with 11% of the population suffering from post-traumatic stress disorder, depression, panic disorder, and a variety of phobias."[37]

A full list of environmental hazards to human health is long, detailed, scary,[38] and beyond the scope of this book. It is clear that environmental hazards of many kinds should be treated as public health issues, researched and regulated as public health concerns, and that specific chemicals and compounds should be banned with a system of regulation much more robust and enforceable than currently in existence anywhere in the world. Right-wing "realistic" economic arguments about the costs of solving environmental problems ignore the economic costs that pollution already causes.[39]

More and more studies are showing that people having regular connection to the natural world is an important component of physical, emotional, and mental health. Being able to walk a forest, swim a lake, sit on an ocean beach—these are not luxuries for the few, they can help all humans. Destroying significant parts of the natural world, or altering them beyond recognition, removes the potential for such wildness and nature to provide health services to humanity. This is not something that shows up on balance sheets, on calculations of GDP, on many governmental budgets except for parks and national forests. It is just important to humanity.

Some Pointless Arguments About Climate Change

Climate change preceded human mass production of carbon dioxide emissions. It is a natural process, or rather a linked series of natural processes. However, we are making these natural processes much more rapid and much worse—worse for human beings. Anything we do to lessen our impact will help us, no matter the original or ultimate cause. All we really need to know to make a start is that human production is, at the very least, contributing massively to the problem.

There are differing predictions of when we will hit crucial tipping points; some predict 10 years, some 50 years; some believe we have already passed one or more tipping points. We may have 100 years before the worst massive, most catastrophic negative impacts, though negative change is happening all around us already. But even if the tipping points to environmental catastrophe are 100 years from now, do we want to pass on these environmental crises to our children and grandchildren? Do we want them to inherit a polluted world, inhospitable to human life, undergoing massive negative change in many natural systems, and much more difficult to remediate because of *our* actions or lack thereof? Let us step up our efforts to address these problems before they get to tipping points which we may not be able to predict with exactitude yet but which we already know we don't want to reach, and from which we may not be able to recover.

Other arguments are similarly pointless when used as excuses not to act with all possible speed. Does the most underlying cause of climate change reside in the tropics, in the Arctic, in the ocean currents, or in the stratosphere? Arguing about this will not make a big difference in deciding what we need to begin doing now. The answers are important in the long run, but the only way of knowing is to engage in much more research and action. Only more information, more research, more practice and implementation, and deeper understanding will get us there.

Some insist that the main upcoming crisis is the soil; others believe that water is what we should focus on; others think that excess carbon dioxide is the biggest deal. The point, however, is that these are all interrelated, and working on any of them will at least help ameliorate the others. The world is not often an either-or place, it is a place of cycles, of linked chains, of networks, of patterns, of intersections and interconnections. If global warming is contributing to water resource problems, working on global warming is also working on water resources, and which one is going to be "the" most crucial is not crucial, not yet anyway.

Another set of wrong-headed arguments come from doomsday scenarios promoted by climate change skeptics. They predict, using zero-sum logic, that environmentally-sound production and the necessary limits on growth inherent in sustainable economics would rapidly throw the world economy (or the economy of the U.S., which for them is the same thing) into instantaneous economic depression. For one thing, they ignore the costs of global warming that we are already paying.

More importantly, investing in environmentally-sustainable agriculture and production will create a great deal of economic activity, generate increases in the GDP, and create millions of new jobs. Those jobs and that growth will not be wasteful, unrestrained, unplanned, and resource-intensive, but will be economic growth just the same. They may not generate as much private profit, but will generate much more public good.

An example is the timber industry. Go back a few decades to the battles in the western U.S. over the spotted owl and restrictions on timber cutting. The timber industry was able to convince many timber workers that their jobs were being threatened by those "damn environmentalists." But the timber companies didn't have the best interests of the workers at heart—the companies were focused on unrestrained profit, unrestrained logging, and the cheapest methods of cutting more trees faster. As well, in search of cheaper labor, companies shifted logging to the U.S. South and to Siberia from the Northwest, often using environmental regulations as the phony public excuse for what they were already planning to do.

The reality is that environmentally-sustainable logging requires *more* workers, creates *more* jobs, is *safer* for workers, and is also better for economic development and growth, especially for local communities. It is also better for salmon runs, spotted owls, and erosion rates. Environmentally sustainable logging practices just don't create as much quick profit.

There is a fallacy in the thinking of some environmental activists and writers too. They see production itself, and/ or technology itself, as the problem, and so argue against all industry and technology, and blame workers for needing jobs.

Some environmentalists speak of the so-called "tragedy of the commons," which contends that we have problems because individuals place their own short-term interests over the long-term interests of all people. They supposedly do this because if they change, the pain of change will hit them immediately, but if they postpone change, then the pain to all people is somewhere in the future. Or because individual benefit is immediate, but the social cost is protracted and is not paid by the individual.

The real tragedy is the tragedy of the anarchy of capitalist production, of enshrining individual profit above planned social good. People don't need or want to make negative choices, but sometimes the system leaves them no good alternatives. That is the fault of the system, not of greedy people, human nature, or human short-sightedness in the abstract. When the system leaves people with nothing but bad individual choices about their own survival, of course people will make individual decisions to guarantee their immediate survival. But there are better alternatives.

The Real Scientific Uncertainties About Climate Change

Many opponents of action on climate change wrap their arguments in claims of "scientific uncertainty." In doing so, they exhibit their own flawed understanding of how science works, and what climate scientists are really uncertain about.

Science is never "finished." It will never reach a point of complete understanding of everything, not even of any one aspect of reality. There will always be processes that the collective knowledge of humankind hasn't yet understood.

There are several reasons for this:

1. The world is a complex of many systems, which constantly interact—and that complexity cannot be reduced to any simple proposition.
2. Because those systems are constantly interacting, they are also constantly changing—there is not a static universe which holds still while we analyze it.
3. Science works by developing ever more sophisticated tools to measure aspects of reality, but measurements and scientific understanding of them are never the reality itself; they are just better and better approximations.

We know that the Greenland glaciers are melting faster than predicted, and that the melting into the ocean will impact sea levels. But how much and by when are still a matter of speculation—educated guesses if you will. Estimates are based on measurements, on projections, on computer models, on research into past climate changes, but they are not the melting itself, not the sea level rise itself.

We can already observe the melting of permafrost in the Arctic regions of the world—those pictures of houses collapsing and highways buckling in Alaska are proof that the process is underway. We also know that melting permafrost releases greenhouse gases that have been frozen, in some places for millennia. But exactly how much and exactly how fast remains for us to discover.

There is still much that we do not understand about climate systems and the ways they interact with all other human and natural systems. We know that the world is getting hotter, and getting hotter faster. But we do not know exactly how hot it will get by what date. However, in spite of such uncertainties, climate models and predictions are becoming increasingly comprehensive, detailed, and accurate.

There are many uncertainties about climate change, but there are no uncertainties about whether climate change is taking place—only about its pace and scale. The real debates are about whether climate change will be catastrophic within years or decades, and about whether or not we have already passed crucial environmental tipping points. We can predict with confidence that droughts and forest fires will increase in number and intensity (they have been doing so worldwide for many decades already, with some calling this the "era of megafires") but we can't predict exactly where or when the next drought or forest fire will take place.

Conservatives use these uncertainties as fodder as they seek to undercut support for action against global climate change, for EPA regulations restricting carbon dioxide emissions, and for restrictions on pollution.

While there are many valid criticisms of the ways in which the EPA has historically limited its concerns to regulating pollution after it has already been created, and how it has relaxed standards under pressure from corporations, to eliminate the EPA as many conservatives propose would be a move in exactly the wrong direction.

Many of the conservative arguments made in public against climate change don't make sense. They are based on a rejection, implicit or explicit, of science itself. They ignore or gloss over the changes that are already obviously taking place all over the world. For example, in 2012, the North Carolina legislature passed a bill to forbid the state's ecology department from referring to or studying climate change in their report on changing Atlantic Ocean shorelines.

False Claims

Just because some right-wing politicians make claims that are patently false, that doesn't mean that they themselves are ignorant, though some are. Right-wing politicians stretch truth and reason to find excuses for policies that benefit the owners and managers of fossil fuel industry, their campaign contributors. Just because the reasons given in public for conservative policies don't make sense, that is not the same as saying the policies themselves don't make sense. Such policies "make sense" in that they make money for a few rich people, lots of money. Transforming our energy production will mean some rich people won't make as much as if we just continued business as usual. Limiting carbon dioxide emissions from electricity-producing coal-fired plants would cost the owners of those plants money they would rather put in their own pockets.

The people who make false claims about climate science are the same people who make false arguments against raising the minimum wage, against equal pay for all, against workers' right to organize. They are the same forces who want to fan the flames of anti-immigrant hysteria, who want to gerrymander congressional districts to continue their power a little longer, who are working hard to restrict the right to vote and restrict the continuation of constitutionally-protected abortion rights.

Such policies make sense, for them and for their financial backers. They don't make sense for the rest of us, the 99% who will pay the price for these anti-science, anti-environment, anti-democratic, anti-people policies.

Everyone who makes an obviously false argument is not necessarily ignorant. Part of our job is to understand who such policies benefit, who makes money from sowing confusion and nonsense, who maintains political power longer as a result. Anti-science claims are financially benefiting a few people, which is why the rich and the right-wingers are determined to undermine popular understanding of climate change science—and there is *no* uncertainty about that.

Overpopulation?

Some want to blame population increases as the root cause of our problems. While restraining population increases is indeed part of a comprehensive program, if we cut the world's population but continue the same economic and production systems, environmental crises will still happen. We can't separate any one contributing factor and make that the be-all and end-all of causation. Separating population from how things are produced, from who benefits most from maintaining business-as-usual, from who decides and who uses wealth and power to escape the problems, leaves us with only hopes for magical market solutions, or miraculous technological fixes, or a zero-population growth that will never happen absent a catastrophic epidemic on the order of the Black Death plague.

Justice, fairness, and basic human decency are all affronted by efforts to blame the global warming crisis on "too many people." Blaming the victims is not a path to solutions; ignoring the class divisions in society limits our ability to find long-lasting solutions.[40]

Poverty is connected to increasing birthrates in developing countries, and capitalist globalization is a major cause of poverty, increasing income inequality, distorted markets, oppressive debt, and financial speculation. Countries with a social-democratic orientation, such as Holland and the Scandinavian countries, have succeeded in bringing population growth under control. Countries with a socialist orientation, such as Cuba and China, have instituted policies to make family planning and contraceptive services available to all, and China's one-child policy (now abandoned) brought down the formerly astronomical birth rate there. Even within India, which as a whole still has high birthrates, the state of Kerala, with a communist-led government for much of the decades since the late 1950s, has brought health care, family planning, and a more equitable distribution of wealth to the population with positive results for limiting population growth. Recently, Kerala had a population growth rate of 4.9% versus the rate for all of India of 17.6%, partly as a result of the positive social programs which Communist leadership in the government created.

Some who blame the increase in world population for all our environmental problems urge profoundly anti-human solutions. But the problems lie not just in the numbers of people but also in the technological, industrial, and agricultural methods we use and the unequal and unjust social systems we set up and impose. Just having fewer people but still producing and distributing food and industrial goods in the same ways is worse than no solution at all, because we would have to turn ourselves into monsters, consigning millions or billions of people to unacceptable conditions, even death. And this would still fail to save humanity.

Chapter 2

The Broadest Framework

In order to create a movement with enough power and sophistication to impose fundamental change on a resistant system, we need to look at all these issues and more in the broadest way possible and integrate our scientific understanding with our social and political activism.

How to Weather the Next Few Years of Climate Change

How will we weather the next few years of retrograde U.S. politics about climate change, while watching the oceans rise, acidify, and lose oxygen, at the same time that extreme drought, extreme hurricanes, extreme forest fires, and immense floods slap us upside the head? All while watching various Republicans, coal-state Democrats, fossil-fuel company flacks, and corporate CEOs deny what is obvious to anyone paying attention. While watching agricultural yields drop, and human hunger increase and intensify.[41] While water stress for hundreds of millions of people intensifies[42] at the same time that Nestlé executives argue that fresh, safe water is not a right, it is a commodity for their profit. While listening to various supposedly well-meaning apologists for the capitalist system admit that climate change is real but insist that technological fixes are all that is needed (for example, Al Gore, in his movies, books, and public appearances).

Our world is changing for the worse as we fiddle with climate-change denier nonsense. The reality is that the nonsense is

47

not naturally-occurring, it has been manufactured. Exxon knew long ago, starting in the 1950s, before they started funding climate change deniers, that the world was warming, would warm more, and that the fossil fuels they extracted were the main cause. They knew that such knowledge was dangerous for their short-term profits, so they decided to spread division and uncertainty as a strategy to delay action.[43] They kept making super-profits while getting tax breaks, subsidies, and write-offs from governments to the tune of billions of dollars a year.

As Bill McKibben noted in an interview:

> Internal communications from Exxon Mobil show the corporation took steps to protect its drilling rigs from rising sea levels and increasing severe weather at the same time it was working to block regulations that would decrease carbon emissions.
> "It took me far too long to figure out that we were not in an argument at all," McKibben said, referring to the so-called debate as to whether a warming climate is caused by human impact. "We were in a fight, and a fight is always about money and power. The fossil fuel industry was the richest and the most powerful industry on the planet, and the fact that it had lost the argument made very little difference to it. It was winning the fight day after day after day."[44]

The good news is that the climate change movement is growing, constantly expanding to take on more aspects of the imbalance challenge facing humanity. The divestment from fossil-fuel stocks movement, civil disobedience at proposed pipelines and coal plants, and the integration of environmental issues into electoral campaigns are all growing parts of our movement. Alliances with other organizations and movements are also growing and solidifying—with Black Lives Matter, with the labor movement, with voting rights struggles, with the Fight for $15.

Despite these positive changes, humanity has not yet turned the corner on climate change, has not taken anywhere near enough serious steps to fundamentally change direction. Worldwide, emissions are still growing in spite of decreases in some countries. The Paris Climate Accord commits countries to ambitious goals but doesn't have enforcement powers, and even the steps promised in that agreement will not be close to sufficient. The Keystone XL pipeline was temporarily defeated during the Obama administration but there are more pipeline proposals in the works, and Trump has revitalized the Keystone XL project as well, in spite of a major spill occurring already.

Some people right now are only ready to recycle, and that by itself is not enough. Some people are encouraged that the nations of the world have committed in the Paris Accords to action to keep temperature increase below 2 degrees Centigrade and "aspiring" to a limit of 1.5%, which is positive but is nowhere near enough, especially with no penalty for lapsing or ignoring their promises. Some people are dazzled by the technological transformations already taking place—in energy, production, transportation, agriculture—but those innovations, by themselves, are not enough.

We can predict, based on our growing scientific knowledge, that there will be more bad news and more harmful impacts from climate change in our immediate future—and in our foreseeable future. Dire predictions that were formerly cloaked in scientific uncertainty are now, with further study and proof, turning out to be almost rosy in comparison to reality.

Since the 2000 elections, when challenged by facts, reality, and struggle, right-wing flacks have escalated their rhetoric, their climate change denial, and their false claims that acting to protect the natural world will destroy the economy (meaning: their profits). The next decade promises laughter for those who can get enjoyment from the increasingly ingenious excuses and attacks from the denialists. The bizarre combinations of illogic, confusion, and disinformation would be humorous if it were not that the consequences of delay are so dire. For example, Trump's claim, divorced from reality, that climate change "might reverse itself."

We can confidently predict that, as science gives us more bad news, the politics around climate change will become a bigger issue in elections around the world and that resistance to positive action will escalate in ferocity and denial.

We can also confidently predict that the costs of taking serious action on climate change will rise with every day of delay. Back in 1988 when Dr. James Hansen testified before Congress about global warming, action taken would have cost much less in the long run.[45] Action taken back in the 1950s and 60s would have cost even less.

Action taken only after the next decade will cost much more than if we start now—more in financial terms, more in human lives harmed as well. The longer we wait, the more lives will be disrupted and destroyed by the increasing effects of climate change—fresh water made unavailable, the costs of super storms on homes, infrastructure, and lives, disease ranges spreading, and so much more. We have already begun to feel these impacts. If we don't act, the impacts will become more severe, even potentially catastrophic.

When billions of people take action in their own interests and for their children, that movement can have an impact far beyond just the numbers who turn out for a demonstration. To maintain our own hope—in the face of dire scientific certainty, in the face of political betrayal and cynicism, in the face of inaction and too-limited action—is to be part of that change, part of mobilizing those billions. By our actions we become part of a better future that we create together. Even if we in the U.S. had a different, more progressive government, we would still need to build the same kind of mass movement.

This is the key to surviving the nonsense and harm from the Trump administration and its allies.[46] We can and must build that movement, since the steps that a capitalist government can make under the best of circumstances will not be enough to stave off environmental degradation and climate disaster. The insanity of moving backwards on climate change, on the promotion of coal, on sensible regulation of industry, on trade deals geared to the super-rich rather than the masses of workers, throws into high relief the importance of the work we would have to be doing anyway. The knowledge that we are building a movement for the very long haul is the knowledge that our work is necessary and independent of whichever politician is in power at the moment.

Those we are working to organize are the hope for the future for all humanity.

Chapter 3

Case Study: Arctic Issues

As climate change increases, there are challenges all over the world. These serious warning signs require humanity to act. This is even more true of the Arctic. Changes in the Arctic are more intense than elsewhere, two to four times more—meaning more warming, more melting, and great potential danger to the world's atmosphere from the carbon dioxide and methane still frozen in the permafrost.

The Arctic countries—Norway, Sweden, Finland, Russia, the U.S. due to the state of Alaska, Denmark due to Greenland and the Faroe Islands, Iceland, and Canada—have a shared interest in addressing these warning signs. But thus far they have divergent, competing interests that have taken precedence over the needs of the peoples living in the Arctic, and taken precedence over the needs of all the peoples of the world.

Forces in all of these countries are fighting over rights to drill for oil under the Arctic Sea, fighting over the "right" of some countries and alliances to militarize the region (the U.S., NATO, and Russia), fighting over shipping lanes and ports. Some see in the melting Arctic ice opportunities to drill more,[47] ship more, and to despoil and exploit an already-fragile environment. This short-sighted greed is typical of capitalism, placing short-term financial gain ahead of the survival needs of all humanity. While the official negotiating strategies of many of these countries are harmful, we shouldn't ignore the battles within each of these countries over the need to take a more environmentally-sound approach.

Many small communities are facing forced relocation due to melting permafrost, sea level rise, and extreme storms. Alaska already faces increased melting of glaciers which creates differential pressure on the underlying continental plates and as a result faces increased earthquake activity. Traditional areas for plants and animals are shifting, in some cases disappearing. Alaska faces a much higher increase in average temperature than the globe generally, as is true for the entire Arctic.

There has been a long-term struggle over drilling for oil in Alaska's far north. This battle takes on increased significance as the impacts of climate change become clearer. We need to leave fossil fuels in the ground in order to limit global warming, and there is absolutely no reason to drill for more oil in the most difficult, treacherous, fragile environments on earth.

Oil companies have been lobbying the U.S. Congress for years to allow them to drill in the Arctic National Wildlife Refuge (ANWR) and off the Alaskan coast in the Arctic Ocean. Shell Oil managed to get permission to drill in the Arctic (not in ANWR) some years ago, and over the past several years they have made efforts to implement their plans. However, they have run into major problems. One is that the harsh winds and seas they must traverse have caused all the ships and rigs they have sent to crash or suffer serious damage.

Another problem that Shell has run into is public opposition and demonstrative actions. Port districts have been pressured to not allow Shell to use their facilities. Cities have been forced to retract permits. And there have been innovative demonstrations to protest Shell. In Seattle, there was *kayaktivism*—a kayak flotilla which surrounded and delayed one of Shell's ships.[48] In Portland, protesters dangled off of bridges, hanging low enough to make it impossible for large ships to navigate.[49] While ultimately unsuccessful in stopping Shell vessels in these particular cases, the demonstrations, and the videos and photographs of them, galvanized world opinion against Shell. The cry of "sHell No!" rang in these ports of the Pacific Northwest and around the globe.

The efforts underway in many parts of the Arctic to drill for oil are especially distressing for those who have studied oil spills from tankers, oil rigs, and deep-sea oil wells. Even under much milder conditions, the BP Deepwater Horizon oil gusher in the Gulf of Mexico exposed how totally inadequate our current level of oil-spill cleanup knowledge and technology is. Companies claimed to have plans for cleanup, but these plans were at best out of date and inadequate, and at worst absolute fabrications.

In the exponentially more difficult Arctic seas, thousands of miles from major facilities of any kind and rimmed in many places by pristine wilderness, spills may prove impossible to clean up and may well be lethal to wildlife and plant species, in addition to the direct impacts of a major spill. As we know from the Exxon Valdez spill, such man-made catastrophes result in lost coastal jobs in addition to the immediate harm done to the environment.

Opposition to drilling in the Arctic needs to be worldwide. There are multiple U.S. corporations which own leases to drill off the coasts of Alaska. A Spanish oil company, Repsol, and companies from Canada, Russia, Norway, and others are studying the potential profits they could make from drilling for oil in the Arctic, even if that means threatening the environment with spills, adding carbon dioxide to the atmosphere, overwhelming or destroying indigenous communities in the process, and despoiling wildlife habitat.

However, some companies have already abandoned drilling leases, due to extreme exploration and drilling costs and fearing public condemnation and anti-corporate demonstrations. The economics of energy production are changing rapidly in favor of renewables. Many investors are learning about the economic risks to their portfolios of depending on fossil fuel companies which rely for their stock valuation on "proven" reserves of fossil fuels—which must stay in the ground. No matter the home country of a corporation, the environmental costs will be borne by all humanity.

Of particular importance for the Arctic are "black carbon" and the albedo effect. The albedo effect is a result of the Arctic ice sheet melting, which causes the darker water underneath to absorb more heat, instead of being reflected back into space by the ice and snow. Crucial to slowing global warming in the Arctic is decreasing the amount of black carbon. This comes from forest fires and diesel engines and results in a layer of soot settling on ice and snow, decreasing reflectivity and increasing the amount of heat absorbed in the area. These phenomena are also called *arctic amplification.*

Another lesser-known impact of global warming is that insect species move as the climate changes, and areas formerly immune to insect infestation can face new and devastating outbreaks. This has happened already in the Pacific Northwest, where pine beetles are attacking trees in areas where the insects formerly had difficulty surviving harsh winters. Major areas of forest in the northwest United States and British Columbia in Canada have been devastated by fungal diseases like white pine blister rust, over 60 million acres since 1990, and this particular problem will continue to move northwards as the climate warms.

Other Arctic challenges brought on by or exacerbated by global warming are ocean acidification, water and air pollution, disappearing species, erosion, as well as rapacious development practices, which most Arctic regions do not have the governmental infrastructure to limit or police.

These challenges and developing crises are not even the worst-case scenarios—these are the impacts that are happening already, with more guaranteed to come. There are even more dangerous possibilities, doomsday possibilities, which could affect the whole human race.

Another piece of the puzzle is that, as Greenland glaciers melt more rapidly than predicted, they are dumping massive amounts of fresh water into the North Atlantic. This has the potential to affect weather patterns in the Americas and in Europe, and the even more dire possibility of slowing or temporarily stopping the Gulf Stream, one of the major drivers of global ocean circulation.[50] This would bring much colder winters to all of northern Europe, affecting weather, growing seasons, agricultural productivity, and disrupting long-established ranges and conditions for agricultural products. Additionally, with warming oceans comes more evaporation, which leads to higher precipitation in some places, which can add even more fresh water to the North Atlantic. This is not a future danger, it has already started to happen.[51]

Climate change is a major stressor posing difficulties for Arctic indigenous communities, but it is not the only one. Traditional fishing and hunting grounds are changing and disappearing. Multinational corporations are bludgeoning these communities with unplanned, over-the-top development. At the same time, NATO and Russia demand the right to militarize the region.

Even in regions with relatively low populations such as the Arctic, it is people that we need to organize. Linking Arctic issues to the broader issues of environmental challenge is the key to organizing enough people to protect the Arctic from the worst excesses of capitalist development, from the rapacious drive to extract fossil fuels at any cost to nature and humanity in general.

Environmentalism must in part be about survival for the polar bears, but it must be more about the well-being of billions of people in both small and large communities. Looming extinction for various species is an important warning to us and represents tears in the fabric of life, but billions of people are who we need to reach and organize. All living things are part of the ecological web. But people are the only ones who can organize to consciously create change.

The problems already being experienced in the Arctic show the rest of the world what is headed our way if we don't make basic changes and make them quickly.

Chapter 4

Capitalism Can't Solve It

Humanity in general is not causing these problems. However, capitalism is, for the most part. Short-term, short-sighted profit as the sole measure of value underlies many of the crises which affect humanity as a whole. Capitalism, in addition to its exploitation of human labor, relies on ever-expanding markets, ever-expanding production of commodities, ever-expanding development, and ever-expanding private profit, all of which are root causes of the current imbalance between humanity and the rest of nature. Increasing capitalist globalization means a huge increase in the transport of goods, which results in huge increases in the burning of fossil fuels to run the ships, trucks, and airplanes that transport globalized commodities.

Capitalism is the root cause of most of the environmental problems we face, and the biggest obstacle to finding real solutions. Capitalism operates on a number of deadly environmental assumptions:

1. nature is "free,"
2. natural resources are limitless,
3. the waste-absorbing capacity of nature is infinite,
4. the waste-absorbing capacity of nature is free of cost,[52]
5. economic activity and the natural world are separate,
6. capitalist economic growth can be infinite on a finite world,
7. short-term profit is more important than long-term sustainability,

8. economic profit can be reasonably calculated while ignoring the social and environmental costs borne by society as a whole, and

9. the production of more commodities without end represents real progress.

These are in addition to the human exploitation and oppression that capitalism engenders and profits from.

To counter the power of the capitalist class and its control of the levers of power in much of the world, the organized power of the working class is an essential part of the force necessary to save humanity from capitalism and environmental devastation. Of course, the working class by itself is not enough. Broad alliances are necessary with all progressive forces and with other social strata such as self-employed professionals. Any analysis that ignores class divisions and capitalist shortcomings limits itself from the start.

As science fiction author Ursula Le Guin said, "We live in capitalism. Its power seems inescapable. So did the divine right of kings." Capitalism is based on a paradigm of infinite economic growth, but we live in a world which is finite, and finite and infinite are not a match. As well, capitalism is based on capitalists paying as little as possible for the production which creates their profits, and that leads most of them and their managers to ignore the needs of nature to be able to reproduce itself. Capitalist ideologues try to portray capitalism as the culmination of human history, but economic systems are not natural laws.

As students are taught in most business schools, the purpose of a corporation is to maximize value (read: profit) for the owners and shareholders. Period. Some business schools have courses in business ethics, but both in teaching business economics and in the real world, profit and shareholder value reign supreme. This is a feature of the capitalist system, not a bug. A few writers and businesspeople try to buck the trend, like Paul Hawken[53] and Nick Hanauer,[54] but they are drowned out by the cacophony of millions of business deals, millions of speculative stock transactions, and the accumulated weight of real existing capitalism.

Capitalism is the root cause of most of the environmental problems we face and is also the biggest obstacle to finding real solutions. Working class power is the only force capable of saving humanity from capitalism and creating a sustainable economy and sustainable environment.

These are class issues, and they need working class solutions. They don't rely on some magical market to solve problems for us. Working class approaches look to fundamental problems, fundamental causes, and fundamental solutions. Developing working-class consciousness is a key aspect of these solutions and approaches.

Supposed solutions which ignore the class divisions in society can at best only postpone the worst impacts of global warming, the spread of persistent organic pollutants all over the world, and other environmental crises that face humanity. Without the organized force of the working class, we are stuck with an unstable and unsustainable economic system which will cause ever-increasing environmental catastrophes.

While there is a need for more serious study to look at the details of how to make an energy transition, for example, a big factor left out of the calculations is the movement of millions for change. No plan which leaves out the necessity of winning a majority of workers and poor people to actively support change can hope to fundamentally address the complex of environmental problems which face humanity. Technological change won't help unless it is adopted by large numbers of people; conservation, unless adopted by millions, won't make much of a dent by itself; political change won't happen except by the active struggle of millions—billions around the world.

The Paris Climate Accord was a new start on international action, a significant improvement on previous multi-national efforts. Most importantly, for the first time all countries in the world agreed except Syria and Nicaragua at the start. Nicaragua at first didn't sign, stating that the agreement didn't go far enough fast enough, but after some months did sign on. Syria has been in the middle of a civil war, but finally decided to sign the agreement. That would have meant that all countries had signed, except that the U.S. under Trump has announced its withdrawal. All signing countries pledged to limit emissions to some extent, to continue to participate in international efforts to limit global warming to 2 degrees Centigrade, and even to try for 1.5 degrees of increase. But this agreement will not be enough. We should welcome these efforts, without having illusions about their effectiveness, taking full account of their limitations.[55]

As Naomi Klein argues in her book *This Changes Everything*,[56] the climate crisis and other environmental problems offer yet another reason to work for a fundamental transformation of our economic system, to build a sustainable economy that harmonizes with nature, to recognize the real limits and constraints that the earth places on industrial development.

The fundamental transformations we need will not be possible on a large scale if we depend on capitalists to engage in this transformation out of their own immediate financial self-interest. Just as only one person engaging in recycling doesn't accomplish much nor create fundamental change by itself, so too waiting for each capitalist in each industry to engage in a total redesign and the consequent investment in new equipment, processes, and products will not accomplish fundamental transformation. Of course, where individuals recycle and where businesses reinvest in redesign, we should encourage, support, and celebrate these victories. But we shouldn't buy into the illusion that individual steps by themselves will create basic change.

Individual change is most effective when harnessed to campaigns that spread the movement to millions or billions of people. Recycling will be more effective if it is adopted by millions of people. Products need to be redesigned so that when their active life is done they become raw materials for new commodities, and so that when packaging is redesigned to create less waste in total and much less that is not biodegradable. The synergy created by doing all these at once will have a much bigger impact than any one action by itself.

International Class Aspects of Environmental Issues

There are two obvious international class aspects that should be immediately apparent to anyone seriously considering the issues.

One, while the primary per capita emitters of greenhouse gases are the U.S., Australia, Japan, and Western Europe, the main victims, and among the earliest, are the masses of people in the poorest countries, who are primarily people of color. Those poorest nations are the most negatively affected by capitalist resource extraction, by imperialist oppression, by the history of European colonialism, by the problems of international debt (which benefits the major capitalist banks), and by living closest to the edge of survival already. Sometimes portrayed as a "North-South" issue, this really follows identically the centers of financial power and the current pathways of international trade. Acknowledging this is just basic humanity, but it is also class reality—the international corporations did the most to create the problem, benefit most from the way things are, and most of them are also among the main obstacles to seriously tackling solutions. Real solutions will hurt their bottom line and challenge their power and control over production decisions, hence they fight all such threats to their power and profits.

These poor nations, most affected by climate change, will also be the predominate source of climate refugees. The refugee problem in the world is already exploding due to wars, civil wars, extreme weather events, and the resource conflicts we are experiencing, and the numbers of refugees are predicted to grow exponentially. The worse the effects of climate change, the worse the world's refugee crisis will be.[57]

Two, in any class-divided society, the rich and powerful use their wealth and power to escape the consequences of any type of crisis, including environmental crisis. They seek to place the blame and the burden on workers and poor people. They seek to find ways to profit from human suffering. The rich and powerful have the largest vested interest in continuing to profit from maintaining unsustainable industry and resource-extraction.

The struggle over implementing real solutions to environmental problems is also a struggle over control—control of resources, control of institutions, control of decision-making, control of production and industrial processes, control over land and land-use, control over development, and control over the political process. These are class issues too.

The world and its people need a sustainable economic system, which includes sustainable agriculture and sustainable industrial processes. Humanity needs this for our survival. Issues of power to save the planet from environmental devastation are issues of democratic power for the majority, meaning power for workers, their families, and poor people, who together make up the overwhelming majority of all societies.

Part of the struggle is over the meaning of "sustainability." The keys to human sustainability are not gross economic measures but scientific and humanistic ones: people and nature must be the measures of sustainability, not profits. Real sustainability does not involve figuring out how to keep making profits, even excessive super-profits, from endless development and endless production of more commodities.

Sustainability is all about human survival at a level of advanced production and health. All humans have a powerful self-interest in their own survival and that of their offspring. However, when a few powerful capitalists maintain their power and enrich themselves by ignoring the need for immediate action or by obstructing positive action, it is foolish to expect them to do anything that would challenge their power and wealth.

There are differences between real solutions and PR campaigns. Changing our industrial production so that it runs on different kinds of energy in order to not create pollution in the first place is not the same as "green marketing." Major government investments in improving the efficiency and affordability of solar power are not the same as ads from British Petroleum claiming that it is now an energy company rather than an oil company. Figuring out how to better insulate our housing stock so that less energy is wasted is not the same as figuring out how to make money by speculating in carbon credits.

The reality is that the world can no longer afford the current energy system, nor the current industrial system. They both must change in order for the balance of humanity with nature to readjust to sustainable levels.

The world especially can't afford the rich anymore. The only force which, if organized, is capable of taking power away from the rich is the working class. This too is why environmental issues are working class issues. "Solutions" which ignore the class divisions in society can at best only postpone the worst impacts of global warming, and of an unsustainable economic system.

Any serious discussion of environmental solutions points to more social decision-making and to more social control over what is produced, where it is produced, and how it is produced, packaged, distributed, consumed, and disposed of. Society's ability to implement solutions requires change in political power, change in governmental structures, and change in national priorities.

Real solutions require taking power away from corporations, from the managers who run them, and from the capitalists and stockholders who profit from them. These are not just economic or scientific questions, they are questions of class power, of class exploitation and oppression, of democratic control through representative elections but also democratic control of economic decisions.

Organized workers have the potential power to wrest control of production decisions away from the capitalist class; they are the only force potentially capable of doing so. The environmental movement needs workers and alliances with and participation from unions. Unions do not only represent their members; the best ones also represent the interests of the working class as a whole. For example, the teacher's strikes in 2018 in West Virginia, Oklahoma, and Arizona demanded not only better pay for workers who have suffered years of cutbacks to their compensation, they also placed the needs of their mainly working class students for books and enrichment programs as central to the teacher's struggle. They were not fighting for themselves in a narrow way, they were fighting for themselves and the students and the communities they serve. The environmental movement needs these workers and their unions as essential elements of the fight for a better world for all of us.

Environmental issues, like issues of nuclear war and peace, are class issues but also affect all humanity. As a result, it is possible and necessary to gather, around working-class forces for change, broad coalitions that include cross-class elements. This is not a substitute for working class leadership and organization, but can complement it and bring additional strength to the movement for an environment that can sustain all humanity.

A No-Growth Economy?

When world leaders met in Paris in December 2015 to negotiate a new international climate change agreement, major media finally, for a moment, paid more attention to climate change issues, covering studies, acknowledging demonstrations around the world, and reporting the major climate change encyclical issued by Pope Francis.[58]

Increasing numbers of scientists, commentators, and environmental activists have come to the conclusion that humanity needs a no-growth economy to stave off environmental catastrophe.[59] Various studies and projections show that, based on reasonable assumptions about the potential to shift the energy industry to a more sustainable path and assumptions about population growth, huge changes in production, consumption, transportation and human reproduction are essential.[60]

This viewpoint is based on a basic problem faced by capitalism: the fundamental design of a capitalist system requires constant and endless economic growth, and that design is at odds with the reality of a finite world. This is a conundrum that capitalism and capitalists cannot solve—it doesn't depend on political will or on the intentions, good or otherwise, of individual capitalists. Even with the best of plans and intentions, unlimited growth on an earth with limited resources cannot work much longer without even more serious negative consequences. Many complementary strategies need to be adopted simultaneously to prevent climate disaster.

There are several problems with the analysis offered by these no-growth commentators and studies.[61]

Little or no account is taken of conservation efforts to protect existing rainforests, to save wetlands, to expand passive land and parks, or to protect fresh-water resources. Conservation, adopted on a mass scale, can reduce human impact on earth—conservation can be one of a range of powerful options which can work together and reinforce each other— renewable energy[62], industrial and agricultural redesign, plus many more.

Projections based on current economic factors can lead to major mistakes—for example, previous projections about the economic viability of solar power were based on the assumptions of the time. Those projections were based in large part on the then-current costs and limited efficiency of solar and on conservative assumptions about technological improvement. Those projections have proven to be way off—the price of solar has fallen dramatically, due to economies of scale as production ramped up, due to rapid technological progress in the efficiency of solar cells and due to improvements in production processes.[63] So making dire predictions based on such assumptions can lead to false conclusions and to bad decision-making. Based on the projections of a few years ago, many assumed that increasing nuclear power rapidly was the only path to low-carbon energy, even given the risks and given that no one has figured out what to do with radioactive waste. Those calculations today look very different.

Some of the assumptions of the argument that population growth is the main cause of environmental problems are based on what is politically and economically feasible at this specific time in the U.S. But that too is likely to undergo major changes as the costs of business-as-usual and the damages from climate change escalate. Assumptions based on maintaining capitalism can also be off by several orders of magnitude, especially as we get decades into the future. While it would be foolish to expect fundamental changes in a short period of time, the closing window on the time humanity has to create solutions to the climate crisis will force more radical changes to our economics and politics.

No-growth scenarios mostly focus exclusively on economic consumption. This means that consumption and therefore standards of living would of necessity decrease.[64] Bill McKibben claims that, *"we might choose instead to try to manage our descent . . . we might aim for a relatively graceful decline."*[65]

But focusing more broadly on ways of increasing human satisfaction without increasing production would enable us to envision a better way—we could decrease the production of commodities for sale at the same time we increase creative opportunities, cultural and educational enhancement and life-long learning, eliminate oppression of many kinds, and generate a much more equitable world. We could eliminate the luxuries of the wealthy and distribute necessities, essential appliances, and services much more broadly.

One of the claims used to support no-growth arguments is to point, correctly, to all the ways in which industrial production harms health. This ignores that much of the harm from industrial production comes from the changes in industry which followed World War II. Just as industry decisions made those changes, production could be changed to more environmentally-sound practices. Specific kinds of production changes are responsible for the most harm to the environment and to human health. We *don't* have to stop expanding every single kind of production to improve our balance with nature. We *do* have to require that the public health and public environmental interests play a predominate role in production decisions.[66]

Too many environmental studies and paradigms (such as the widely used "carbon footprint" calculations) use per capita data that ignores huge income disparities and hence the huge disparities in consumption. Capitalists, especially the super-rich, are personally responsible for much more overconsumption of goods, for the disproportionate impact of luxury goods, and for cheating the poor of their fair share of the consumption of essentials by distorting economies. For example, some countries in Central America which used to be self-sufficient in food are now forced to import more expensive food due to the large areas of agricultural land that have been converted to production of export goods like cut flowers—driven by the need to pay down the international debt forced on them by international banks. There are no reasons, except profit and imperialist power, that this could not be reversed. According to some studies, the top 10% of the population worldwide accounts for approximately 50% of greenhouse gas emissions.[67]

Another way that using national averages confuses the issue is that decision-making power and authority are not evenly distributed—most people get no vote on whether or not to build a coal-fired power plant. Bad economic and environmental decision-making is much more the fault of the super-rich and their bought-and-paid-for politicians and managers.

In one major way, these studies understate the environmental problems we face. Climate change is the largest, most threatening, and most comprehensive set of problems we must deal with, but it is far from the only environmental crisis that is looming or already here. Climate change studies often focus on economics and energy production, but ignore other environmental problems, including acidifying oceans and fishery collapse, the spread of organic pollutants which affect human and animal reproductive systems, decreasing soil fertility, increasing water stresses of many kinds due to many causes, deforestation and increasing forest fires, and many more. Adding these into the mix argues for more fundamental change more quickly. A comprehensive look requires consideration of agriculture and diet,[68] sensible population limitation measures, transportation, construction, social and health programs, pollution of many kinds, and more.

The proponents of no-growth environmental economics are correct, but only as long as we limit ourselves to the way capitalism functions, only if we accept the limitations and assumptions of the capitalist system. Capitalism will reproduce the same basic problems due to elevating private profit into a god and endless economic growth as a dogma.

If we instead picture a future with more equality of income and opportunity, with non-economic needs factored into our measures of human satisfaction and happiness (rather than just gross GDP averages), where societies promote conservation as a way to decrease production and energy wastage, then we can begin to see a way that human life for the vast majority can be improved without increasing harmful production or burning more fossil fuel. If major countries invest more in research and development to solve technological problems and then capture the economic benefits of their discoveries such that the benefits spread to all of society and to all countries, even more is possible.

Everything is Connected, Including Human Social Systems

Ultimately, we need a socialist society (see Part 5). But we can't wait for socialism, we must act now. We must make a start right now, even given the capitalist system's domination of the world's economy. We can:

- change accounting systems to include so-called "externalities" in corporation profit considerations,
- adopt aspects of the Chinese-initiated "green GDP" calculations or Bhutan's measures of "gross National Happiness," though these too have limitations,
- increase tax rates on polluting companies,
- adjust the price of goods to include disposal costs,
- grant tax credits to companies that adopt large-scale environmental improvements,
- change industrial processes to eliminate the production of pollution (in some cases creating more profit in the process),
- trade elimination of international debt in exchange for maintaining existing rainforest stock, and
- use public pressure campaigns to force corporations to change practices such as the over-cutting of timber and illegal anti-union campaigns.

Anti-sweatshop campaigns, corporate accountability campaigns, NGO-sponsored international boycotts against environmentally-destructive corporate practices, restrictions on the free flow of capital which is used to evade labor and environmental standards, will all help. Simply enforcing existing U.S. environmental regulations and laws would help, especially if the EPA is funded to hire enough investigators to do the necessary enforcement.

Finding ways to trade elimination of international debt in return for maintaining existing rainforest stocks is one innovative idea. Though the rainforests of the Amazon, Siberia, and Indonesia are a resource for the whole planet, the people of the whole planet do not pay for the resource. So those who live in and near the rainforest, stuck in dire poverty, are often forced by bitter, immediate necessity to cut down trees for charcoal, clear land for farming and housing, and sell to large corporations who cut forests by bulldozing massive amounts of land for grazing cattle. If we find a way to compensate the people who live there for maintaining the resource for the benefit of the whole planet, we can change the equation that now works against the rainforests.

Any of these steps can contribute to the solution. But the problems are fundamental, so the overall solutions need to be fundamental—band-aids and antiseptic creams can't heal cancer. Solutions to collective problems must be collective solutions. Solutions to worldwide problems must be worldwide solutions.

Such solutions require marshalling all available resources because of the scale involved:

- to gather the massive capital investment to redesign industry to end the production of greenhouse gases and other pollution,
- to fund the huge outlays to alter our agricultural systems to use less water, deplete less soil, feed local populations first,
- and to fund the up-front investment necessary to change to more sustainable, labor-intensive, organic, less monoculture farming.

These investments are mostly not going to be profit-making in the beginning; they are just necessary for human survival.

Even when changes will be profitable in the long term, that is of little interest to capitalist investors who only see their desire for short-term excess profits. What we see instead is increasing rates of extraction, because that pays off more in the immediate future. This is pennywise but pound foolish, and capitalism thrives on this approach because the immediate profits go to a few, while the long-term costs are borne by the many. Sooner or later, all non-renewable resources are going to run out, so we need to begin to slow down the rate at which we are depleting them; that is simple common sense.

Only a system that puts the needs of people and nature ahead of profits will ultimately work, a system that uses measures of human survival and the greatest good for the most people, rather than using measures of the short-term profit of the few at the long-term expense of everyone, including the capitalists themselves. We need humanitarian ways to measure social and economic progress, rather than using "the market" and only the market as an all-encompassing framework, because that imposes limits incompatible with many of the changes we need to make for human survival. The capitalist system is an obstacle to the solutions our survival requires.

Fundamental economic, social, and political changes are also necessary because without them, our countries and economies will become more unequal as they come under more stress from changes in nature. Without justice and equality for all, this will lead to social cataclysms, to destructive warfare, to repression. It will lead to battles over water that destroy water, battles over fossil fuels that destroy some of the limited fossil fuels left, battles over food that destroy food, battles over land that destroy the agricultural capacity of the land, and battles over survival that will kill many more then are "saved" on the "winning" side.

Chapter 5

What is the Working Class Anyway?

Some environmentalists think that since environmental crises threaten all humanity, we should address all humanity as our audience, that it "should" be sufficient to just appeal to good people everywhere. Since everyone is affected, everyone has a self-interest in fixing the problems. While this may be a truism, it doesn't correspond to the way the political and economic worlds work. Confronting a system resistant to change, with entrenched political and economic powers eager to maintain their "profits-as-usual" way of operating, requires a counter-vailing organized power to institute change.

The most powerful element of that countervailing force resides in the working class, the vast majority of humanity which works for a living, which under capitalism has to subordinate itself to the often-dictatorial commands of corporations. The ability of workers to stop working and thus bring the economy to a halt is a tremendous power. The potential political power inherent in the position of workers in the economy is exactly the power necessary to transform our current economic and political reality to one based on providing the greatest good for the greatest number of people.

What is the working class? The working class is made up of all who work for a living, who make the preponderance of their income from a job, no matter their level of income or skill. The working class is the vast majority of all societies. The working class is not defined by income level but by people's

main relationship to the means of production, to the ownership or lack thereof of the companies that employ them.

In the U.S., the working class is often hidden behind an
obfuscation of income categories. Most mainstream statistical
breakdowns of the U.S. population, and typical poll categories, focus on the "middle class." A huge amount of discussion in U.S. national political campaigns and public discourse
singles out middle-class issues—middle class income,
middle class prospects, why the middle class is declining, tax
rates for the middle class. But almost all those categorized
as middle-class work for a living. Many of them, like most
lower-paid workers, are only a few paychecks away from
abject poverty.

The phrase *middle class* obscures more than it elucidates.
People who have what is called a middle-class income are in
reality just somewhat better-paid workers, and sometimes not
that much better paid at that. People who work for a living
are workers, no matter the level of their income. Higher-paid
workers are still workers and have much more in common
with lower-paid workers than with top-level managers,
owners, and major stockholders. Service workers are workers,
entry-level workers are workers, highly-paid engineers are
workers. Doctors are starting to unionize, discovering that
their high levels of education and training don't protect them
from the impositions of health care and insurance companies,
which are in fact often huge corporations more interested in
the financial bottom line than in human health or in decent
working conditions for health-care professionals.

Ownership of all the equipment and machinery in the
world accomplishes nothing without workers to run it—even
computerized machinery which hones metal to high toler-
ances needs workers to design, manufacture, and assemble
the computers, engineers to design the programs, program-
mers to find and fix the bugs. Robotization is moving ahead
at a rapid clip, a process that will only speed up, but it still
takes people doing work to make everything run. All of the
worries about robotization displacing workers are really
worries about capitalism. If the benefits of technological
improvement were shared by society as a whole, robots and

computerization of the workplace wouldn't be a threat but rather a bonus for all workers.

One sign that middle class is a fictional social category is that no one agrees on exactly what constitutes a middle-class income. Different economists and statisticians place the barrier between lower-paid workers and middle-class workers at radically different levels. It is not a scientific category with a clear definition; it is a way to avoid talking about the common interests of workers of all incomes.

What Do All Workers Have in Common?

They all work for a living, they all work for bosses, they all have to give up at least some of their rights (sometimes implicitly, sometimes explicitly) in order to hold a job. They are all subject to company discipline, they all have at best a limited say in decisions which affect their lives, they all have part of the value of their labor appropriated to pay the high salaries of CEOs, to fund stock dividends, and to pay interest to banks on business loans. Almost all workers, except for a few who work for co-ops and worker-owned enterprises, work in dictatorships—there is no democracy on the factory floor or in the kitchens of fast food outlets, unless workers unionize and demand a say. Even then, the democracy is limited and almost always under attack. Capitalists claim that socialism won't work because it is a command economy, but all major capitalist enterprises are command economies, with top-down leadership, imposed policies, and work organization geared to maximize profit. Wal-Mart is but one extreme example of an international, top-down, tightly controlled command economy.

All workers also have a unique power—the power to stop working. When one worker stops, it may not mean much, but when workers unite and stop work together, it matters quite a bit. They can, through collective action, stop production, or stop providing service, or stop selling whatever is being sold. When key workers, like longshoremen or teamsters or railroad workers, threaten to strike, it is seen as a national crisis requiring the intervention of the country's political leaders to bring it to a resolution. Truman nationalized the railroads to stop a strike; Bush personally intervened in a longshore dispute which threatened to shut down all major ports on the West Coast. When truckers in France go on strike, it brings much of the economy of the whole country to a stop. This ability, to band together and stop work, is the basis for all union power. It is the stick on the union side in all negotiations, paired with the carrot of continued profits for the company if work continues or resumes. Political and social crises can cause an uproar, but don't bring the economy to a screeching halt. Only workers can do that. That power is at the root of why the environmental movement needs workers, because the environmental movement confronts and threatens the power of the corporations and needs the countervailing power of the working class to transform the entire economy.

Environmental approaches that blame "all of us" ignore the class divisions in society, ignore the predominant role of money, wealth, and power in governmental and economic decision-making, ignore that the financial benefits from the economy as currently constructed go disproportionately to the top few percent of the population (in other words, to the biggest capitalists), and ignore who within society has a vested interest in preventing change.

The slow and ineffective responses following Hurricane Katrina in New Orleans and the equally slow and bungled response in Puerto Rico following Hurricane Maria[69] prove the existence of widespread poverty in the U.S., prove that the government and government agencies (i.e. the U.S. Army Corps of Engineers and FEMA) often act against the interests of poor and working people, prove that the oppressed and exploited do not share in the benefits of our "high standard of living" (which has been going down or stagnating for the majority for decades), and prove that staggering levels of inequality and injustice exist within a supposedly "rich" society.

Such class divisions within developed industrial countries show that the conflict is not between the "rich North" and the "poor South," it is between capitalists and rich landowners the world over on the one hand, and workers, family farmers, and poor people the world over on the other.

International divisions between countries and continents are really class issues, and divisions inside countries are class divisions too. But the class angles of global warming (and other environmental crises) don't stop there. In any class-divided society, the rich and powerful use their wealth and power to escape the consequences of any crisis. They seek to place the blame and burden on workers and poor people. They seek to profit from human suffering.[70] They have a vested interest in continuing to profit from business-as-usual, and have a vested interest in preventing progressive change and any fundamental shift in social power dynamics.

Many who understand that fundamental change is needed nonetheless ignore or dismiss the working class as the main force for accomplishing that change. Some propose vague ideas of environmental activists not directly connected to any actual class struggle implementing fundamental change, just because we need change: a version of "all good people should just get together." These are forms of utopianism, advocated by people who have good intentions and reach for optimism.

But unfortunately, change doesn't happen just because it "should" or "must." There have to be real and powerful organized forces which propel that change. Social change starts from small groups of people, but has to reach, inspire, lead, activate, and organize millions (billions when we speak of worldwide change). Only such a force has the potential power to implement fundamental change. In our times, that is only the working class, which worldwide is larger than it has been at any time in history (though this is not to suggest limiting environmental struggles only to workers).

Another confusion that some spread about the working class is that, because the composition of the working class in the U.S. is changing, that means that workers are no longer important. We have a service economy, or a new economy, or an information economy, as if all such work was no longer performed by actual workers. It is true that there are more service workers than ever in the U.S.; it is true that robotization and computerization are eliminating many traditional jobs. But internationally, the industrial working class is larger than ever before. These workers may work in smaller, decentralized industries, may not labor in massive factories with tens of thousands of workers, but they do the work on which all the economies of the world are based. And they are not disappearing.

In order to reflect reality, our definition of who is part of the working class must be very broad, even as the composition of the working class changes. The working class is not only made up of white male "blue collar" workers, it is racially, nationally, ethnically diverse, made up of people of many ages, genders, skill levels, education levels—everyone who gains the main financial means of survival by working for someone else.

As we redefine the concept of quality of life to include more cultural and artistic work, this will be performed by artistic and cultural workers, who will be workers nevertheless, an integral part of the working class. Lifelong education requires workers to teach; health care for all requires well-equipped workers who are often highly-trained specialists; workers such as longshoremen who have organized to win significantly higher pay than most are still workers. Intensive organic agriculture requires more agricultural workers, some of whom may help ameliorate the problems of rapid urbanization around the world by moving to rural areas as more rural jobs become available. All of these workers still work for a boss, for a corporation, and experience attacks on their rights and living standards. These workers have in common with all a need to unite to fight for democracy, both political and economic on-the-job democracy.

Workers of the World, Unite to Save the World

From the start, Communists and most socialists around the world have prided themselves on international solidarity, on placing the needs of the working class as a whole above the needs of any one section of the class. They have boldly proclaimed that workers represent the solutions of the future in the struggles of the present.

Marx and Engels, in the Communist Manifesto, wrote:

> The Communists are distinguished from the other
> working-class parties by this only: 1. In the national

struggles of the proletarians of the different countries, they point out and bring to the front the
common interests of the entire proletariat, independently of all nationality. 2. In the various stages
of development which the struggle of the working
class against the bourgeoisie has to pass through,
they always and everywhere represent the interests
of the movement as a whole.

This approach has renewed relevance for the posture that
communists, socialists, radicals, and progressives take on
environmental issues.

Climate change, along with other environmental issues. has
increasing international importance in determining the future
of humanity, of which workers and poor people are the vast,
vast majority. The need for a future with clean air, clean water,
for ecosystems free of persistent organic pollutants, and for
sufficient food, shelter, and health care, is threatened by the
continuing growth in greenhouse gas emissions, by our current agricultural practices, by the current systems of production, distribution, and waste disposal.

A step forward in the process of building international labor
solidarity could be to develop international unity around
issues of occupational health and safety, a concern for workers
everywhere. Unions already have some international programs and relationships in place, and building links between
unions, sharing information and strategies, and waging joint
campaigns, possibly industry by industry, can create unity
among workers around the globe. This can bring unions into
aspects of environmental struggles, utilize the growing body
of science about workplace safety, and link health and safety
issues on the job with health and safety struggles in working
class communities.

The mining, production, and transportation of coal provides a contentious set of issues. President Obama, while he
spoke about the importance of addressing climate change,
also supported continued growth in coal production and
the expansion of fracking. This so-called "all-of-the-above"
energy strategy ignores the reality of the growth in green-

house gas emissions and ignores, as Bill McKibben put it in a major *Rolling Stone* article,[71] the basic math of how much fossil fuel is left in the ground and how much greenhouse gases can be emitted in order to stay within the margin of safety for humanity. Short-term jobs and GDP growth can increase with more fracking, but that would decrease our chances for limiting global warming and would increase the number of earthquakes in regions which had very few before fracking, such as Oklahoma.[72]

There are a variety of struggles taking place about coal. These include struggles over the building of new coal-fired electrical plants. They include struggles over whether or not some West Coast ports will expand their facilities to enable a dramatic increase in rail traffic to export huge quantities of coal to China. They also include struggles over mine safety (coal companies often ignore mine safety laws, sometimes resulting in many deaths) and mining practices such as mountaintop removal and the disposal of toxic waste, especially contaminated water, from the mining process.

Any serious environmental program must include provisions for job retraining for displaced workers, for job creation in new energy production and conservation, for addressing the damage to local communities when large-scale changes are made in areas dependent on the coal industry. Environmentalists must find common cause with workers who suffer environmental hazards on the job (such as black-lung disease), suffer environmental hazards in the communities where they live (the bursting of "waste containment" holding tanks and pools into drinking water, for example), and suffer the general environmental challenges facing all people.

Coal miners are not the enemy. They face the most direct negative health effects on their jobs, with high rates of asthma and other respiratory diseases, and have only such safety regulations and health care as have been forced on the mining companies by the federal government.

But the short-term need for jobs in a particular area cannot supersede the long-term needs of the entire working class or of humanity as a whole.

The progressive left of the political spectrum must project a program that addresses the needs of the whole working class, alongside other democratic demands. When the Left or the union movement ignore or downplay how serious our environmental challenges are, they can only project short-term policies that are counter-productive to building the necessary unity.

To give the working class a "choice" of jobs all of which will harm humanity in the long run is no choice at all, and no favor to those workers either. And the long run is increasingly right here, right now. Many of the predicted effects of climate change are already happening, already changing our world, already making it a more difficult place, already placing many in harm's way.

It is essential that the movement for environmental progress be coupled with demands for environmental justice and for living-wage green jobs, retraining, extended and expanded unemployment insurance, and health care for all.

The needs of humanity must take precedence over the short-term interests of one group or another, and over one country or another. This is not just a matter of theory or ideology, it is a matter of science and survival.

To have a strategy which can encompass all this complexity requires a consistent philosophical approach, one that is principled, persistent, and realistic, based on an understanding of how change happens in the real world. Such a philosophical approach is the subject of the next section.

Part Two:
The Philosophy

Chapter **6**

Radical Environmental Philosophy

Dialectics, Very, Very Briefly Defined

Marxist philosophy is called Dialectical Materialism. It attempts a nuanced study of patterns of change rooted in objective reality. This outlook presents a unified view of human activity and nature, of which humans are an active part.

Dialectics is the study of change, of how and why change happens, and of the observable features and patterns of change. Everything is actually a process, so dialectics views the world as a complex of processes which constantly change and constantly affect each other. Any phenomenon we observe represents only a temporary equilibrium of opposing material forces, a momentary "snapshot" in a process that came from change and leads to more change.

When water is heated, there is a slow accumulation of small quantitative changes, until the critical threshold of 212 degrees Fahrenheit is reached, the water boils, and water transforms into steam. When water is heated, there is a struggle between forces trying to keep water molecules bonded to each other and forces trying to pry them apart. The difference in the water between 180 degrees and 181 degrees is minimal, but the accumulation of heat, one degree at a time, ultimately leads to water's tipping point and transformation to a new phase of matter, steam.

All processes have points at which they change to a qualitatively new state; however, we don't always know where those points are with the precision and predictability of water becoming steam, or transforming into ice at colder tempera-tures. All processes are also subject to the pressures of other systems—for example, the exact boiling point of water changes depending on what elevation you are boiling it at, due to vari-ations in atmospheric pressure.

Everything changes and in the process goes through phases during which small changes accumulate relatively slowly. These changes have both internal and external causes. At some point (exactly which point is different for each process), as a result of those accumulated quantitative changes the existing equilibrium breaks, leading to *qualitative* change, to a revolu-tionary leap to a new state of existence.

Human systems don't stay the same any more than the systems of nature. Human systems also have contradictions; among them are contending classes which drive change.

Dialectical materialism helps us understand the paradox of why, in a class-divided society, scientific, technological, and industrial development leads to increased poverty and income stagnation rather than to shared improvements in the living standards of all people, why exponential increases in the world's productive capacity and food supply have not elimi-nated poverty, hunger, or homelessness. It provides us with the means to understand, and ultimately reverse, the deep-ening hunger, poverty, and social crises caused by capitalism. It helps illuminate the causes, interactions, and potential solu-tions of the growing environmental crises faced by humanity.

Human consciousness is the combined social and indi-vidual reflection of reality, and builds on accomplishments and understandings that grew from previous human activity and thought. The reflection of reality in human conscious-ness inevitably lags changes in reality; this lag alone can cause errors in human thought and action. Time, effort, and activity are essential parts of the process of understanding and knowing. Understanding takes time and effort and grows not only from study and abstract reasoning but from the process of doing.

Dialectics is a way of thinking about the patterns of dynamic change in the real world. But dialectical laws are not mathe-matical formulae. Dialectics can't function as an equation that gives us a simple solution based on straightforward computation. Dialectics can't tell us exactly where each tipping point is, because it is different for each process and changes over time and in relation to other pressures. Dialectics won't somehow automatically illuminate all the details we don't yet know about nature or how all the processes of nature interact.

Dialectics is a series of propositions about how to think about the world and its interacting parts. It suggests questions to ask and patterns of change to look for in any process. There is a structure, an architecture, of all change, which plays out in unique ways in each process.

Dialectics is not a series of "truths" to memorize, but rather a way of thinking that helps us get to root causes, to the fundamental nature of whatever we are trying to understand better. Dialectics is a method to use to reach understanding, *not the understanding itself.*

We always need to look at the interconnections of a process with the rest of the world, look for the essential quantitative and qualitative changes taking place, look for the history and trends of the process, and look for the intersections between human and natural processes. We must always look to the connections of any issue with both smaller and larger systems, and pose questions so they are big enough to get an answer that fully addresses the issue. Dialectics tells us that the truth is always the dynamic whole, not merely in the parts considered in a linear or mechanical fashion.

Static, mechanical approaches and constructs don't fit the natural world; they can't flow with the interacting evolution of multiple networks of linked living organisms. Analysis based on appearance and form, rather than essence and content, is always superficial. We need to understand processes more deeply if we want to make informed decisions that result in real progress based on understanding matter in motion.

For example, some scientists locked themselves into studying the fertility of the soil as if it was only a matter of chemical processes, identifying which chemical needed to be boosted to increase agricultural yields. "Their research increasingly zeroed in on the individual parts of the soil, losing sight of it as a complex biological system. Soil biology and soil fertility came to be viewed as consequences of soil properties, rather than as key influences on them."[73]

Processes are connected across any boundaries we see or construct. Human biology is a socialized biology—the significance of something depends on its social and natural context. Organisms select, transform, and define their own environments even as they are limited by those environments. Ideas become an active part of human nature and society, interacting to change the social conditions that helped bring the ideas into existence in the first place.

Things are the way they are, but they haven't always been that way and they won't always be that way. We need to not only see what things look like now but also learn what they used to be like, what their trajectory is, what their connections to other changing processes consist of, and what external and internal contradictions and forces drive each process.

Studying Marxism is one part of developing the understanding necessary to create change. As Michael Parenti put it:

> Marxism is not a science in the positivist sense, formulating narrow hypotheses and testing for predictability, slicing up bits of reality for microscopic examination. It is a science that shows us how rather than what to think, how to conceptualize systematically and systemically, moving from the particular to the larger forces that are at work, from surface appearances to deeper things, so better to understand how social relations and class structure interact, and how they shape human experience.

He goes on:

> Marxism is also a holistic science in that it recognizes, rather than denies, the linkages between various components of the entire system, be it the mass media, criminal justice, Congress, racism, transportation, sexism, housing, military intervention abroad, unemployment, elections, or whatever, we will see how that part reflects, within its own particularities, the

nature of the whole, and how in its specific dynamic
it serves the larger system—especially the system's
overriding class interests.[74]

Many questions that climate change raises relate directly to
aspects of Marxist philosophy: the interconnectedness of all
things; the world as a complex of interlocked processes; "tipping point" qualitative transformations that arise from seemingly small quantitative changes; the unity and struggle of
opposites including within the natural basis of life; the back-
and-forth exchanges between the processes of nature and the
activity of humans. Dialectical thinking is the cure for mechanical, linear models which limit our appreciation of the multiple
complex adaptive system interactions which surround us.

Environmental examples illustrate dialectical principles,
and dialectical thinking illuminates the interconnectedness of
human systems with the processes of the natural world.[75] This
section is not intended to be comprehensive about either, but
to be a start at integrating these concepts.

What's Wrong with Either-Or Thinking

Dialectical thinking corresponds more accurately to how
nature works than either-or, mechanical thinking. If we are
going to adapt to nature rather than have nature adapt against
us, we need to learn to think in the way that natural systems
work, seeing complexity, multidimensionality, contradictory
aspects, and both slow and sudden changes. Change is contradictory, multidimensional, and multidirectional.

Much of the history of logic, science, and philosophical
systems has been plagued with linear, either-or, reductionist
thinking. Either something exists or it doesn't. Either one
thing is true or its opposite is true; they can't both be true. This
kind of logic can be useful when considering abstract ideas
and propositions. However, it doesn't correspond to the way
the world actually works.

In the real world, contradictory things are often true. They
are often, oddly, mutually reinforcing. What may logically

seem like mutually exclusive opposites can both be true at one and the same time, can even be mutually necessary. For example, global warming is causing the edges of the ice fields in Antarctica to shrink. At the same time, warmer water and a warmer atmosphere lead to more moisture in the air, which leads to more snowfall in colder areas, which leads to a thickening in the middle of some ice fields. Warmer weather on average and more snowfall in some places are both occurring. Although a few ice fields and glaciers are expanding, most around the world are shrinking at historically unprecedented rates. Global warming leads to melting ice fields which leads to colder water in the oceans, which flow to temperate zones, temporarily chilling them, delaying the full warming process. We are experiencing more severe floods *and* more severe droughts.

We need to learn to think dialectically, to understand the contradictory nature of processes and relationships, to understand the constant change that flows from contradictory struggles, to understand that small constant changes cause processes to reach tipping points where some aspect of nature "flips" to a new state.

Another limitation of some scientific study is a tendency to postulate an artificial barrier between "closed" systems which do not interact with the rest of the world, and "open" systems which interact outside themselves. In reality, the differences between these two types of systems are matters of degree, not of kind. Supposedly closed systems react outside themselves too, just at different paces or scales. There is no totally closed system, and while research can sometimes develop knowledge by acting as if a system is closed (to limit complexity and highlight which factors are most crucial within that system), science must recognize that such limits are limits of knowledge and research, not limits of reality. These perceived limits are due to our incomplete understanding of reality.

Many of the recent efforts to develop a science of complexity seem as if these scientists (such as the work of the Santa Fe Institute[76]) are rediscovering the laws of dialectics. Webs of interactions, patterns of non-linear change, structures of interconnection, network effects, patterns of change and interaction that replicate in natural systems at all scales and that replicate in human systems, communication systems, and electronic systems—all these reinforce the importance of dialectical thinking. These efforts are adding to and integrating important related concepts such as emergence, self-organization, clusters and hubs, and also providing mathematical, biological, and sociological proofs.

The Necessity of Theory, the Primacy of Practice

Reality is the test of our theories, the measure of what we are doing to save our environment and how well and quickly we are doing it. There is much we don't yet know about how all the natural processes on which our lives depend will react to more carbon dioxide in the atmosphere, to rising sea levels, to changing weather patterns, to the overuse of limited fresh water. We have theories, which many climate scientists have used to create computer models, but none of these can fully anticipate real life developments in all their complexity. There is great uncertainty in climate science; there is much to learn before we have it all "figured out."

Reality trumps theory, but without theory, we have no way to understand reality. Theory without practice is empty; practice without theory is blind. Theory is often required to figure out the right questions to ask. We need theory to inform us about where to start. In the process, we will make mistakes or ask the wrong questions for a time. But we will discover new aspects of reality as we go, and improve our theories in the process.

Break It Apart, Put It Back Together, and Understand Time, Place, and Circumstance

To understand any phenomenon, we first have to divide it, classify its constituent parts, and learn to understand which internal processes have the greatest impact. This much scientists have gotten very good at—fragmenting reality into ever-smaller segments and specializing in understanding the details of each piece. The trick is then to put it back together, to understand how the different parts stand in relation to each other and, even further, to understand how one particular phenomenon interrelates with and impacts other processes.

Oddly, this problem has been exacerbated with the rapid growth of scientific knowledge, leading to increased specialization. As soil scientist Sir Albert Howard noted long ago, some scientists seem "intent on learning more and more about less and less."[77] This has led to neglecting the essential work of generalizing and integrating new knowledge from many fields. The truth is not only in the details, it also lies in connecting the details to the grand patterns and processes of the whole world.

We can't look at any one system abstracted from the organic natural setting in which it exists, not if we seek real understanding. If we only look at systems in their separateness, it can result in solving one problem at the expense of creating new, worse problems. Our solutions have to mesh with each other, and mesh with all the intersecting systems which give rise to an integrated series of problems. Linked systems co-evolve, so fixing one without working on the rest can be self-defeating.

An example is the introduction of multiflora rose shrubs as a natural hedge for grazing lands in the 1950s in the eastern U.S. The shrubs aggressively invaded farmer's fields, leaving little room for cattle to graze. It is now outlawed in certain states, with penalties for people who do not remove this plant.[78] Some tried to solve one problem but ended up creating a worse one.

Time, place, and circumstance matter—they are dimensions of the interactions between systems and processes and affect those interactions. For example, there have been times when small atmospheric changes resulted in small climatic changes and other times when the same small atmospheric changes triggered major climatic transformations.

This can be applied to our understanding of the very origins of life on our planet. A paradox which stalled our understanding of the origin of life was that under present-day conditions, life could not have arisen on earth. It would have oxidized before it had a chance to get started. In the 1920s, a Soviet biochemist, Oparin, showed that the present environment on earth is in part a product of life. The pre-life earth had a different atmosphere which was conducive to the start of life. But once life developed, the existence of life added great amounts of oxygen to our atmosphere, altering it in ways that facilitate the continuation of life rather than its origination. Sometimes called the Oparin-Haldane theory, it was developed independently by British scientist and Marxist J.S. Haldane. While it appears that several of the assumptions they made, for example about the nature of the atmosphere while life was developing, may be incorrect, it was an important step forward in understanding the development of life. More recently, there have been several other theories about life's origin[79] as well.[80]

Constant Change, Matter in Motion

We easily observe patterns of change on the scale of human life: we all are born, mature, decline, and die. Every one of us goes through this process, unless we die before we have the opportunity to mature.

But just because change is not always observable on a human time scale doesn't mean that what we see is permanent and unchangeable. Everything we see, feel, and experience is in a process of either coming into being, maturing, declining, or passing out of existence. Everything. No exceptions. All of existence is matter in motion, from the internal quantum particles inside atoms to the movement of planets and even solar systems. All changes in things and processes affect other processes and relationships. Everything exhibits this progression, some at a faster pace, some progressions change much more slowly.

We are now able to measure the small accumulations of pressure in tectonic plates which lead to cataclysmic geological change. Continents spilt apart due to the action of the earth's crust. Mountains arise from volcanic action, thrusting up into seemingly permanent form, until, like Mt. St. Helens, they erupt again and collapse partially or completely. Rocks are worn away by water until they break up and disintegrate. Microorganisms in the earth break down rock particles to create the mineral elements in soil. The continent of Australia is moving fast enough, in relative terms, that it causes problems for accurate GPS system tracking.

No matter how permanent some phenomenon appears to be, there are internal processes going on within it, and changes due to outside pressures from its environment.

The human history of the last 10,000 years has taken place during a largely warm period within the much longer history of the earth's climatic transformations. Just because the climate and most geologic systems haven't fundamentally changed during the last 10,000 years, we have no reason to think the same will be true in the years ahead of us. Many weather and geological events that operate on cycles of thousands of years are going to happen again, even if it has been thousands of years since the last occurrence. Cycles related to the earth's orbit, tilt, and wobble operate on cycles of approximately 22,000, 40,000, and 100,000 years,[81] and that isn't something we can or should try to change. Changes in these cycles affect earth's climate, and humans can either recognize that reality and adjust to it or ignore it at our peril. Though totally catastrophic change is not likely in our lifetime, we have to prepare future generations for the realities they will confront. Our choices now will help determine whether those realities will be better or worse, will help determine if future choices will be easier or more difficult.

We are starting to understand that evolutionary changes are going on around us all the time. Evolutionary change is accelerating even in remote parts of the globe due to pollution, global warming, changes in vegetation and animal life, altered growing seasons, etc. Evolution is not some ancient process long finished, it is an active force in today's world, even if the only changes we can see thus far are smaller quantitative ones. We know that those will lead to larger, qualitative changes, even if we can't predict the exact timing of such leaps.

The basic irrevocable, unchanging law of nature is that everything is always changing. The only thing that doesn't change is change itself.

Everything is Connected to Everything Else

Water is related to rainfall is related to ocean temperature is related to Arctic warming is related to ice formation is related to . . . and on and on. The natural world is one big web of inter-penetrating processes, each affecting all the others in sometimes unpredictable ways, or rather in ways that we are not able to predict because we don't yet understand the complexity and multidirectional impacts of all these interconnections.

As climate change increasingly affects us, we learn in direct ways that humans are not separate from their environment, that what we experience in one region of the world is intimately connected to what people experience elsewhere. We are learning that it is not just an interesting fact that the earth rotates elliptically on a slightly wobbly tilted axis—this macro-reality determines major aspects of our lives, affecting climate cycles and ocean currents, and dictates that global warming is having its earliest and heaviest impacts at the North and South Poles.

Pollution that is blown away from us is blown away to somewhere else, to affect somebody else; it doesn't just disappear. The currents in the Indian Ocean are not separate from the cycle of monsoons, are not separate from the temperature of the ocean waters swirling around the Antarctic, are not separate from the temperature in the North Atlantic, are not separate from how we heat our houses, produce our food, and transport ourselves and the goods we produce. To understand the chains of cause and effect we must understand these networks of interrelationships.

Because all things are really processes and all processes are related to each other and have mutual impact, things are complicated, and we can get stuck with unintended consequences. For example, in some areas of northern India and Bangladesh, the UN financed the drilling of wells to help people whose lives were at immediate risk due to groundwater contamination. They did not bother to test the water from the wells because, after all, it was natural and obviously an improvement over the stagnant water people had been drinking that was killing them, and because drilling wells had been a solution elsewhere. Only one problem—the water they pumped out of the wells was contaminated because it had drained through rocks containing naturally-occurring arsenic. Slow lethal poisoning was substituted for quick death by water-borne disease.

"When one tugs at a single thing in nature, he finds it attached to the rest of the world," wrote John Muir. To consider things and processes in isolation from their real natural settings leads to mistakes.

For example, when European settlers came to Australia, they found massive forests and assumed those forests functioned like the forests in their homelands. So they cut the forests, expecting them to grow back within a century. The problem was that appearances were deceiving—the Australian forests grew on nutrient-poor soil and had taken about 400 years to grow, rather than the 80 to 100 years that a European forest took. Once the trees were cut, the poor soil was exposed to the elements and massive erosion took place, foreclosing even the possibility of forest regeneration in many areas.

Human Processes Impact the Processes of Natural Life

If we don't pay attention to human processes at the same time as we study the processes of natural life, we can miss potential solutions and make bad situations worse. We can make things worse by focusing too much on only one problem, no matter how important that problem is.

For example, some scientists and environmentalists are rethinking their stance on nuclear energy. By focusing exclusively on the excess carbon created by our energy systems, they conclude that nuclear energy is part of the solution. It is seen as one way to keep producing more energy without constantly increasing the carbon load in our atmosphere. This has led people to ignore or discount the catastrophic potential of nuclear accidents and ignore the reality that we do not know how to safely manage nuclear waste. There are already 80,000 tons of radioactive nuclear waste, which will remain potentially lethal for tens of thousands of years. Some nuclear waste at Hanford in Washington State, for example, has a half-life of 4,000 years, yet it is buried in containers that will disintegrate within 150 years or less, and those containers are already leaking, endangering the Columbia River.[82]

It has become clear that the mining of nuclear fuel exposes workers and local communities to extremely dangerous radioactivity, dramatically increasing the incidence of many types of cancer in miners and in surrounding areas. Also, the calculations about the carbon dioxide impact of nuclear power ignore the emissions from the construction of the plants and from the manufacture of the massive amounts of concrete used in construction. The arguments in favor of nuclear power have been jumped on by companies interested in avoiding the regulations and oppositional movements which have restricted the development of nuclear power plants in the U.S. over the past several decades.

The radioactive leak in Japan at Fukushima in 2011 following an earthquake and subsequent tsunami, while not instantly catastrophic except for the immediate area, proves that potential dangers are not completely within human control. The radioactivity from this nuclear plant malfunction, years later is still spreading around the world, creating unintended consequences.[83]

It is not enough to accept the assurances of the nuclear promotion industry about safety. That has to be decided scientifically by independent sources who have nothing to gain economically from promoting nuclear power, who consider all the ramifications for the long-term health of workers, communities, and the natural systems that will be affected. One important consideration, often ignored, is that since nuclear plants are such massive undertakings, are so expensive and complex, construction time is a significant problem. Solar and wind installations can be constructed much more expeditiously. Hence, a program of renewables can have a quicker, cheaper impact on lowering emissions.

Some people insist that all industrial and energy-producing processes involve trade-offs. True enough, but we need to understand what the *real* trade-offs are in order to make informed decisions. These trade-offs are not simplistic equations of jobs versus environmental regulation costs in the present, they include the costs to future generations, the potential of catastrophic yet unexpected accidents, and the impacts on aspects of complex life we do not yet understand. If our efforts to solve global warming create massive amounts of nuclear waste, we jump from the frying pan of global warming into the fire of nuclear contamination.

Biofuels are another example of an illusory solution. Using naturally-growing plants for energy rather than hydrocarbons sounds logical, almost warm and fuzzy. How much more natural can you get? However, there are a few problems.

First is that we need all available land and water for growing plants and feeding animals in order to feed the growing world population. Second, agriculture as now practiced needs massive amounts of water, so growing biofuel exacerbates the demands on water systems—water we desperately need to feed people, to sustain humanity, and to replenish the land and the aquifers. Third, large agribusiness monoculture crops for growing biofuel will not only absorb increasing amounts of water (pumped by burning fuel, decreasing the efficiency of the replacement energy), they will require increased use of pesticides, will deplete the soil over some years of growing cycles and hence require more land, and this will displace rural populations. Burning biofuels also releases greenhouse gases into the atmosphere, so it contributes to global warming.

If we jump on the biofuel bandwagon to the exclusion of other necessary efforts we will be cutting off our noses to spite our faces. Instead, we need to improve automotive mileage, substitute mass transit for individual transport, use improved rail systems for long-haul transport of goods, research other alternative fuels, and design cities and human support systems that aren't dependent on moving resources over great distances.

Biofuels may have a place as one part of a system of solutions, when the raw material comes from recycling waste products such as used cooking oil or waste fat from chicken processing, or, as in Brazil, if it comes from the scrap leaves and stalks from sugar cane harvesting. But this is not a magic bullet, not a complete answer to the problem of depleting fossil fuels nor excessive carbon dioxide emissions. Growing crops for fuel on a large scale is dangerous for food security, for water conservation, for sustainability, for biodiversity, and for keeping the price of basic foodstuffs like corn affordable for poor people. A rapid escalation in corn prices a few years ago already caused serious problems in Mexico, resulting in both hunger and riots.

Another way in which social, economic, and environmental problems are linked is that some of the poorest countries, kept that way in large part due to imperialism, are also the places which will be hit earliest and hardest by global warming. Global warming will cause more drought and famine in Africa, will cause more flooding, higher storm surges, and drought in much of Southeast Asia, will negatively impact agriculture in many countries where masses of people are barely surviving now.

Change in One Process Affects Other Processes

When humans divert water from a river for irrigation, the river's normal flow changes. What happens downriver changes and the amount of water absorbed by the ground changes. Check out the Rio Grande, often barely a trickle when it reaches the Gulf of Mexico.[84] When governments decide to construct a dam to produce hydroelectric power, they consequently determine (intentionally or not) what is going to happen to salmon runs, to the fishermen and women who depend on the salmon, and to the price of salmon in the supermarket. They often unintentionally cause significant increased evaporation from the huge lakes that build up behind massive dams, wasting the very energy they are trying to capture and decreasing the total amount of water available to sustain agriculture. Change in one place in the chain affects the whole chain.

When an ice field melts enough to break off and float away into the ocean as an iceberg, that exposes darker land or water underneath, which absorbs more of the sun's heat energy, since the ice no longer reflects as much of it back into space. Deglaciation (glaciers melting away to nothing, exposing the darker ground or water underneath—known as the *albedo effect*[85]) affects the heat absorption rate of the planet. This is in addition to the direct effects on water levels and the short-term cooling (from floating and melting ice) and longer-term warming (from more absorption of heat) and acidification (from the absorption of carbon dioxide) of the ocean water.

The heat and salinity of ocean water affect its mass and also affect ocean currents. In the North Atlantic, cold, saltier, heavier water sinks to the ocean floor, drawing warmer water north, which is a major engine of global ocean currents (the "conveyor"[86]). We are seeing signs that this ocean current system could slow or even potentially shut down.[87] As the massive amounts of fresh water stored in Greenland's glaciers melt, this decreases the salinity of this part of the ocean, lessening and potentially stopping the cold water from sinking and drawing warmer water north. This engine of the worldwide ocean currents is threatened.

Without warmer water being drawn north, Northern Europe will get much colder on average and face more floods and droughts,[88] even as it experiences hotter summers (another hotter/colder climate paradox). One problem with the prediction of when this might occur is that heat in the oceans lags atmospheric heat by several decades, so even if we stopped all human creation of atmospheric carbon today, the oceans would continue to warm for several more decades.

Everything is always changing, and every change ripples throughout the interconnected natural systems. Each change affects humans and their systems because we are dependent on nature for our existence. For example, when humans overfish a fishery system, we increase the retail cost of the shrinking supplies of fish, drive fishermen and women out of business, decimate the economies of fishing villages, destroy a formerly renewable source of the protein humans need, and alter the ecological balance of that region in unexpected ways.

When we deplete the soil or poison it with salt due to over-irrigation, the very projects set up to increase our food supply also set in motion processes which will destroy part of our food supply.

All Processes Contain Struggles Within Themselves

As Richard Levins and Richard Lewontin say in *The Dialectical Biologist*, "Things change because of the actions of opposing forces on them, and things are the way they are because of the temporary balance of opposing forces." The contradictions within processes drive development, and all processes are unities of opposing internal forces, struggling against each other but also mutually dependent. As a long-standing stable situation becomes unbalanced, dramatic change can occur.

Within the atmosphere of earth, there is quite a bit of naturally-occurring carbon. Without carbon, the earth can't hold on to enough of the sun's heat for us to survive, so we need carbon in the atmosphere. Maintaining the balance of carbon relies on the actions of many different systems, some of them opposites. The atmosphere is dependent on processes which create carbon, processes which absorb carbon, processes which store carbon, and processes which transform carbon. Trees take in carbon and give off oxygen, so whether forests are growing faster than they are being cut down affects the amount of carbon in the atmosphere.

Oceans capture carbon in various ways, and store it in various ways—in the water, in the shells of living creatures, in the collected shells of dead creatures that have sunk to the ocean floor. Many things can change the ability of the oceans to absorb more carbon—the relative amounts of salt versus fresh water, ocean currents, and ocean temperature, to mention some. How much land is covered by growing plants, how much by paving, how much by forests, how much by ice, all struggle and interact to increase or decrease the amount of carbon in the atmosphere. Major changes in any of these interlocked systems affect all the other parts as they penetrate and impact each other.

We need carbon, but too much carbon can make it too hot for parts of the environment and ultimately for us. Too much can trigger enough heat that the permafrost starts to melt, which will lead to more carbon being released into the air, making a feedback loop that could lurch beyond any possibility of human control. Too much carbon can upset balances on which life depends.

Our dependence on natural circumstances partially beyond our control is one of the greatest weaknesses of human life. It is also one of our greatest strengths, due to the human ability to adapt to changing circumstances and to radically different environments. But that adaptability is not without limits.

There are numerous examples throughout history of environmental crises forcing large-scale human change. Norse

Greenland, the Roanoke Colony, the Mayan Empire, and many successive Mesopotamian agricultural societies were either destroyed or forced to move when their environments changed, either from natural causes like the Little Ice Age, or multi-year drought, or due to direct human causation such as soil depletion, erosion, or over-irrigation.

The crises that threaten us are not just environmental; they are also crises of our social, political, and economic systems. They will accelerate social and economic problems, generating more social instability and conflict. The adaptability of human social systems is even more limited than general human adaptability.

When oppressive, class-divided societies are stressed, whether by war, economic crisis, shortage of resources, or impending environmental collapse, the ruling class first transmits the main burdens of that crisis to the oppressed classes, using money and power to escape the consequences as long as possible. For example, "Versace is building a new hotel in Dubai . . . but the beach sand now gets so hot that guests burn their feet. Solution: a 'refrigerated beach.' As the hotel's founder explained, 'We will suck the heat out of the sand to keep it cool enough to lie on. This is the kind of luxury top people want.'"[89]

Global warming leads to warmer temperatures, but it also leads to more extreme weather, more intense storms, even more snowfall in some places. Process and change are not unidirectional; they can exhibit as opposite phenomena resulting from the same change—more rainfall, more floods, *and* more droughts.

One pattern of change is periods of extreme variability as tipping points get closer (and sometimes due to increased efforts to stop change and reassert the old balance). The qualitative leap is then often followed by specialization, by successive adaptations to the new balance.

Change is Both Reformist *and* Revolutionary

The phrase *tipping point* is the current jargon of choice when discussing the potential of major sudden changes in our environment. All that *tipping point* means is that points come in every process when a leap to a new state, a new balance, is made. This is a principle of dialectics, known as the transformation of quantitative change into qualitative change.

Stephen Jay Gould, noted evolutionist, described this phenomenon as "punctuated equilibrium."[90] He observed the slow accumulation of changes in species, the slow development of small genetic changes, which upon reaching a tipping point (combined with ecological and climatic changes) burst forth as if from nowhere into massive genetic changes in a relatively short period of time, historically speaking. This happened during the Cambrian Explosion.[91] A system might seem to be in general equilibrium, but it is actually in a state of creative tension during which the pressures for change build up.

Other sciences use their own jargon to describe this pattern—*phase transitions, hinge points, event horizons, threshold effects, critical junctures.* They all describe similar aspects of phenomena and processes, observed in all places we have studied deeply enough thus far.

Earthquakes are another example of quantitative change leading to qualitative change, driven by contradictory forces. Opposing tectonic plates push against each other, building up great force and tension, until a quake releases that pent-up energy in a massive realignment. Then the process of incremental movement and building up of pressure starts over again. This cyclical, repetitive transformation never returns the plates to exactly where they were before the quake. As a result, which fault lines are under the most pressure changes following an earthquake-driven realignment, creating quake dangers in different areas.

Nature Works Slowly and Incrementally, *and* Works Swiftly and Decisively

Even without human intervention, the planet has gone through major changes from one state to another. The danger we face today is that the results of human activity (burning hydrocarbons, depleting rivers and aquifers, creating pollution, depleting soil) will push nature's processes faster and more decisively to shift to conditions that humans can't survive well under, if we can survive at all.

Some of the models that scientists are developing to help understand global climate change are flawed. They focus on quantitative, protracted, linear changes to the exclusion of looking for tipping points which could cause big, quick changes in the atmosphere, in the oceans, in the formation or loss of ice fields. If we ignore either the slow accumulation or the dramatic shifts, we will develop flawed solutions based on flawed understanding.

Based on the slow incremental accumulation of small changes, all systems, natural, social, and economic, reach tipping points when they transform to fundamentally different systems. The sky is not falling, and the world economy won't collapse tomorrow or the day after tomorrow. But it is foolish to ignore the possibility that we could overload nature past the point of no return for the conditions humans require, especially when many, many signs point in that direction already.

Tipping points happened at the end of each ice age, happened to mountain ranges, happened with slave systems, happens to tectonic plates, happened with feudalism, happened to ancient empires, happened to agriculture in some areas which through over-farming and soil depletion (along with changes in weather systems, rainfall, and soil salinity) became deserts where rich agriculture had existed.

Archeological discoveries about ancient societies in the Middle East show cycles of settlement followed by abandonment, followed by resettlement in some cases. For instance, there was a widespread desertion of cities in Mesopotamia around 2200 B.C. following weather changes, drought, and soil depletion. Some of the causes came from weather systems beyond human control, other causes were the direct result of human agricultural practices depleting water and soil and increasing soil salinity.

The World as a Series of Gigantic Feedback Loops

We can study the Arctic and Greenland glaciers and ice sheets as they are affected by global warming, learning how and when they will melt and break up, and at what pace. This is an important aspect of the scientific research we need. But if we study these in isolation, we make a big mistake.

Earlier studies of the Greenland ice sheets focused, for obvious reasons, on what was happening on the surface. We now know that just as important is the study of what is happening at the base of the ice sheets and glaciers, where melting water seeps to the bottom and lubricates the path of a glacier as it moves to the sea, speeding up that motion. When ice melts, other events occur as a result. When major sections of ice at the poles begin to melt, more of the heat which ice reflects back into space is instead absorbed by water, land, and vegetation, increasing the heat absorption of the earth. In turn, this can accelerate the melting of huge areas of permafrost.

Ripple effects eventually result in a new equilibrium, but will that equilibrium always be hospitable to humans? If all the fresh water contained in glaciers and ice fields, like those on Greenland and Antarctica, is released into the oceans, that can result in the rise of sea levels by several hundred feet, swamping many cities built near the water. This is not imminent, but that's the direction we are headed. All that fresh water also changes the density of water, which can change the ocean currents, disturbing the process of monsoon activity in South Asia, which can result in no rain for crops, leading to mass famine. Again, all this won't happen tomorrow, but we can see that developments are moving in that direction, and would be foolish to ignore the longer-term consequences of the changes we see in the present.

Glacial melting can have other effects too. As a glacier melts, it loses a massive amount of weight. The decrease in glacial weight eases pressure on the tectonic plates far underground, making it easier for them to move. This results in increased earthquake activity, as is already happening in some parts of Alaska. Global warming doesn't *directly* cause more earthquakes, but it contributes to conditions that result in more earthquakes.

Similarly, it seems as if global warming, while not increasing the incidence of hurricanes, is contributing to the increased intensity of hurricanes. As the ocean absorbs more carbon dioxide from the air, the water warms, and warm water is what provides the fuel for the force of hurricanes. Additionally, the warmer atmosphere causes more evaporation, resulting in the massive amounts of rainfall which accompany hurricanes now. Not only are hurricanes gaining in intensity, they are impacting land that has been increasingly deforested, paved, eroded, and otherwise robbed of natural protection against the effects of storms. Taken together, these further amplify the impact on farms, animals, hillsides, rivers, towns, and people. Too many wetlands (nature's safety valves which allow safe drainage for flooding) have been drained and developed. As well, since global warming causes more evaporation and thus more humidity in the air, hurricanes are bringing massive rainstorms along with their destructive winds, causing flooding, increased storm surges, and inundations which overwhelm infrastructure designed for our old normal, not the still developing new normal. Sea walls built to withstand storm surges of 10 feet are easily overwhelmed by a 13-foot storm surge.

Once a major global process reaches a tipping point, there is no turning back, not on a time scale needed by humanity.

New States of Being Transform Previous Balances

The climate of the earth has "flipped" from one state to another numerous times over the millennia it has been in existence. Warming periods followed Ice Ages and were in turn followed by Little Ice Ages, followed again by relative warming. While within each period there were significant variations in temperature, once a certain tipping point was reached, the main climate systems transformed to a new balance, a new relative equilibrium. Each of these transformations was not only of temperature, but also of ocean currents, sea levels, ice formation, precipitation, and other linked phenomena.

These changed conditions led to changes in animal life and vegetation that affected regional climates and even human agricultural development. This affected where and when humans were able to begin agriculture and the domestication of animals. And now, human alteration of nature is challenging its ability to find a new balance compatible with human existence.

As these systems flipped, they reached a new balance, one fundamentally different from the previous balance. In time, the new balance was itself transformed. And the process repeats. Nature *will* survive. Nature *will* reach a new equilibrium. The question is whether or not our species will be able to survive that new balance. And if we do, will that new balance be compatible with developed human existence, with the existence of human sustainability at a level of technological and cultural advancement and agricultural and water sufficiency? We don't know the answers yet. The challenge is: are we willing to do what it takes so that we stop playing dice with all other forms of nature for the benefit of the few, the rich, the exploiters? Will we continue on this path which is transforming the relationship of humanity and nature in ways that harm humanity? Or will we find a new path?

Internal and External Causes

You can swat a fly with a flyswatter, but no one would use that flyswatter to try to stop a stampeding rhinoceros.

Whether or not a rock breaks when force is applied to it depends on what kind of rock it is and how brittle it is, but also on what kind and size of force is applied to it. The same amount of force that breaks one kind of rock may leave another kind unscathed.

To understand any process, we have to know its internal makeup, know what pressures it is subjected to, and also know what pressures that process subjects its environment to. Learning about the interaction of internal and external causes helps provide real understanding.

Human life also contains such internal and external causes and interactions. History includes wars and invasions which started for often complex reasons not always acknowledged at the start. Outside pressure, such as military attacks, force reactions, but how a country responds also has to do with internal pressures, struggles, and contradictions. Looking at the struggles in the United States about whether to enter World War II, whether or not to confront fascism, all while some industrialists signed contracts to provide fascist Germany with goods, shows that U.S. entry into the war was not just a matter of right or wrong, not just a matter of one or another decision, but was a field of contention between many opposing forces, both internal and external.

Whether or not a union strike is victorious depends on the workers and their level of organization, determination, and alliances, but also on the financial state of the company, on its corporate culture, and on the reading of the general political and economic situation by both sides. A strike that inflicts financial damage to companies to the tune of billions of dollars usually wins. However, some years ago, a four-month long grocery strike in Southern California inflicted about two billion dollars of damage from lost business due to large-scale public support, as well as ongoing losses as customers learned to shop elsewhere. But the companies were prepared to pay the price, due to the competition they expected from Wal-Mart (and Wal-Mart's less expensive and less humane—and most often non-existent—health care benefits and overall compensation). So the companies refused to change their contract proposals, and hired (very expensive) substitute workers (scabs). The companies were prepared to pay the price of a massive amount of lost business. By all standard measures, the union and workers should have won, but instead they were forced to accept a contract with serious concessions, including a two-tier wage system.

Such struggles need dialectical understanding, not just arithmetic calculations.

Scale Matters

For many centuries, few believed that the continents had once been connected, because no one had seen continents move. We didn't yet know how to measure continental drift; we didn't even know there was such a thing. Continents were looked at as separate from each other, because humans didn't yet understand the history of geological change. When we look at the transformation of continents, we are talking about a scale of millions of years, and periodic rapid change over "shorter" periods of hundreds or a few thousands of years. Compared to the time scale of human life, such change seems like it takes forever. Only relatively recently have we started to be able to measure the small changes which in time led to fundamental transformations in the continental plates. We have begun to understand that these transformations include long periods of slowly accumulating pressure and faster periods of cataclysmic change.

Scale matters, too, in the nature of the different ecological problems we face. A rapidly rising sea level would be disastrous and would harm innumerable humans, but is something humanity could recover from. It is even something we can ameliorate the worst consequences of by preparing and changing now. But fundamental alteration of the atmosphere has the potential to challenge the existence of our species. If the air becomes too polluted for human health, we can't simply breathe something else. If an area becomes too hot for human survival, that area will no longer be habitable, adding to the refugee crisis.

You can't get rid of cockroaches in a single apartment—you have to tackle a problem at the scale on which it exists, an entire building or neighborhood in such a case. This is why regulatory reforms that aim to limit pollution one factory at a time after it has already been produced are at best stop-gap measures, and at worst just public relations efforts to justify the continued production of pollution. Scale matters.

Manure, in modest amounts, can be a key ingredient in boosting the fertility and vibrancy of the soil. However, when capitalism creates massive factory farms for animals, massive amounts of manure are created, and at this scale, this waste becomes toxic. Factory farms for animals are bad for the conditions for the animals themselves; they also function at a scale which creates a huge waste problem. At the smaller scale of a few farm animals on a family farm, the same manure was a valuable resource. Scale matters.

When a set of problems has an array of causes, then a coordinated set of solutions is required. Small changes in the personal habits of a few people won't help much. Market solutions such as "trading pollution credits" (also known as "cap and trade" programs) are counter-productive unless part of a comprehensive set of solutions. Otherwise, they are just a fig leaf to let companies claim they are "paying the price" while continuing to create more pollution. Such programs can slow the increasing rate of creating pollution but will never result in ending pollution or excessive carbon-burning.

The world is a complex system, like a giant network or web. The more complex the equation, the more that small differences in inputs can ripple throughout the equation, resulting in big changes down the line. This is sometimes called the "butterfly effect" for the way a butterfly's wings flapping in China could theoretically ripple through the system to result in a hurricane in some other part of the world. This holds for both problems and solutions. The more solutions we put into place, the more we will learn; the more we work at improving all the factors we possibly can, the better chance we have of avoiding the natural cataclysms that otherwise await us, from intensifying storms to rapidly rising sea levels.

Scale matters when we talk about the part that individual humans play in global climate change. On the scale of an individual day in an individual life, it doesn't make much difference if someone drives or doesn't drive, if someone composts and recycles or just throws everything into the trash. What one person does on one day makes little difference, but when combined with the actions of many other human beings over time, the cumulative impact is huge.

The same can be applied to measures to solve environmental problems. The scale on which humans make change matters. My little bit less of water use or driving less or buying a more efficient car will not help much by themselves, but if we change production, packaging, distribution, sales, tax credits, and education to help millions do the same, the total will make a tremendous positive difference. We won't get very far if we leave it on an individual basis only, but if we connect individual efforts with social and economic changes, we have a much better chance of making serious progress. We in the developed world, especially the U.S., are the heaviest consumers of energy and resources and thus have a special responsibility to act, to take it upon ourselves to lead in efforts to create positive change.

Form and Content, Appearance and Essence

What we see on the surface of things is rarely fundamental truth. Appearances can fool us. For example, in 1816, there was a volcanic eruption that spread a dark cloud of particulate matter over the earth, causing a cold "year with no summer." That could happen again, driving temperatures down, making it seem that the earth was no longer heating up. But most such one-time events don't change the basic course of climatic developments, not permanently (there are a few important exceptions like giant meteor strikes). So even while global warming is going on, there may be short-term reverses, clouding the issue. We have to distinguish surface appearances from underlying developments. Both affect us, but the underlying developments affect us for much longer and in more basic ways.

Form also often resists change from smaller quantitative accumulations (the resilience of a system measures this), until a qualitative leap forces changes to both form and content. For example, in massive global systems like ocean currents, there are huge amounts of inertia which slow down change. But for that very reason, once basic change starts in these systems, it is very hard to stop.

While content is more basic than form, there is a constant interaction between the two, in which form determines limits and choices for content. The form of liberal democracy interacts with the content of capitalist economics, at times working in harmony as far as the capitalists are concerned, at times with democratically-won victories limiting what capitalist enterprises can do. The public sphere of liberal democracy provides an arena within which workers can contend for power, can fight for controls on capitalist power, can win victories which restrict capitalist prerogatives. The capitalist class in the U.S. has relied on liberal democracy to hide its dictatorial economic rule and to work out conflicts between different sections of the capitalist class. These interactions between form and content are examples of the unity and struggle of opposites.

Chapter 7

The Basic Challenge

The fundamental reality of all human life is that our existence is based on food, water, and resources that come from nature. In turn, the ways in which we create and distribute food, drink, clothing, and shelter impact the natural world we depend on.

The basic question remains: *Will we restructure our social, political, economic, agricultural, and industrial systems to work more in harmony with the natural world?*

Looking at patterns of change in the real world can help answer this question.

The longer we wait to change our approach, and on a scale significant enough to have real impact on the scale of the problems, the more expensive the changes will be. The longer we wait the more severe the adjustments we will have to make, the more social and economic dislocations will be involved, and the more pain and misery will be inflicted on millions of people.

The history of human life has been a series of successive entire ecosystems appearing and then being replaced either due to external events or due to human impact on the environment. A cycle is observable in nature following human abandonment: after a cultivated field is abandoned, there is usually a rapid colonization by grasses, vines, and annuals. Under their shade, bush and tree seedlings sprout and may squeeze out the early colonizers, only to be replaced in turn by slower-growing shade-tolerant trees. Each negation is in turn negated, but none of this happens instantaneously, and none of it happens on the time scale that humanity requires.

We need to keep multidimensional change ever-present in our minds and focus on the interconnectedness of all phenomena or else our "solutions" will end up creating new and potentially worse problems. The interconnection of all processes must inform our actions.

A single-minded focus on global warming and greenhouse gases can lead us to ignore other crucial environmental challenges:

1. the increase of persistent organic pollutants (POPs) everywhere in the world,
2. the abuse of antibiotics to maximize profit in the meat industry which helps lead to super-resistant diseases,
3. the use of inadequately tested genetically modified non-reproducing seeds,
4. the dumping of toxic chemicals,
5. the poisoning of water systems,
6. the imbalances and dangers of monoculture agriculture,
7. and many more problems.

These are all threats to humanity's sustainable balance with the rest of the natural world. These problems already contribute to the premature death of many, to more disease and famine.

Our changing environment affects the vulnerability of organisms to disease, and creates new habitats for germs. The organism causing Legionnaire's Disease is found all over the world but has always been rare in its human impact until relatively recently because its food requirements are so complex and unusual. But that organism can tolerate heat and chlorine by getting inside of a protozoan. Industrial heating columns and water systems kill off the competitors of this organism and also create a biofilm that enables the organism to thrive in hotels, rest stops, and other gathering places. As well, the fine spray of modern shower heads can carry it to the deepest corners of our lungs. So human change can intensify natural threats to humans in ways we can't always predict.

"New" diseases come from somewhere, and we can't prevent them in advance of knowing about them. When such diseases hit growing urban populations around the world, many of which have inadequate water and sewage systems, the stage is set for epidemics. As well, diseases such as malaria, which used to be mostly restricted to the tropics, are spreading farther north and threatening new populations, due to the limited global warming we're already experiencing. Animals that have been frozen in the permafrost can contain the organisms of ancient diseases we haven't confronted in all of recorded human history, which get released once the carcasses have thawed.

Climate change leads to lower rainfall in many agricultural lands causing food supplies to plummet, and ultimately contributing to increased famine. The same climate change is already leading to rising sea levels which threaten to increase flooding in densely populated areas such as Bangladesh, Indonesia, the Philippines, the Netherlands (a world leader in ocean rise amelioration and land protection), and much of Florida, Louisiana, coastal California, and the coastal Carolinas. This can lead to increasing the already severe refugee problems the world is experiencing. These interconnections can exacerbate each problem, intensifying the negative impacts on human populations and agricultural systems.

Acid rain has more than one cause *and* more than one effect. In the first place, acid rain injures trees. Bark beetles can then penetrate the cracks in the bark, carrying fungus spores with them that kill the trees. Killing some trees can weaken an entire forest ecosystem. The problem is not only acid rain, it is the chain of consequences that follow in its wake.

Small changes in wind patterns in the Indian Ocean can affect whether the monsoons that Asia relies on for rainfall to grow crops will happen or not, and that affects the pressure on other water systems. "Green revolution" crops which rely on massive amounts of water can have the unintended result of farmers using ever-deeper wells to drain the water table many feet below the surface. This is being done at such a rapid clip that water is pumped out much faster than rain replenishes the underground aquifers, and as a result this particular source of water becomes a non-renewable resource (this is happening to the Ogallala Aquifer in the U.S. West, in Yemen, and in India). In effect, some farmers and communities are "mining" water. Solving a food problem by creating a water problem is short-sighted, and will ultimately cause another, potentially worse, food problem. Natural systems have all evolved to work together, and there is no magic by which humans can separate one process out of this natural web.

Another example is the Dust Bowl during the 1930s. It illustrates how a problem, once started, causes other problems: accelerated erosion leading to dust conditions leading to changes in weather patterns leading to the collapse of agriculture in the region, leading to large-scale human migration (and leading to extra exploitation of and discrimination against "Okies"). These conditions were reversed in some areas, but not in most and only with great difficulty and over a long period of time. There has been a return to dust conditions in some places.

"Green revolution" varieties of seeds increased yields per acre, but they also created dependence on a whole array of pesticides, herbicides, fertilizers, irrigation, and mechanization (which only some farmers could afford). This led to soil depletion, erosion, draining water tables, and undermining the long-term productive capacity of the land. A supposed solution turned into a problem. A short-term victory added to a long-term crisis.

We tend to take soil for granted. Like water, soil too can be turned into a non-renewable resource when soil depletion and erosion are accelerated by human activity to the point that they overwhelm soil formation. There used to be topsoil up to 21 inches deep over much of the U.S. Great Plains region. Now in most places it is less than 6 inches deep; in effect, we have been mining the soil. Chemical fertilizers can boost output, but only temporarily—the soil begins to act like a heroin addict, requiring ever larger doses of fertilizer to get the same effect, depleting the soil faster in the process, and increasing run-off which chemically contaminates streams, lakes, rivers, and creates massive dead zones in bodies of water such as the Gulf of Mexico.

Soil and water can replenish and regenerate, but this process can take decades or hundreds of years if left to nature alone, and then can only happen if human-caused erosion and deforestation haven't stripped the land back to bare rock, or if humans massively drain an aquifer, in which case replenishment can take thousands of years.

When human societies are under the pressure of food crises, they tend to exploit resources even faster in a desperate but vain drive to catch up to the problem, resulting in a self-reinforcing cycle of environmental degradation and destruction. The interactions between human-driven climate change, water overuse, and the degradation of soil can overwhelm the ability of natural systems to support human and animal life, first in areas that have long been teetering on the edge of agricultural collapse, then in a more generalized fashion throughout the world.

Marx noted, "All progress in capitalistic agriculture is a progress in the art, not only of robbing the worker, but of robbing the soil; all progress in increasing the fertility of the soil for a given time is a progress towards ruining the more long-lasting sources of that fertility."

Exploitation is Bad, Including Environmental Exploitation

Human life is threatened when the natural conditions which permit life become altered in basic ways. Humans depend on oxygen, water, and on photosynthesis in plants which feed humans and animals. Together, plants and animals provide us with essential sustenance. Take any of these away for long enough (and it doesn't take very long, especially with oxygen and water) and human life ceases to exist. Negatively impact any one of these and, sooner or later, that will have negative impacts on all the others, and negative consequences for humanity.

Virginia Brodine, in *Red Roots, Green Shoots*, offered the following definition of environmental exploitation:

> The exploitation of the environment is the expropriation of land, natural materials, and energy sources at one end of the production process and of the

waste-absorbing capacity of the environment at the other end, without paying the cost of maintaining the capability of the environment to continue supplying the one or to continue absorbing the other.

If we compromise nature's ability to regenerate itself and the materials we need for our survival, we compromise our own ability to survive. We can't just take and take from nature without adjusting ourselves to nature's need to replenish itself and to absorb, integrate, and detoxify waste products. We depend on nature for our survival: if the air becomes too polluted for human health, we can't simply breathe something else. We can't endlessly alter the balance of natural systems such as the atmosphere without suffering the consequences of that alteration.

There are direct human costs of capitalism, rooted in the exploitation of human labor for profit, but there are also serious environmental costs, as capitalist production and agriculture exploit the non-renewable resources we depend upon in an ever-speedier race to catastrophe, all in the endless pursuit of short-term maximum profits.

A massive movement is needed, worldwide in scope, to fight defensive battles against environmental degradation and exploitative development. Then the movement can proceed to fight for long-term fundamental transformation of our economies. This movement requires protracted struggle, building a resistance infrastructure, uniting many kinds of organizations and approaches. In the process, we need both principled stances and practical compromises.

But how do we decide what is a principled compromise, and what is unprincipled? How do we judge the different options available? How do we pick and choose with whom to side? Applying this philosophical outlook to the environmental struggles we face, the environmental movement which we must build, and the ways in which we can build unity are the subjects of Part 3.

Part 3:
The Movement

Chapter 8

Movement Lessons

A Positive Tipping Point for the Environment

The most crucial tipping point has been ignored by most writing on the climate crisis—the environmental movement tipping point. Although environmental movements have the support of billions of people, actual environmental organizations and campaigns have been confined to much smaller groups of people. The environmental movement, and the other organizations and movements it allies itself with, have not yet reached critical mass. The environmental movement can and must become the crucial tipping point, helping create the political power to make change.

The environmental movement tipping point is a positive counterweight to the negative change taking place around us, the event horizon which will signal a movement large enough, united enough, powerful enough, sophisticated enough, experienced enough, and militant enough to challenge the system which is creating or exacerbating the many environmental crises we face.

There is no shortcut around building a massive, worldwide movement for fundamental transformation of all aspects of society. Solutions to environmental challenges that work just by fiddling at the edges of the system are not solutions to the fundamental challenges that face us. If it were possible to create fundamental transformation without billions of people being actively involved, that would be easier—but there is no benefit in wasting time searching for shortcuts that do not and cannot exist.

Component parts of this broad movement are already active and growing. The movement to address climate change, the movement for environmental justice, the movement for a decent future for humankind, are already broad, already reach all parts of the world. But the broader movement does not yet have a unifying strategic outlook capable of winning the additional billions of people that the cause needs, and is not yet capable of uniting the diverse tactics which different groups advocate into one massive movement.

Each of these component parts of the environmental movement, while acting on the almost daily new political and environmental challenges and crises, must also develop a long-range view of the struggle, of what is needed to accomplish its ends. Together, they can reach the environmental movement tipping point on which our shared future depends.

The movement we need, one powerful enough to create fundamental change, will be a coalition of coalitions, an alliance of alliances, a movement of movements. Within the environmental movement itself, there are many coalitions already—scientists working to understand climate change, activists fighting specific environmentally dangerous development projects, national organizations sponsoring national demonstrations and promoting legislative solutions, broad public awareness, media coverage of weather disasters linked to climate change, and so many more.

We start with a look at some of the mass movements in U.S. history which offer important lessons for all who work to make change.

Lessons of the Civil Rights Movement

We should again listen to the still fresh soaring rhetoric and moral outrage of Dr. King's famous speech to the March on Washington (and of the other speeches, not as well-known but equally part of the history and impact of that day). We should reflect on many lessons from that struggle.

The Civil Rights Movement holds lessons not just for the civil rights struggles of today, but also for the environmental movement. Just as the 1963 March on Washington was the culmination of years of much difficult and dangerous struggle and led afterwards to more struggle and change, saving our planet will not be a single event or a single kind of change. Just like the Civil Rights Movement needed and won allies in the labor movement as it fought for jobs as well as freedom, the environmental movement needs to build those alliances with labor and workers and to fight for jobs as part of our own struggle for human survival.

Like the Civil Rights Movement of the 1950s, 60s, and 70s, the environmental movement is one that has both moral and practical aspects. It needs a strategy that unites both inside and outside struggles and goals. It must unite diverse elements around a common program that recognizes and acknowledges that diversity—diversity of many kinds of struggles, of related but distinct organizations, of legislative efforts and policy goals but also of educational programs, community organizing, popular demonstrations, civil disobedience, legal challenges, and electoral efforts.

The Civil Rights Movement taught us that while we can't rely on the political system to somehow automatically self-correct, we do need the political system to pass laws and enforce them.

Like the Civil Rights Movement, this struggle must be waged on intensely local issues that immediately and directly impact people's lives, and must also be waged on the national and international stages. It must involve individual, personal change, in the emotions, thoughts, and the actions of each of us, one by one, and also involve political, social, legal, and economic changes on the scale of millions, even billions, of people. It must involve compromise and concessions, street militancy, and also the most strident denunciations of the immorality of business as usual.

The changes we need are so fundamental, so complex, and touch on so many areas of life, that any one-track approach is ultimately doomed to failure. Only a strategy that finds ways to unite these diverse and sometimes seemingly contradictory strands into one mighty movement has any hope of success.[92]

The movement needs to welcome all levels of change, struggle, and participation. The success of such a movement, and the strength to create, even impose, that success, requires the understanding and activity of millions of people, some of whom will dedicate their lives and others who will limit their participation to voting. If we fall into the trap of condemning those who recycle because recycling by itself won't be enough, we cut ourselves off from millions who want to do the right thing and are ready to take the first steps within their personal control. If we sneer at those who engage in political campaigns since there are inherent limits to what can be accomplished through the political system right now, we cede an entire crucial arena of struggle to the deniers and right-wing pontificators and lose opportunities for mass education and mobilization.

Those who seek to pit personal responsibility and personal change against social and legal change, from either direction, fail to see how much effort, how much struggle, how many sacrifices are needed from so many people and on so many fronts, fail to search for ways to unify and to bring people into struggle who are just starting to engage.

The Civil Rights Movement was able to win victories because it united a moral vision and moral outrage with local and national organization, with public opinion, with political pressure. Regular citizens were able to activate themselves in intense local struggles, alongside national campaigns to change laws and policies.

Central to the Civil Rights Movement was the fight for voting rights. It was understood as the key to breaking the stranglehold of reactionary politicians on power in many parts of the South, as well as in some Northern cities. It was the key part of the battles for full citizenship, for full civil rights, for a share in the political space where decisions are made that affect the lives of poor and oppressed people.

Without forcefully placing the moral issues clearly before millions, we will not inspire and involve the youth of today. But if we rely *only* on moral persuasion we will never build the necessary organizational muscle, never build strong and lasting institutions of resistance, never build the political power necessary to challenge and replace the entrenched economic interests which play an outsized role in our politics. Convincing people to act, to take on the hard and difficult tasks of struggle and sacrifice requires appealing to their moral sense of right and justice, and their own self-interest in survival. But making change actually happen, in society, in production, in transportation, in agriculture, in distribution, and in consumption, requires organizing those who are personally inspired into effective political and economic campaigns.

We need wild places and polar bears and campaigns to save the bears and preserve the wilderness, but those by themselves won't save humanity from untold suffering—we also need to address the daily living needs of billions of people, for food, for water, for living-wage jobs, for shelter. We need to create options so that workers don't have to take jobs where short-term survival needs force them to work against the long-term survival needs of humanity.

The enemies of labor rights are the enemies of voting rights are the enemies of women's rights are the enemies of health care for all, are the enemies of immigrant rights, are the enemies of environmental laws and regulations, wildlife, and wild lands. Creating fundamental change requires unity across many kinds of struggles and organizations, building bridges of understanding across many issues. It requires street heat and militancy and also requires electing officials who must compromise at times. It requires recognizing the difference between tactical compromises and abandonment of principles. It requires unity that is multi-racial, multi-national, multi-gender, multi-generational, as well as uniting believers of all kinds with those who are not religious at all.

People in all progressive movements and organizations need to understand that environmental catastrophe threatens them too, if not today then soon. It might be a hurricane like Katrina or Maria; it might be a multi-year drought such as California recently experienced, or a water crisis across many states, or forest fires of extreme intensity. But we are all threatened, and we all need to unite. The solutions to any limitations of the environmental movement will come from addressing the real problems facing all humankind, including immediate economic survival needs.

The Civil Rights Movement was a protracted struggle over many decades, which built on many previous decades of resistance and activism. There were boycotts, non-violent resistance, voter registration drives, legislative and legal efforts of many kinds, sit-ins, marches, religious coalitions, and the Freedom Rides. There was participation from sections of the labor movement. A crucial factor was bringing the reality of segregation home onto TV screens nightly, forcing Americans to confront racism and wrestle with its moral and political implications. There were organizations which both cooperated and competed (NAACP, SCLC, SNCC, CORE, and many more, including many strictly local groups), leaders who cooperated and sometimes offered competing strategies (A. Philip Randolph, Reverend Dr. Martin Luther King Jr., Malcolm X, Fannie Lou Hamer, James Farmer, John Lewis, Stokely Carmichael, Medgar Evers, Bayard Rustin, Whitney Young, Ella Baker), and groups which broke away or stood aside from the main part of the movement to focus on armed self-defense rather than principled non-violence (The Deacons for Defense and the Black Panther Party, to mention two—and not to lump them together; they were different in many ways) or espoused a form of go-it-alone nationalism (The Republic of New Africa, the Nation of Islam).

When Dr. King decided to speak out against the War in Vietnam in 1967, he was roundly condemned by many civil rights leaders for taking the movement into an area which they thought should be avoided in order to keep as many liberal and centrist allies as possible. In 1967-68, others who had been close allies did not want to follow Dr. King into the Poor People's March movement, which was aimed at addressing economic and social as well as racial inequality.

Michael Honey, writing in *The Nation*, tells us that King understood the importance of linking civil rights with struggles for economic justice:

> Remarkably, given the brutality that people had faced in the civil-rights struggle, King warned that the second phase of the freedom movement would be even harder. "It is much easier to integrate a lunch counter than it is to guarantee an annual income," he said, and the resistance from capitalist elites as well

as Southern sheriffs would be much worse. Yet King insisted that the country needed a moral revolution that would "raise certain basic questions about the whole society." Like Malcolm X, he saw the agenda for organizing as global and revolutionary.[93]

Honey goes on:

It might also be time to dispense with the standard notion of King as a top-down leader and the Student Nonviolent Coordinating Committee and the New Left as the bottom-up movements of that time. Movements require many kinds of agitators, organizers, and leaders. We should embrace the many different movements fighting for rights and freedom today—women's rights, immigrant rights, LGBTQ rights, peace and nonviolence—as well as people of all ethnicities. But we should also bring labor issues and union rights to the forefront of our concerns, as Coretta Scott King did after her husband's death. Advocating for a federal holiday in his memory, she pointed out that it would be the first one to honor an American who "gave his life in a labor struggle."

The lessons of the 1963 March on Washington and of the Civil Rights Movement, of the years-long struggles lead by Dr. King, include that successful movements for change require broad unity with many forces, require the active participation of millions, require building coalitions and unity across many organizational lines, require consistency and persistence in the face of determined opposition, and also require soaring poetic visions of what must and can be, like the preaching, speaking, and organizing of the Rev. William J. Barber II.[94]

The Civil Rights Movement also illustrates that the course of struggle is not a simple matter to predict. Entering into a struggle never comes with a guaranteed outcome. History looks very different in the rear-view mirror, once we know how events turned out. Looking forward, in the middle of a struggle, it is never certain how events will unfold. Struggle doesn't come with guarantees. When Dr. King was sitting in jail composing his *Letter from the Birmingham Jail*, he didn't do so expecting that it would still be read decades later. When he drafted his speech to the 1963 March on Washington, he was focused on speaking to the needs of the movement at that time, not planning to write a speech that would become one of the most quoted ever.

Another key lesson from civil rights struggles is that any progressive movement must attack racism. Racism has been central to the economic and political development of the U.S. and is intertwined with many aspects of society. Without rejecting racism, without including a critique of racism as part of its program, no movement can build the necessary unity. The ways that the Civil Rights Movement attacked racial segregation, educational inequality, legal discrimination, and housing and job discrimination helped to inspire the Farmworkers, Native American struggles, the anti-war movement, and the women's movement, as well as the anti-apartheid movement in South Africa.

Lessons from the Anti-Vietnam War Movement

We can look to the anti-Vietnam War movement for other important lessons for how to wage difficult struggles that have real impact, lessons about how to build broad-based unity, and also for lessons about what strategies and tactics to avoid, which strategies and tactics get in the way of unity.

Most discussions of the anti-war movement focus on the much larger demonstrations of the late 1960s and early 1970s. The "forgotten" history of the anti-Vietnam War movement actually started in the early 1960s. Those first anti-war demonstrations took place at a time when U.S. involvement was "limited" to several thousand "advisors." These small demonstrations, often of only forty or fifty people, proved prescient about the dangers of U.S. military engagement in Southeast Asia, about the likelihood of escalating numbers of U.S. troops, and about the false or empty claims used by mainstream politicians to justify the U.S. role in a foreign civil war.

These demonstrations were small, composed mainly of left-wingers and pacifists. They were dismissed by the political mainstream and media as irrelevant, in much the same way that early warnings by some scientists about a potential global warming catastrophe were dismissed as hyperbolic and irrelevant to public policy and to economic decision-making. The problems caused by the U.S. War in Vietnam for the U.S. economy and the U.S. military were present in those early days, but only in embryonic form. As the war grew, as the number of U.S. troops increased, as costs as well as death tolls went up, these problems became more and more apparent to more and more people. The struggle against the war escalated alongside the escalating war. It took many years for the problems caused by the war to occupy center stage in U.S. politics, but once a tipping point was reached public opinion never swung back to supporting the war.

The anti-war movement played a key role in ending U.S. involvement, but we shouldn't exaggerate its impact. The movement succeeded in turning a majority against the war, but that did not result in either an immediate end to the war nor in a fundamental shift in U.S. foreign policy. Even with a majority against the war, Nixon won re-election in 1972 in a landslide. U.S. foreign policy under both Democratic and Republican presidents continued to be aggressive, to rely on the use of U.S. military might as a threat or an actuality, to focus on the commercial interests of major U.S. corporations, and to seek to further the geo-political interests of U.S. capital. However, for many years after, U.S. foreign military action was constrained for fear of massive internal opposition—and breaking this "Vietnam Syndrome" was a key objective of Reagan's military adventurism in Panama, Grenada, and Lebanon.

The anti-Vietnam War struggle was a multi-year, multi-faceted struggle that involved massive marches (though they started out small), electoral politics, congressional hearings, civil disobedience, picket lines, weekly vigils, teach-ins, draft resistance, media exposés, an exponentially growing student movement, whistleblowers, GI resistance, and millions of people learning the truth from their own experience that their government was lying to them.

Ultimately, the anti-war movement included a wide variety of social and political forces and relied on a wide variety of tactics, from peaceful marches and demonstrations to organized mass civil disobedience to petitions and election campaigns. While not all allies participated in all forms of tactical actions, this great variety of actions played a role in building an effective movement.

The GI resistance organizations played an important role in helping millions to learn the duplicitous nature of government and military actions and pronouncements.[95] An example of the intersectionality of struggles was the powerful message sent by Muhammed Ali refusing the draft, going to prison rather than fighting in an imperialist war against other people of color.

The movement had two competing anti-war coalitions resulting from a forced split (engineered by the Socialist Workers Party, a Trotskyite group), many kinds of organizations, and many independent activists. Nearly everyone came together for the biggest marches, but there were competing strategies (single issue versus multi-issue), multiple slogans and chants (*Set the Date, Stop the War, Resist the Draft, Bring the Boys Home, Ho-Ho-Ho Chi Minh—the NLF is Going to Win*), and internal conflicts and disagreements of many kinds. Some wanted the broadest movement possible, others wanted breakaway civil disobedience. Some groups degenerated into anarchism or violent resistance, others were slow and steady all the way start to finish.

The "Weathermen" Fallacy

Illusions about how much a mass movement can accomplish can lead some activists to disillusionment, to despair, to responding positively to efforts to constantly "up the ante." This was a feature of the Weathermen, an offshoot of the anti-Vietnam War and student movements, which carried out the self-destructive "Days of Rage" in Chicago in 1969, as well as several bomb plots and other dead-end schemes. The futility of such supposedly more radical tactics in service of a strategy that was no less than suicidal in the end (to the group and to some of the individuals involved) is obvious to those with a long involvement in struggles, but it can appeal to those looking for a shortcut around the protracted slog of movement building and reaching and winning a majority.

The actions of the Weathermen and of various anarchist groups—breaking windows, planting bombs, making exaggerated, self-righteous claims that they were going to "bring down the war system"—drove away potential allies. Such actions not only did not succeed in building the movement, they did not succeed at their stated goal of bringing the war machine to a halt. They made it easier for government forces to plant agents provacetuers who incited actions aimed at weakening public support for the anti-war efforts. They provided the government security apparatus with excuses to surveil and persecute all anti-war activity.

Preventing new activists from being trapped in this kind of blind alley is the reason to pay attention to similar fringe efforts now. Because of their overheated rhetoric and media-coverage-grabbing violent tactics, the Weathermen set the broader anti-war struggle back. Their tactics drove potential allies away. Their super-militancy ended up separating them from the mainstream movement, provided an excuse for repression, focused them inward, and placed their emphasis on personal commitment to what they perceived as the "higher" stages of struggle and personal self-sacrifice rather than on winning a majority of people.

Understanding these problems leads to the need for a growing movement to recognize and address the radicalization that happens. Often, new activists experience frustration when change doesn't happen as quickly as it should or as people want it to and thus they can be seduced by harmful tangents. We need to win the entire movement to a long-range strategic outlook within which to situate tactics.

A movement needs a generally accepted goal and unity around that goal, while enabling individuals, organizations from local to national to international, and the public in general to engage at whatever level of activity they are ready to engage. A deeper understanding of history, where we've come from, what we have won in the past and how, helps provide perspective.

People change their minds for a variety of reasons and in a variety of ways, but seldom from radicals preaching at them, shouting at them, trying to make them "pay" for their opposition to necessary change, or from small groups breaking a few windows. Principled civil disobedience is often a useful tactic, as is the related tactic of non-violent resistance. But militancy for the sake of proving you are more militant than anyone else turns most people off.

This way of understanding how and why people change leads to another insight: while education, morality, and logical exposition all play necessary and important roles, people learn most and best by engaging in action themselves. In part, people entering struggles learn that they need more education and analysis. Once they begin to engage in struggle, they begin to hunger for deeper thinking, deeper knowledge, and a strategic outlook. This doesn't come from "turning up the volume" on protest, but from convincing people to take the first step.

There is nothing more radical than reality. We need to rely on reality to be our ally. Some of the most impactful participants in the anti-Vietnam War movement were veterans themselves and the families of those killed during the war. They could speak powerfully from their own personal experience. That experience exposed the lies in the official story, countering it with individual stories that had the weight of personal morality, personal suffering, and direct involvement with what was actually happening. Connected to the movement, these personal stories provided testimony from eyewitnesses which spoke powerfully to those who were wavering or uncertain. The personal testimonies of those who have suffered through extreme weather events such as Hurricane Sandy and the devastation in the Philippines from Typhoon Haiyan are worth at least as much as another homily on climate change from a theoretical perspective.

The political power and impact of a movement comes from a combination of elements, not from any single magic bullet, any specific strategy or tactic. Personal stories and experiences, mass demonstrations, Congressional testimony, widespread organization, civil disobedience, petition drives, legislative efforts, grassroots organizing, theoretical work, educational efforts like teach-ins, religious witnessing such as weekly vigils, draft resistance, attempts to publicly shame those who profit from business as usual, coalition-building linking issues and activists, all are part of the struggle, and no one aspect by itself leads to victory.

Those who, for organizational reasons or from ideological conviction, try to limit the movement to one or another tactic do the broader movement a disservice. Those who want to build a movement without the component of moral outrage drain a key aspect of vitality and outreach. Those who rely only on moral outrage or on spontaneity alone prevent the movement from building the kind of organizational muscle required for protracted movements.

The anti-Vietnam War movement, which lasted well over a decade, needed flexibility, needed to adapt to changing circumstances. Public civil disobedience, so effective at the height of the anti-war demonstrations, would have been counter-productive at the start of the movement—though there were particular kinds of civil disobedience early on that did help grow the movement, for example those few soldiers who refused orders to go to Vietnam such as the Fort Hood Three.[96] But when, after years of demonstrations which grew bigger in size and scope yet didn't stop the war, to limit the movement to demonstrations and reject civil disobedience would have limited the movement. A movement can't and won't grow in a straight line, using only one tactic over and over.

Early efforts called for Congressional action, but the struggle for various legislative solutions both partial and more far-reaching changed once Congressional Representatives and Senators started to take public anti-war positions and respond to the movement in the streets with actual legislation. Taking advantage of such splits in the ruling circles required flexibility, compromise, and a tolerance for contradiction—for example, Senator Fulbright played an important role in the anti-Vietnam War efforts in Congress while at the same time playing a retrograde role on civil rights issues.

Lessons from the Labor Movement

The U.S. labor movement has a long and tumultuous history. In recent years, it has been shrinking as a portion of the U.S. working class. Nonetheless the labor movement remains one of the most successful and protracted mass movements in U.S. history. The labor movement has its own specific challenges in the present, but all movements can learn from the successes and limitations of labor struggles. The decrease in union membership over the last 40 years especially has also had a negative impact on U.S. national elections, on growing income inequality, and on institutional resistance to the corporate agenda.[97]

The first and most important lesson from labor is that when engaged in sustained struggles, organizational muscle makes a difference. The labor movement was and is not just made up of like-minded people—unions are a form of coalition, uniting people of diverse views and cultures who share a common bond, one that can reach far beyond the ranks of union members to unorganized workers and to society as a whole.

But accomplishments like the weekend, the eight-hour day, winning unemployment insurance, and ending child labor happened in large part because unions are institutions of struggle. Unions provided the Civil Rights Movement with financial support, organizational support, and turned out members for demonstrations, contributing greatly to the successes of that allied struggle. Labor could do that because of the money, experience, and the institutions it created. It was no accident that Walter Reuther, head of the United Auto Workers, was in the front line of many national civil rights marches alongside Dr. King, Rev. Abernathy, and others from SCLC, the Southern Christian Leadership Conference.

There is a need for ongoing organizations with actual budgets. Some demonstrations can now be pulled off with only a handful of organizers and paid staff, due to the ways in which the Internet and social media can amplify their efforts. But that doesn't always work, and does not always lead to a sustained movement. Regular membership, standing leadership bodies, budgets, fundraising, publications, strategies, plans, and other features of established organizations enable them to last through the ups and downs, the ebbs and flows, of movements, to keep going when moments of spontaneous mass success are gone.

In 1981, in response to the taunts from Reagan and his breaking of the PATCO strike (the air traffic controllers union, which had endorsed Reagan during the election campaign), the AFL-CIO sponsored Solidarity Day, a mass demonstration in Washington DC that brought about 500,000 people into the streets. As part of that, organizers faced problems of getting that many people around the city, avoiding an impossible crush of buses. Because they had a budget, their solution was to rent the entire subway system of the city for the day, making it free for all to ride. That kind of financial wherewithal is of great benefit when it comes to mass mobilization.

The labor movement, with structure, membership, organization, and infrastructure, is built for the long fight, for winning continual improvements, for sustained organizing. With resources, it can last through both the ebbs and flows of struggle.

Some environmental organizations have sought ways around their financial problems by pandering to corporate sponsorship to provide the funds for paid staff, but end up compromising their principles in the process, providing cover for greenwashing efforts.

The history of the labor movement also teaches that militant fights can inspire and galvanize a mass movement—it happened with the San Francisco General Strike of 1934, which started as a longshoremen's strike and spread after police murders. It happened with the Flint Sit-Down Strike in 1936-37.[98] This occupation by workers of their factory challenged the owners, confronted public and private police forces, and captured the attention of the country and of many around the world. It was a high point in the efforts to establish industrial unionism in the U.S., a high-water mark of militancy, and a turning point towards victories which, though limited, were real and offered lasting improvements for millions of workers.

The U.S. labor movement also offers examples of how restricting the labor movement to "bread and butter" issues limited its ability to build mass coalitions with others—having a grand vision of what is needed helps inspire, energize, and activate.

When, in a morally bankrupt concession in response to the anti-union, anti-Communist Taft-Hartley Act, the mainstream of the labor movement kicked the radicals out of leadership and in some cases even membership during the McCarthy period, it robbed the labor movement of its beating heart. It lost much of its experience of organizing real struggles, much of its connection to wider progressive movements. This led to selling union memberships as if they were nothing more than insurance policies, as if the union was an agency selling a service, not a struggle organization. These practices became known as "business unionism."

When the tide turned sharply against labor in the 1980s, much of labor had to move away from the business unionism straightjacket, had to relearn how to organize struggle. The labor movement had to relearn how to participate in and lead coalitions. That shift back to a struggle orientation is still going on today, and the labor movement is still suffering from this partially self-inflicted wound.

While attitudes towards unions are changing, particularly among young people, the union movement itself needs to radically change if it is to reverse the downward trend in membership and union strength. The 2018 West Virginia teachers strike shows that workers are capable of waging a determined, persistent battle for their own interests and for the interests of the communities they serve. Too often, unions over the past decades have only gone on strike when forced to do so, as defensive last-ditch efforts against the attacks of the employers on wages, benefits, and working conditions. Too many unions remain mired in insular craft unionism, business unionism, and have neglected their need to address society-wide problems. The labor movement needs to transform itself, needs to meet the challenges of the moment. That includes representing the needs of the whole working class and of society as a whole, by building alliances, by uniting with many progressive movements including the environmental movement, by moving away from a "professional representation" model to one that places the rank-and-file members at the center of mobilizing, organizing, and decision-making.

There are on-going debates in the labor movement between using an organizing model or a mobilizing model, a polling model or a structural test model, a pressure campaign or a member-centric campaign.[99] The reality is that all of these are needed; they only become a problem when one is presented as the best or only strategy to the exclusion of the others. They all can be useful elements of moving the labor movement back into struggle mode in difficult times, but often a union will "choose" one model as if it is the solution. As with the environmental movement, there is not just one tactic, not just one style of organizing, which will fit every circumstance.

However, all models are not equal. Strategies that don't include the direct mobilization and empowerment of the members automatically limit their effectiveness and long-term impact. Unions that still use a business-unionism model, selling the union as if it was an insurance policy, doom themselves to sitting on the sidelines of the main battles that impact workers—battles that take place in the public square, in the political and electoral systems. Strategies that include organizing the membership to place workers as the decision-makers multiply the impact of any other tactics they use.

Another long-term lesson from the history of labor is that whatever you win will be under constant attack—victories are not secure until society reaches a basic tipping point. Advances such as Social Security, Medicare and Medicaid, unemployment insurance, the forty-hour week and eight-hour day, the right to have a union, the right of organized workers to participate in the political process—all have been chipped away at by the agents of the system. Even major victories will be challenged and threatened. This will be true as long as the private profit system maintains its death grip on the levers of political power.

The capitalist class often engages in violent attacks against workers' struggles. The history of labor strife is filled with examples of agent provocateurs, of state violence against strikers, of murders and beatings by private militia. For just one example, check out the history of how the Ford Motor Company was organized during the 1930s. The workers ran up against the determined opposition of Henry Ford, a Nazi sympathizer. He hired thugs to murder union organizers and activists, he tried to get the state to crush union picketlines and demonstrations, he bought media and public officials to propagandize against the union. He also funded anti-Semitic, anti-immigrant campaigns. In the face of this, rank-and-file union members persevered and eventually won.

A more recent example is from an ILWU strike in Longview, Washington, where the union faced legal threats, vicious police attacks, private security forces, teargassing, up to and including tying members of the women's auxiliary to railroad tracks and then spraying them in the face with Mace.

The struggles of workers to wrest power away from employer prerogatives parallel and complement the struggles of citizens to wrest power away from private property prerogatives. The struggle for real democratic control over the economic decisions that affect our lives relates directly to the struggle for real democratic control in communities over the economic decisions that now produce pollution, environmental degradation, reckless development, and other challenges to a sustainable balance between immediate human needs and the long-term human need for a healthy environment.

The labor movement is at its best when it fights for the working class as a whole and for programs that provide for the public. Many programs fought for and won by the labor movement, in alliance with many others, benefitted society as a whole, not just union members. Social Security, unemployment insurance, the eight-hour day, all were victories for all workers and for a just, humane society for all.

An approach that unites union members' needs with the interests of the broader society wins more for workers. For example, when grocery workers in the Pacific Northwest planned to work on a ballot measure to increase the minimum wage for all workers, they found that their polling was much better if the fight for a $15 minimum wage was paired with the requirement of sick leave for all workers. When food service workers, grocery workers, and health care workers don't have adequate (or any) sick leave, that can affect the health of the entire population, and much of the public understood that.

Fighting for such job and social demands in a linked way can make each struggle stronger and more appealing.

A little-understood fact about the labor movement is that, even in its reduced state as a smaller proportion of the working population, it is the predominate organizer of more people, and more kinds of people, than any other organization. With many millions of members, the labor movement is much more diverse than often portrayed. There are more women in the labor movement than in the organizations of the women's movement. There are likely many more African Americans in the labor movement than in all the national civil rights organizations. There are likely more gays and lesbians in the labor movement than in the official organizations of the LGBTQ movement. The composition of the labor movement represents a cross-section of the united movement we need. It trains leaders and activists uniquely qualified to cross many organizational and social boundaries. Some union members stand at the intersections between movements, participate across those intersections, and provide a bridge to building unity across movements.

This reality defeats many stereotypes about who belongs to unions. 46% of union members are women, 36% are people of color. 12.5% of white workers are covered by union contracts, while 14.5% of black workers are. Over 40% of union members have a bachelor's degree or higher.[100] The labor movement represents the entire U.S. working class—it is not just limited to a fictional blue-collar "white working class" that many pundits pontificate about. The U.S. working class is multi-racial, multi-generational, multi-gender, multi-national. It already has in its membership a cross-section of the population. Of course, the labor movement can do better by organizing more workers, promoting more youth, women, and people of color into leadership, and speaking even more to the needs of society as a whole.

A short-sighted focus on environmental problems to the exclusion of the economic framework that creates and maintains those problems is as self-defeating as a short-sighted focus on global warming and greenhouse gases to the exclusion of other environmental threats. The environmental

movement needs workers and needs alliances with and participation from unions. Because organized workers have the
potential power to wrest control of production decisions away
from the capitalist class, they are an essential element to the
fight for fundamental change.

Another class issue is that workers are among the first to
be victimized by toxic chemicals on the job. Later, those toxic
chemicals are dumped in ways that affect all of us. Workers
in the factories and workplaces die, contract environmental-
ly-induced diseases, and get a double dose of pollutants, being
exposed both where they work and where they live. Just as
many corporations fight against environmental regulations,
they have mounted serious campaigns against efforts to pass
"right to know" laws requiring companies to inform their
workers of the toxic chemicals they are exposed to at work.

Corporations are no more hesitant to hurt their employees
than they are hesitant to hurt the communities where those
employees and many others live. This is not a new phenomenon; coal miners and their communities have suffered severe
respiratory problems for hundreds of years, and efforts to
ameliorate those problems have been resisted by the companies at every step. Owners now declaim against a supposed
"war on coal" but the mining companies have been waging
war on coal miners, their families, and their communities for
centuries. Coal is actually no longer economically feasible, no
longer the cheapest method of producing energy.[101]

Some Texas construction workers are now waging a fight
to demand that the guarantee of regular breaks is honored
and adequate hydration provided, because when they are
working outside in the escalating heat with no breaks, that can
be life-threatening.

Working class solutions don't limit themselves to considerations of carbon footprints or individual recycling. They don't
rely on some magical market to solve problems for us. Solutions are based on understanding that technology is a tool, and
that technological solutions and improvements must go hand
in hand with social and economic changes to be effective.

Workers need to work in safe workplaces, free of toxic chemicals. They need to live in neighborhoods and houses which

minimize energy loss due to inadequate housing construction and endless commutes. They need to live free from toxic waste and industrial pollution. They need sources of clean, safe water. They need healthy, affordable food supplies that don't use chemical pesticides and herbicides, and don't rely on carbon-burning transportation over huge distances. They want and need to know that their descendants will have the possibility of living healthy lives in a world where all people have choices, opportunities, and democratic political and economic power.

Workers need to shoulder their share of the costs of change, but they don't need to shoulder the share of the capitalists. Capitalists, with their luxuries, their conspicuous consumption, their arrogant use of power, and their resistance to change need to shoulder the main burden of the costs of fixing the system that has brought them so much. Instead, they resist any effort that challenges their "right" to make excessive profits and to use short-term profit as the measure of all things.

Unions are beginning to address global warming, beginning to resist attempts to place the burden of the crisis on the backs of their members and other working people. They are holding conferences and participating in coalitions. Many unions are demanding that candidates they support address global warming along with other issues of concern to workers. Many unions and workers understand that the corporations that attack the environment also attack workers' rights, workers health, and unions. Efforts to build support for environmental issues inside labor go back years, to Tony Mazzocchi, a leader of the Oil, Chemical, and Atomic Workers Union, founder of the Labor Party in the 1990s.[102]

Increasingly, there are coalitions between unions and environmental groups, "Blue-Green" coalitions, and projects like the Apollo Alliance. The pacesetter for these joint efforts is the "Blue-Green Alliance" founded by the Sierra Club and the Steelworkers Union, which is putting out an advanced program to create "green jobs" which has already influenced election debates and has been joined by other unions and environmental organizations.[103] The West Coast Longshore union (ILWU) participates in the Coalition for Clean and Safe Ports, another intersection between the labor and environmental movements. The example of the ILWU taking action on issues beyond just the immediate on-the-job ones, shows one of the ways in which unity is built—the ILWU has organized shutdowns in West Coast ports over divestment from companies which did business with apartheid South Africa and against handling cargo from South Africa. In 2017, the ILWU staged a one-day walkout protesting the Nazis and white supremacists who marched in Charlottesville, one of whom killed an anti-Nazi protester.

Efforts are being made to organize port truckers, who are forced to spend hours idling their trucks while waiting for cargo, harming the health of the drivers and the community, creating significant pollution and wasting gas. Some Teamster locals have been in direct coalition with environmentalists to promote better pay and working conditions for these workers.

Some environmentalists condemn the labor movement and workers in general for being somehow backward at tackling climate change. They see workers as part of the problem rather than seeing that workers are essential to the solutions we need. The working class, in the U.S. and also internationally, is the only force which, in alliance with others, has the potential power to create the fundamental changes we need.[104]

Some of the same scientists who very clearly see the role of constant change and development in the natural world have a strangely static view of the working class and its unions. They don't see the labor movement, and the broader working class, as changing, as always being in motion, as capable of understanding their long range interests.

At their worst, both the labor and environmental movements focus narrowly on their own immediate issues, to the detriment of both. At their best, they can make more progress together.[105]

We can't pretend that conflicts between environmentalists and unions aren't real and can be very challenging. When workers pile into town meetings to support power plants or pipelines which environmentalists oppose, that causes immediate problems for building unity, for creating trust, and for finding working-class solutions to environmental issues.

When unions, for example many building trades unions, have knee-jerk reactions against anything and everything the environmental movement proposes, that can end up harming building trades workers. When environmentalists demand that workers to make an impossible choice between either feeding their family in the here and now or doing the moral thing and immediately quitting their jobs, that creates disunity and division.

Such difficulties won't vanish but can be solved more easily if the environmental movement unites with labor to propose and fight for living-wage green jobs as part of a massive public works program to rebuild infrastructure, retrofit and insulate building stock, transform the energy industry, and create millions of jobs in the process.

Issues of workers' rights are international, in ways very similar to the international aspects of environmental challenges. The need to build international unity within labor, within the environmental movement, and between both movements, is an urgent task.

International capital has already figured out how to, in many cases, escape international borders. For years now, it has been a truism that Exxon-Mobil has its own foreign policy, not tied to the U.S. or any other country, placing their own profit interests ahead of those of the people of the world. The labor movement and the environmental movement need to build international cooperation against the depredations of multinational corporations. International labor was divided for many decades by vicious anti-Communism, and has taken too long to adjust to the international role of capital, the ability of companies to export jobs and factories, to play workers in one country off against workers elsewhere.

Lessons from the Anti-Apartheid Movement

There was a rash of serious depression among progressive activists following the 1984 re-election of Ronald Reagan. There was a period of uncertainty about how to proceed, about whether or not there was much hope of stopping the right-ward wave in U.S. electoral politics. But within days, the anti-apartheid movement began a series of demonstrations outside the South African Embassy in Washington D.C., with many arrests including of civil rights movement veterans, members of Congress, union leaders, and individual activists.

There proceeded to be a years-long campaign involving demonstrations and arrests at South African Consulates all over the country, bills in Congress condemning apartheid, educational and divestment campaigns on many campuses, in religious denominations, and over the investment strategies of public pension funds. Combined with a massive worldwide movement, and with heroic and determined struggle within South Africa itself, apartheid was finally defeated.

The organizers of that first demonstration understood the need to be bold, to seize the initiative, to make protest public, to force clear moral issues front and center in the public discourse, to expose the horrors of racism and oppression. Their approach not only inspired anti-apartheid activists around the country, it also inspired progressives to act on many issues, to kick themselves out of their depression and take action, to fight the system.

The struggle against apartheid in the U.S. was protracted. It went on for years, it combined legislative action with stockholder protests, with local actions at South African Consulates, with educational efforts, with organizing speaking tours for South African leaders and activists, with legal challenges. It was not a one-shot deal. And the struggle in the U.S. was united with a worldwide movement engaged in similar actions and struggles.

The anti-apartheid movement had to reject the anti-communist rhetoric, the anti-terrorism claims, of right-wing politicians who sought to divide the movement, to drive a wedge between the movement and the broader public. They had to reject the racism inherent in many of the arguments of the opponents of divestment, and reject the "it's only business" arguments of multi-national corporations. They had to reject efforts to demonize and discredit the leaders of their movement, such as the work of the CIA to track Nelson Mandela and then report on his activities and location to the South African authorities who proceeded to arrest him and then incarcerate him for 27 years.

Lessons from the Existing Environmental Movement

We already have many decades of experience in the modern environmental movement. Rachel Carson is often credited with initiating the modern movement with the publication of her book *Silent Spring*. There were simultaneous efforts to popularize the negative effects of radioactive fallout from nuclear testing, led in St. Louis by the Committee for Nuclear Information founded by, among others, Barry Commoner and Virginia Brodine. From the first Earth Day in 1970 to the People's Climate March in 2014 to today's resistance to the efforts of the Trump administration to scuttle climate action and environmental regulation, the existing environmental movement has won some victories, lost some battles, and has been working its way to the forefront of people's awareness.

In the process, we have learned that it is not enough to have science on our side, though that is essential. Education and explanation are both important and necessary but not sufficient. Just testifying to Congress about looming environmental disasters is not enough to overcome either the inertia of the system nor the active resistance of industries hell-bent on protecting their short-term profits.

We have learned that stopping or controlling pollution after it is already created is difficult, expensive, and considerably less effective than stopping it before it is produced in the first place.

The struggle to pass legislation can only be one part of the movement. Limiting the struggle to legislation and regulation limits the appeal to average people and limits how they can participate, places a damper on the radical edge of a movement, avoids real mass action, stunts grassroots organizing, restricts the movement to "acceptable" channels. That said, rejecting all legislative and regulatory struggles limits the ability to win partial but immediate demands.

The environmental movement must fight for jobs, jobs, and more jobs—otherwise, we force workers to choose between now and later, between short-term personal survival and long-term human survival. Barry Commoner asked:

> Why should environmental activists be in favor of economic growth, when this seems to fly in the face of the argument, often advanced by some environmentalists, that high rates of production and consumption are the chief *cause* of environmental degradation? That view is based on the assumption that production is *necessarily* accompanied by pollution, so that these two processes rise and fall together. It reflects a prevailing myth that production technology—the high-compression engine, the nuclear reactor, or genetic engineering—is simply the practical application of scientific knowledge and is therefore no more amenable to human judgement or social interests than the laws of thermodynamics, atomic structure, or biological inheritance. The environmental experience has shattered this myth. The high-compression engine and the nuclear reactor were built in response to *human* decisions and their linkage to smog and radioactive waste can be readily broken by building electric vehicles and photovoltaic cells instead.[106]

People learn from struggle and are inspired by victories, even partial ones. This is an other reason for diversity of tactics. No matter how apocalyptic the dangers we see, we must have a "progress not perfection" attitude. We need to understand that solutions require fundamental transformation of our political, economic, and production systems. But we can't wait, and we can't get to such basic change without immediate partial changes (the "possible right now").

Passion for protecting the earth, animal and vegetable life, and the quality of human life is essential, but that cannot substitute for organization. Just because change is right, that does not automatically lead to sufficient action to bring about that change. We are in a power struggle with well-entrenched interests which are intertwined with our limited democracy. It is not enough to be passionate, to be right, to be prescient. We need a movement that has persistence and power. The movement itself must be sustainable.

Any and all environmental struggles quickly run up against the capitalist system. This can lead to environmental activists beginning to understand the need for basic systemic change.[107] Environmental struggles are a new path to socialist consciousness, a new way to understand the need for fundamental economic change.

Bill McKibben plays a vital role in the environmental movement. He has written several important books, including *The End of Nature* and *Eaarth, Making a Life on a Tough New Planet.* He founded 350.org, an Internet-based organization which has sponsored worldwide demonstrations calling for a return to no more than 350 parts per million of carbon dioxide in the atmosphere, which is essential if the planet is to avoid the worst effects of climate change. 350.org plays an important role in coordinating and publicizing many divestment struggles. As a polemicist, activist, and thinker, McKibben's contributions have international significance.

But his analysis hasn't always met the needs of the moment in three major ways.

First is that he has sometimes placed the struggle against Democrats as the central one for environmentalists. He is correctly worried about how often many Democrats waver, procrastinate, and obfuscate, some of them on all environmental issues, some on one or another particular issue.

Second, McKibben sees people in general as his target audience. This is certainly understandable, since people in general will all be negatively affected by environmental problems and should see their self-interest in solving them. But to create fundamental change requires winning a majority of workers and building real connections with their unions. That requires campaigns that place a green jobs program as central to environmental struggles. Blaming unions in part for the delay in raising automobile emission standards, while it has an element of truth, is not the strongest way to win an argument for the labor movement to fully engage in alliances with environmentalists.

Third, McKibben has sometimes placed climate change struggles in competition with other struggles, arguing that action on global warming should take precedence over other struggles, like the one to create universal health care coverage. Rather than making an argument for the connections between climate change and other environmental struggles, he places them in competition—a sure way to discourage allies whose main focus is and will continue to be those other struggles. McKibben has moved more towards building broader-based unity and alliances in recent years, stressing the movement's participation in coalitions as key to fundaméntal transformation.

Of course the environmental movement and its allies need to pressure Democrats and any politician who works to block progress, but they are not the main obstacle to action on climate change—the right-wing and its science-denying propagandists, funded by fossil fuel companies, are the source of the problem, the source of the main opposition to action. Obama's actions on the environment were mostly positive and useful, even as they didn't go far enough. To build the broadest movement requires winning millions who were part of the successful Obama election and re-election victories. Placing an attack on Democrats as *central* to progress is not designed to win their base but to push that base further away from their potential allies in the environmental movement.

People in general can accomplish much. They can demonstrate and protest, sign petitions, write letters to Congressional representatives and newspapers, blog, vote and canvass for votes, educate and convince neighbors, and connect worldwide environmental issues to local issues; the list goes on. We must encourage all people to take action—the activity of millions of individuals can powerfully impact politics, policies, and the public discourse.

But only workers have the power to shut down the economy. Only workers, when organized, have the power to alter the economic system. Workers do the daily work at all the crucial chokepoints of the economy, and perform the services that keep the economy running relatively smoothly. The power of workers to bring the economy to a halt is a powerful and essential tool to create fundamental change.

All progressive struggles have an environmental component, and successful alliances have been built by joining environmental programs with jobs programs, uniting environmental concerns with economic ones, uniting environmental and labor organizations. Environmental and civil rights organizations can find common ground in fighting environmental racism. Worldwide environmental issues can be joined with struggles for peace and justice worldwide; international environmental struggles can be linked to international labor struggles.

This holds true for the other sides of these coalitions—they too need to reach out and make alliances with environmental organizations, rather than characterizing them as against jobs, as against making progress on other issues, as primarily white not only in membership but in concerns. Of course the environmental movement needs to expand and diversify, needs to reach out, needs to build alliances, but so do all these other groups. It is up to all of them to find common ground and to engage in mutual support.

In many struggles, in the U.S. and around the world, indigenous activists, tribes, nations, and spiritual leaders are providing initiative, leadership, and inspiration. Participating in demonstrations against pipelines, such as the Keystone XL or the Dakota Access pipeline (DAPL) for two examples, offer a way to move more people into action and for many people from all parts of society to join with environmental activists. Struggles against mining on reservation land, for water rights, for tribal sovereignty over their own land and what lies under it, are opening the eyes of many to the racism inherent in corporate efforts to steal from Native Americans. The DAPL struggle in particular offers lessons for today's struggles in how to use social media, how to reframe the public discourse in more favorable terms, how to use of drones to monitor what company and government forces were doing, and building breakthrough solidarity with tribes and supporters around the entire country.

Unity with many other movements and struggles is the road to victories for the environmental movement. The movement needs to incorporate legal and legislative efforts with broad coalitions, demonstrative actions, community organizing, civil disobedience, public education, and other forms of struggle. "Green marketing," greenwashing, and various advertising/ labeling schemes are not the solution. Making clear that short-term job growth which forces workers to engage in work that is harmful to their own long-term survival is wrong and that there are better ways to create jobs is the path for the environmental movement to take to win allies for the long-term struggle.

The Left must be among the advocates of the importance of environmental issues. Public awareness and knowledge are growing, especially among young people. Within the environmental movement, there is growing awareness of the need for alliances and coalitions, of addressing issues of poverty and inequality as part of how we address global warming, of building a mass movement capable of implementing change. The environmental movement must acknowledge and address the more deeply felt and immediately disastrous impacts on the poor in general and on communities of color, as well as on less-developed countries, primarily populated by people of color.

The role of the environmental movement is undergoing a transformation, from an over-reliance on legal and advocacy strategies, to a more active engagement in the political process and in coalition-building, alliance-building, and trust-building with labor and other movements. Solving the serious environmental problems that confront humanity requires a broad-based, majority movement. Environmental issues are growing in importance. There is a growing majority consensus around the world, both among the public and among elected officials, about the necessity of addressing major environmental problems.

Mainstream Environmental Organizations

The strategy of some older environmental organizations to seek and accept funding from major corporations, and limiting struggles to legislative and legal efforts, is not sufficient.

There have been a number of disputes over the strategies of various "mainstream" environmental groups. Some claim that they rely too heavily on an oppositional, confrontational approach, fighting with corporations when they could have a bigger impact by seeking cooperation. Others condemn mainstream groups for taking any corporate money at all. And often many national environmental groups focus on raising money and engaging in publicity campaigns rather than on building organizations of struggle. Others rely on media-catching staged protests geared to getting coverage rather than having an actual impact on policy. Headline-grabbing protests can be inspiring, can bring crucial issues to the attention of millions who otherwise would not be aware of them, but by themselves such tactics are nowhere near enough.

These debates miss the point that all these strategies are necessary aspects of the broader struggles that the environmental movement must engage in. There is not one single strategy which fits all circumstances, not one single tactic that fits all situations.

Similarly, a focus on lobbying for better regulations and laws is an essential component of the struggle to wrest control of issues that affect all of us away from the hands of private, profit-seeking managers and owners. It is part of the struggle for democracy, to make our political system address the needs of the vast majority. But such efforts, such as doorbell-ringing fundraising, when not backed up with the organizational muscle of on-the-ground organizing and mobilizing, will be doomed to minor successes at best.

The efforts of the mainstream environmental groups, while insufficient by themselves to reach real, long-term solutions, must be seen as part of the broader movement, complementary to the organizing, mass demonstrations, and local efforts of grassroots groups. We can see these mainstream organizations as allies without subscribing to the entirety of their limited or limiting strategies.

International Aspects of the Environmental Movement

Some environmental organizations are already international, such as Greenpeace. McKibben's group, 350.org, which is mainly an online vehicle for organizing rather than a "bricks-and-mortar" organization, has promoted worldwide demonstrations on more than a few occasions. Every time there is a United Nations Conference on Climate Change, there is a "shadow" conference of environmental activists, scientists, and organizations, with attendance sometimes numbering in the tens of thousands, with linked mass demonstrations that are much larger.

The environmental challenges we face are international in scope, affecting people in every country, on every continent. Fighting for international treaties with enforceable commitments is an important part of the environmental movement, and this approach has won some victories. However, even those victories are partial, such as the Paris Climate Accord, signed by all countries but the U.S. The U.S. withdrawal by Trump is the only case of a country dropping out of the Accord, and even so the withdrawal will take three years to accomplish, giving us time to reverse the decision. Two countries which had not signed it have now done so—Nicaragua had not signed it originally because the agreement had not gone far enough, and Syria had not due to the raging civil war. It set ambitious goals, and many countries have promised even more stringent goals for themselves. But even if all those commitments are fulfilled, that will not be enough to reach the stated aim of one and a half degrees of warming, forced on the negotiators in part by small island nations facing imminent threat of disappearing beneath the waves, and before that with the contamination of their drinking water. The Accord was a major step forward, but nowhere near enough. Such international agreements will never adopt a goal of fundamental economic transformation.

Unity requires recognizing diversity, not only ethnic, national, racial, and gender diversity, but also diversity of the challenges faced in different locales. The international environmental movement must build organizational alliances around the world, must recognize that the impacts of climate change are not identical in all places, and that all countries do not have the same resources for adaptation, mitigation, or extreme weather recuperation. Unity requires addressing those differentials in our understanding, in our demands, and in our actions.

Some, unconsciously imbued with the illusion of American exceptionalism, may think that the environmental movement in the U.S. is the world leader, the most important part of the world movement. Such unintended (in most cases) arrogance ignores the strength the U.S. movement can gain from the struggles elsewhere, from the inspiration from intense struggles around the world, from the victories that are won.

For example, Bolivia has enshrined the needs of nature in its constitution. Indigenous peoples around the world are waging and leading struggles against mining interests who seek to despoil their ancestral lands, and are finding new ways to build unity. A U.S. example is the Cowboy and Indian Coalition, which began in conservative Nebraska to fight the Keystone XL pipeline.

It is impossible to seriously consider solving the problems facing millions of people in Africa without looking at all the major factors affecting them, including:

- increased drought in many places,
- accelerating urbanization without adequate municipal systems (water, sewer, etc.),
- the AIDS crisis,
- crushing international debt, deformation of development driven by the policies of the World Bank and the IMF,
- the massive transfers of wealth to international banks over many decades,
- the drive to control resource-extraction by multinational corporations,
- rising ocean levels and water temperatures,
- excessive demands on limited water systems,
- the legacy of colonialism which encouraged and depended on intertribal rivalries and warfare to control vast populations and suppress popular struggles for sov-

ereignty, and which imposed artificial borders, massive poverty, and internal and external refugee populations.

All these are linked together, and no one of them can be solved in isolation, without simultaneous actions to solve the others. Environmental battles are happening all over the world, people everywhere are taking action on climate change, people are fighting important local battles that should resonate with the world movement.

For example, a recent UN report says, "Competition over oil and gas reserves, Nile waters and timber, as well as land use issues related to agricultural land, are important causative factors in the instigation and perpetuation of conflict in Sudan." Flooding, deforestation, overgrazing due to explosive livestock growth, and decline in rainfall caused by regional climate change have been stress factors. It continues, "Long-term peace in [Northern Darfur] will not be possible unless these underlying and closely linked environmental and livelihood issues are resolved."

Another problem is that nature is letting us know in no uncertain terms that the development path which Western Europe and the U.S. took is not available to other countries, not without hurting everyone including the vast majority of people in the less-developed nations themselves. All of humanity needs developing countries to take a different path to industrialization; just creating more of the same will not help the people of less-developed nations. All of humanity *also* needs the U.S. to transform its industrial production and transportation systems (if the U.S. just cut back its carbon emissions to the level of Western Europe, that would make a significant contribution to buying time for the whole world). It is not one or the other, it is both simultaneously.

These international issues go far beyond just environmental concerns but can't be separated from them. Social justice is hard or impossible to achieve when there is not enough food, water, or income for even subsistence living. Improving the lives of billions of people who live on the equivalent of one or two dollars a day must be seen as linked to environmental struggles.

To Catastrophize or Not

Sometimes, controversies erupt among environmentalists and scientists over whether or not to explain exactly how bad the environment could get for all humankind if we do nothing. Some argue that we need to project positive approaches that encourage people to think that their efforts can and will make a difference. Others argue that only a clear exposition of the catastrophes that await if business-as-usual continues will shock people out of their inertia,[108] will break through the din of denialism, will clarify matters in the midst of confusion and disinformation. Others claim that catastrophizing distracts from the main issues[109]or discourages people from taking action, fearing it will be a waste of time and energy.

Such arguments miss the point that we need both. People need to know just how bad life on earth could get. People need to understand the consequences of inaction. Some people need to be shocked out of complacency. Not everyone, but some people.

All of us *also* need to know that we can make a difference, that our actions matter, that taking action is not hopeless and futile. We need to know that we are not alone, that millions of others are seeking answers and ways to make a difference, just as we are.

Just as we need many approaches and many tactics, many efforts to educate the public will help, and that education can and must take many forms. Exposing the role of corporations is one piece; explaining the dangers that might await humanity is another piece. Making clear what we can do, how we can build a positive movement that can create the political and economic space to improve life for us and our descendants is another.

And the reality is that thus far, in spite of many kinds of progress being made, for example in shifting to renewable, clean energy, greenhouse gas emissions continue to rise, continue to accumulate in the atmosphere. These emissions continue to "bake in" negative consequences for humanity on the earth in our shared future. That is part of the truth, and needs explaining, just as the potential for progress and improvement need explaining. It is not one or the other; both are needed.

Lessons from Science

Creating fundamental change is not just about telling the truth in public, not just about defending science against attacks by the ultra-right; to be successful it must also be about creating political power. The challenges are so basic that the solutions must be basic too. It is not enough to get the science right, we also have to get the movement right.

Scientific research is part of the solution but insufficient by itself, as has been shown by the experience of those scientists who thought they only needed to explain the problems in order to bring forth the political will to create change.[110]

We have seen that providing information to the public is not sufficient—scientific knowledge is crucial, but it is not enough. Knowledge, understanding, factual details, morality, and passion need to be paired with effective communication with the whole public, and need to be linked to ongoing mass organization. Technology is also part of the solution, but technological innovation must be adopted by millions to have sufficient impact and can't be predicated on continuing and reinforcing a system that relies on overexploitation of the earth's resources. We also can't limit technological change to only technologies which will be profitable in the short run.

Some lessons from the early environmental movement in the U.S. include that:

> Environmental pollution is created by production, and eliminating pollution requires fundamental changes in systems of production
> Scientists have a social responsibility to make their work relevant and understandable to the public
> Sound political strategy in the environmental field must be based on sound science, and
> Sound science is a-disciplinary science—traditional academic disciplines prevent the kind of "systems thinking" that leads to truly fundamental solutions to social problems.[111]

Scientific understanding of constant change needs to also be applied to understanding social, political, and economic change. As is true with the climate, everything in the world has tipping points, including political movements and economic transformations. Seeing natural change but not social, cultural, and political change is a limitation on the contributions we need from scientists. Scientists need an holistic approach not only to science but to the interface between science and the political, economic, and social worlds.

With the growing movement for science, for reality, for facts, an important new strain of the movement against the Trump administration and against the climate deniers has swung into motion. It must learn to be partisan, not in a narrow political sense but in the sense of being partisan to the truth—and that partisanship has to affect how scientists are politically active. The role of scientists in the movement is not limited to educating people about scientific truth, it must also include running for office, organizing demonstrations, participating in struggles at all levels. It is a positive sign that this is already happening, in part in reaction to efforts from the Trump administration (and the Bush administration before it) to muzzle scientists, to prevent government scientists from studying climate change or, if they do manage to study it, prevent them from even using the words "climate change" when they report their findings.

A basic science lesson is that there is no substitute for research, for discovering the actuality of what is happening and why. To fix any problem, it needs to be understood. Research, testing our partial knowledge to gain more knowledge and deeper understanding, and advocating to the public are linked tasks of the scientists in the environmental movement. This is why the Trump administration is working hard to defund research, to muzzle scientists, to avoid knowledge.[112] Scientists are engaged in other forms of struggle that might not be recognized as such by many: whistleblowing on agency efforts to muzzle them, leaking damaging memos, and working to save data collected by government scientists who were paid by taxpayer's money, data which belong to all of us but which the Trump administration is trying to remove from the public domain.

The anti-science approach of the Trump administration and the willful ignorance embedded in the public justifications offered for many of his administration's decisions is leading more scientists to run for office, to bring scientific understanding into the halls of political power. This positive development is a sign that more and more scientists are understanding that their public responsibilities don't end at the laboratory door.

Lessons from Management Theory and Practice

We have massive engineering and organizational tasks ahead of us, and we will need all the tools we can get.

Our movement has lessons to learn from management theory and practice, as counterintuitive as it may seem for a Marxist to advocate. Though management theory is most often used to streamline the exploitation and oppression implemented by corporations, some of the principles can be applied to a scientific study of how to create change. We should not reject the tools themselves just because they have been used in an immoral way. When used to help implement positive changes, such tools can have great value.

One such principle is that "if you can't measure it, you can't manage it." Detailed plans are necessary, with targets, checkpoints, checklists, and program management to help achieve real goals, including PERT analysis.[113] They provide a way to implement accountability. Even though the most important reasons for protecting the environment aren't values we can measure, specific measures are necessary to determine if progress is being made. Tools and methods to measure quantitative improvements can be a useful tool when aimed at the right goals. They can be used to coordinate path-dependent interlocking tasks and processes, dealing with the complexities of fundamental change in many aspects of production, energy, distribution, and materials management.

One reason for measurable goals is so that we can work for and search for continuous improvement, for constant incremental progress. We didn't get into this environmental mess all at once, and we won't get out at all at once. We need big changes and we also need small changes, and incremental change is one aspect of many programs. We also need to distinguish between effectiveness and efficiency. Peter Drucker, management guru, noted years ago in *The Effective Executive* that you can become very efficient at doing the wrong thing. This is another way of saying that while measurable goals are necessary, first you have to make sure that you have the right goals. This is an argument for having a long-term strategy for the environmental movement—to be sure that we are not spinning our wheels in dead-end battles while losing sight of the war we have on our hands, the war with the economic system of capitalism.

An appreciation for management tools can help in transforming our production processes. It can help to manage a shift in public agencies toward the needs of all rather than acting as agents of one or another economic special interest.

Lessons from the Right Wing

After the debacle of the defeat of Barry Goldwater in the 1964 presidential election, and after the Watergate debacle, conservatives were ostracized in many parts of the public consciousness and areas of the political system. Some right-wing billionaires and right-wing theorists saw the need to develop a coherent strategy, to come up with new ways to sell their old ideas, to create, sometimes out of whole cloth, new excuses and justifications for their retrograde policy proposals.

They began to set up or more extensively fund an entire network of institutions—the Heritage Foundation, the Cato Institute, and many others—to offer intellectual cover for their efforts to turn back the clock on the New Deal advances, to fight efforts to regulate more of the economy, to write in secret legislative proposals (the American Legislative Council, ALEC, has done this very effectively) that can be passed in many states. They offered employment to young conservative thinkers and developed public figures and financed electoral campaigns at many levels. This paid off first in the election and administration of Reagan, then in the "Republican Revolution" of Newt Gingrich during the Clinton years. Their work continues today, reaching the height of both farce and tragedy in the election and administration of Trump.

They learned the value of staying focused on a simple message repeated almost endlessly, of crafting a message that had little to do with the reality of what they actually want to accomplish. We can learn from these efforts how to tailor our message in ways that reach people, that break down the divides of region and race and religion, that help accomplish the aims of a livable world with livable wages, without cynically lying to people as the right-wing does.

Frank Luntz, conservative theorist and pollster, has built his entire career by focusing on the language used in public debate, understanding the power of branding and re-branding. The Left can learn from the importance of this focus, as a method to help frame the debate, to set the terms of struggle in ways that most appeal to the most people. A recent struggle example of this is when the Dakota Access Pipeline (DAPL) struggle made a conscious effort to shift from it being a struggle against Big Oil to labeling it as a movement of "Water Protectors."

The right wing cleverly attacks sources of institutional opposition. They attacked ACORN, Planned Parenthood, health clinics, unions and their ability to participate in elections, groups that mobilize to register new voters (up to and including the non-partisan League of Women Voters). All of these groups provided ongoing support for progressive politicians and policies, or even just worked for good governance. This provides two lessons: One, it is necessary to attack the institutional sources of the right-wing movement, and two, the right-wing has provided a template of the kind of alliances we need to build between issues, organizations, and movements; all the groups and organizations they have attacked have a shared interest in defeating these attacks.

The Left needs a variety of institutions—think tanks, advocacy organizations, direct mail campaigns, financial support for demonstrative action, organizing legislative struggles from writing bills to promoting them to passing them, and media with a progressive slant to challenge the right-wing noise machine on a daily basis. The Left must recognize that it is not in this alone—there are positive educational efforts by many, including media coverage that is not in small radical publications but in major outlets, such as the excellent coverage of climate issues by *The Guardian* from England.[114]

Lessons from All of It

There are lessons from all movements, all efforts to fight wrongdoing, to correct injustices, to create positive change. However, this author does not have detailed personal knowledge about all of them. For example, there are inspiring stories and crucial lessons from the immigrant rights struggles which managed to reclaim May Day for the U.S. working class, from the women's movement, from LGBTQ struggles for full legal equality and protection, from youth struggles for a living wage and for free tuition, from senior struggles to protect and extend Social Security and Medicare, from the movements to protect and improve education, to boost teacher pay, to limit class sizes, to adequately fund schools, and to have decent working conditions for teachers.

Environmental change, like all basic change, revolves around questions of power. Workers have the potential power needed to create fundamental change, so there is no shortcut around winning a majority of workers to support a movement.

Successful strategy for the environmental movement (and the other movements as well) involves making connections between movements, organizations, coalitions, struggles, learning from each of those movements, and in the process developing broad-based unity to reach and organize millions of people.

Chapter 9

More Strategic Considerations

The Broadest Basis for Unity

Progressive movements need a commitment to the fight for democracy at the center of their campaigns. This is not strictly an electoral issue, though electoral campaigns are a piece of it. It is also a battle for the right to protest, the right to demonstrate, the right to vote, the right to have your voice heard and your vote count. The attacks on voting rights and the efforts at voter suppression have elevated the importance of voting, of working to reach non-voting citizens, of restoring voting rights to those who have served their time in prison, of demanding full political democracy.

All movements have a self-interest in the battles over democratic rights. If an organization wants to have the option to hold a demonstration, the ability to do that lies in protecting the rights of all to occupy public space, to participate in the public discourse.

These rights are at least partially enshrined in the Bill of Rights—the right to free speech, the right to peaceably assemble, the right to petition for redress of grievances, the right to freely associate. Protecting these basic rights is key to any movement being able to act effectively, to influence public opinion, to work to win masses to their struggle. Extending voting rights is a key part of the fight to engage much more of the public in changing the basic dysfunctional political dynamic in the U.S.

161

The fight for democracy also connects us to deep and profound streams in U.S. political culture. The history of our country is in part a history of working to make the promises of the Constitution real. The franchise was extended from white male property owners to all white males to all males to all females, and then to eliminating obstacles like poll taxes, citizenship tests as a voting requirement, and intimidation at the polls on election day. In some states, there is extended and early voting, in others all-mail ballots or same-day registration. Several states have made voter registration automatic. All of these steps toward a fuller democracy are under attack from the right wing, desperate to find ways, including gerrymandering, to keep their stranglehold on power.

We should avoid illusions about voting and U.S. political democracy. Democracy in the U.S. is limited, just as the Constitution itself was limited and flawed, protecting the state governments of slave owners, counting slaves as less than full human beings, not guaranteeing voting rights to the entire population, enshrining indirect elections for the Senate and President. But failing to protect and extend democratic rights is a failure that would keep masses of people from impacting public policy, from changing the rules, regulations, and laws to better protect us, from protecting the right to protest itself.

Those on the Left who argue that we should stand apart from the Democratic Party, arguing that it is a capitalist party and that there are many examples of hypocrisy by Democrats, miss the point. Even if there is only an inch of difference between Democrats and their Republican opponents, millions of people live in that inch. Even small differences in policies and programs can either help improve real lives, or harm millions. For example, the food stamp program is not a solution to the problems of hunger in the U.S., but having such a program does positively impact the lives of millions, including many children. Small differences in approach matter to millions of those we need to win to more fundamental solutions, and they need to know the Left is on their side, that their lives right now matter to us.

If we set ourselves apart, we also set ourselves apart from the labor movement, many civil rights movements, and tens of millions of people who still identify with the Democrats or see them, for good reason, as the only viable alternative to reactionary control of government. Those movements are not agnostic about battles in the Democratic Party, they understand that it matters to millions of people who the Democratic nominee is, that it can make a difference in the lives of those millions. That does not mean we need to see a Democratic nominee for president as a working class hero or heroine, as an ideal candidate with a perfect program—they have not been and will not be.

The media and many political campaigns want to make elections about the horse race, about who is winning the day, about the personalities of one or another candidate. But politics is more serious than that, and the consequences for the people of the country are much more serious than that. If nothing else, the Electoral College victory for Trump shows that no matter how limited the Democrats are, it can be much worse, our rights can be under more vicious assault, the possibility of protest and even voting can be threatened or even eliminated if the system feels threatened enough. The Democratic Party is not the solution, but it is part of the current political reality in the U.S. To ignore it as if there was no difference between the two major parties is foolish, and amounts to abandoning an important field of struggle to the right and the center-right. To act as if every single Democratic candidate was equally hypocritical is a basic misreading of reality.

The fight for full democracy includes a pathway to citizenship for all who live here including immigrants. Anything less amounts to taxation without representation, one of the key issues of the American Revolution. Residents who work, pay taxes, and participate in our economy, should also be able to participate in making the social and political decisions that govern society.

The fight for democracy includes the right of all to participate fully in the rights of citizenship and residence—including the rights of immigrants to a life free from discrimination, including the right of all to marry, including the right of gays, lesbians, and transgender people to hold jobs free from discrimination, to find decent housing, to be free of violence and oppression.

This also means fighting to guarantee full citizenship rights and full representation for residents of Washington DC. The right to be secure in our homes, the right to be free of intimidation, violence and oppression are important for all, and the environmental movement must participate in struggles to protect and extend civil rights to all. After all, clean air and clean water are, or should be, among those rights. Roosevelt's Four Freedoms, proclaimed during his 1941 State of the Union address to Congress in the lead-up to U.S. participation in WWII, are still democratic tasks which lie ahead of us—rights to freedom of speech, of worship, and to be free from want and fear.[115]

On the Nature of Coalitions

Coalitions are essential tools, ways to build trust and understanding in the process of struggle. They offer a path to larger mobilizations, bigger impacts. But they are not a substitute for ongoing organization, and we should not be confused about what coalitions are and are not capable of doing.

Some of the problems of the movement arise from misunderstandings about the nature of coalitions. Coalitions, by definition, are made up of people and groups which might disagree with each other on some points or which may have different focuses or goals. Or they might have similar interests but work to organize different sets of people. They might come together around a particular issue, event, or campaign, but each organization has its own strategy and its own organizational interests. They might have divergent interests but share one or more common goals. For example, during the First Gulf War some right-wing libertarian groups joined with the primarily left-led coalitions against that war.

Coalitions have both strengths and limitations. They can act as a force multiplier, bringing new social groups and organizations into action on an issue of common concern, while enabling each organization to maintain its unique and independent role. They can create a more positive public impression by making clear how many groups have joined together on an issue or struggle. There are coalitions of coalitions—broad, national groupings that bring together a great variety of mass organizations, some of which are already coalitions on their own. Such formations are most often related to major national struggles over laws and national priorities, such as health care for all.

Some coalitions exist on one issue in one locality for a limited time. These coalitions exist in part because the member organizations do not share long-term goals or strategies but find strength in working together on a limited set of issues. Some coalitions are restricted because their unity is temporary and limited.

National coalitions are often alliances between groups of national organizations, and sometimes those alliances never reach the local affiliates of those organizations. The activities of some of these coalitions are limited to lobbying and public relations campaigns. They result in positive publicity and progressive statements of principles, but sometimes never reach to actual mobilization of their memberships into joint actions. This limits their potential effectiveness, since often the activists are limited to the national staffers of the allied organizations. Not involving the mass membership of the coalition partners is a major weakness of many worthwhile national coalitions.

Other coalitions are relatively permanent, where a group of organizations share many common goals. In some senses, labor councils function this way, uniting many different unions who cooperate on a relatively permanent basis on a wide variety of issues, while still maintaining the independence of each union and its specific group of members. It is important to understand which type of coalition is being built, in order to adopt strategies and tactics appropriate for that type, and to avoid mistaken assumptions and illusions about what can and cannot be accomplished.

Coalitions can't and won't substitute for on-the-ground organizing, for permanent organizations of struggle, for institutions of resistance. The reverse is also true—organizations on their own can limit their effectiveness by standing apart from the compromises and limitations involved in coalition-building.

Coalitions are most effective when they unite a variety of organizations and movements, when they mobilize their memberships into collective joint action, when they reach out to those millions who will spontaneously respond to unity and action, and when they crystalize mass sentiment into mass demonstrations linked to electoral and legislative struggles.

People who are becoming active for the first time can find it easy to overestimate the level of agreement in coalitions which may appear more united than they really are. These new activists may confuse coalition with identity, thinking that because groups are united in a coalition they must share all their goals and strategies as well. For example, during the opposition to the First Gulf War, some individuals proposed to a local coalition that the whole coalition should function together on a precinct level for electoral work, ignoring the significant ideological differences between the member organizations. This confuses the real potential of coalition-building.

A fusion coalition of the kind advocated and led by Rev. William J. Barber II in North Carolina, the founder of the Moral Monday movement, is a living example of the kind of coalition which acknowledges differences, works through issues of trust and division, keeps its eyes on the prize, looks for unity across traditional political lines and divisions, keeps its moral compass firmly at the center of its politics, and unites unions and workers, community groups, civil rights groups, religious groups, and many others.

Their experience also teaches important lessons about persistence—though the Moral Monday movement seemed to burst on the scene, it took seven years of painstaking work beforehand to create the coalition capable of seizing that political moment. Having a coalition already in place, with years of joint work and trust-building, enabled the Moral Monday movement to start out by joining the spontaneous opposition to right-wing legislative efforts with established on-going organization. The existing coalition didn't sponsor the first Moral Monday demonstration in the North Carolina capital knowing that the kind of spontaneous turn-out from many thousands would happen. But they were able to turn that outpouring into several years of weekly demonstrations which addressed many issues.[116]

Environmental Racism

Following the horrific violence in Charlottesville, Virginia by a fascist plowing into a crowd of anti-fascist protesters, killing Heather Heyer and injuring 19 others, the Sierra Club issued a statement, including this:

> Some have asked why Sierra Club would get involved in this issue. To quote Martin Luther King, Jr, "All life is interrelated. We are all caught in an inescapable network of mutuality, tied into a single garment of destiny. Whatever affects one destiny, affects all indirectly." An attack on racial justice is an attack on all of us, as we are all connected in our rights and dignity as human beings sharing this fragile planet. Or, to echo our founder John Muir, "When we try to pick out anything by itself, we find it hitched to everything else in the Universe."

As more environmentalists and environmental organizations come to understand the links between environmental issues and civil rights struggles, making links like these from both sides helps the process of building unity, joining causes and struggles and gaining strength from each other.

Environmental racism is a multifaceted set of issues. The most obvious are the ways in which toxic chemical plants, pipelines, and waste dumps are situated in, on, and near communities of color and Native American reservations, exacerbated by the lack of people's political power to stop such "development." You can see this in Houston's "Toxic Alley," in efforts to situate nuclear waste dumps on or near reservations, in Superfund sites which have low-cost housing nearby, often the only housing that poverty-stricken families can afford.

Another aspect is the lack of minority representation in decision-making bodies both public and private, which facilitates imposing environmental toxicity on predominately non-white communities. When entire communities are disenfranchised, their concerns do not even appear at the tables where decisions are made. When plants are located on reservations, often the residents have no say in the environmental and economic decisions which affect their lives.[117] In addition to facing extra environmental insults in their communities and on the job, these communities are often frozen out of public policy-making at the local and state levels.

Often, the lowest paying jobs are also the ones most subjected to the unregulated use of toxic chemicals. These same jobs are disproportionately filled by women, African Americans, Mexican Americans, and other disenfranchised groups.

The extra environmental load forced on these communities provides the basis for unifying those communities with the environmental movement, making that movement more diverse—and stronger as a result. It becomes a pathway to unify the environmental movement with civil rights and community organizations. It is a clear case of self-interest for those communities to engage in struggle with the opponents of environmental regulation and public control over many aspects of production and waste.

The excess environmental damage to communities of color is piled on top of the already-burdensome weight on all of us. This reality presents both a problem and an opportunity— for those faced with this double and triple burden, the only solution lies in alliance with the entire environmental movement. At the same time, in order to be inclusive and powerful enough to implement real change, the entire environmental movement must ally itself with communities of color and poverty to address their specific additional problems. Both sides of this equation need the other—a strong basis for unity in action.

Environmental Movements Led by Indigenous Peoples

Some aspects of environmental racism and the struggles against it are exhibited by Native American communities, tribes, and nations in the U.S., and by indigenous peoples the world over. In the U.S. as in other countries, native lands are seen as ripe opportunities for exploitation—for pipelines, for water contamination, for waste dump location, for destructive mining practices, for the theft of many kinds of natural resources.

Those attacks are matched by the leadership shown by indigenous peoples to environmental struggles. Tribes, have asserted their sovereignty in the public discourse[118] and in the court system over their own lands and their right to decide for themselves about pipelines and mines and access to water. Unique alliances have developed, such as the Cowboy and Indian Alliance against the Keystone XL pipeline project, uniting tribes, ranchers, and farmers across traditional political boundaries.

Indigenous struggles include civil disobedience to prevent mine development in many parts of the world, opposition to pipelines crossing native lands, and court and political battles over issues of sovereignty. Contingents of indigenous activists from around the world leading mass protests such as the People's Climate March in 2014 are a positive step on the part of the environmental movement, a recognition of the inspirational and practical roles played by indigenous struggles.

Native leaders can speak with moral authority about the harmful consequences of development, of rapacious corporations attacking their rights, land and sovereignty. They can address political processes which at best ignore their input and at worst condemn tribes and nations for trying to have any say at all in decisions which affect their lives and lands.

The New Divestment Movement

Several decades ago, the movement to divest funds from South Africa played an important role in helping to defeat apartheid. This was in part due to the direct effects on the South African economy and companies invested in South Africa, but also because it provided a path for a great deal of public education on the issues, and because it gave many people in many parts of the country and many parts of the economy a tangible way to become engaged.

There is a new divestment movement picking up steam, a movement to divest pension funds and other public monies, and the funds of both public and private universities and colleges, from fossil fuel companies. This movement, just starting to have an impact around the country, will be important for some of the same reasons. It switches at least part of the battlefield from national and international struggles where money and political power hold sway onto smaller battlefields. That is where moral persuasion and moral shaming, local organizing, and political campaigning can have a larger impact. The campaign, initiated by 350.org, has already had some success. As McKibben said in an interview with *Fortune Magazine*, "In 10 months since the 350.org campaign started, seven colleges have already divested including San Francisco State, Hampshire, and Unity College. They have been joined by, among others, religious organizations like the United Church of Christ and the cities of Seattle, San Francisco, and Providence, who say they have plans to divest. The biggest action will be in the states, which control big pension funds. Bills are moving through the Massachusetts and Vermont legislatures to do just that. Internationally, the movement has spread as well. A number of big pension funds in Australia are offering fossil-free portfolios."[119]

This fossil-fuel divestment struggle has already started on many more college campuses, in several cities, and with campaigns directed at boards in charge of public fund and pension investments. It provides a specific way for millions to understand the issues and how they are impacted, and provides a path for people to have real-world impact. It can take place on a single campus, in a town, as part of contract negotiations, as part of a more general public education campaign. It gives people a handle to grasp, when often the issues related to climate change seem impossible, seem too huge to do anything about.

The campaign targets the political and economic power of the fossil fuel industry, which funds climate change deniers, which funds much of the ultra-right in the U.S., and which has a huge vested interest in business as usual. Exxon Mobil is the most profitable company anywhere at any time in history and wants to keep it that way. That requires them to keep their public image as clean as possible, to keep people buying their stocks, and to keep investors from understanding that much of their "inventory" of fossil fuels (which their corporate worth and stock valuation are based upon) must stay in the ground if humanity is to keep climate change from becoming a total catastrophe. As McKibben notes "It is not a flaw in the business plan, the flaw is the business plan." Profiting from the extraction and burning of fossil fuels is profiting from harming the future of all humanity.

Legal Efforts

A growing part of the movement for change is the emergence of important legal challenges to business as usual. While it is necessary to understand that, as with all efforts, legal challenges by themselves aren't a solution, they are a worthwhile front in the broader struggle.

There are several kinds of legal challenges already underway. One is the wide range of local efforts to demand environmental impact statements for all major projects, which companies often try to ignore or do a pro forma statement that glosses over the real issues. Other local efforts sue corporations for evading government regulations, ignoring local and state laws, and illegally imposing costs on society as a whole.

Another is the efforts of some state attorneys general, including from New York State, to sue Exxon Mobil for their decades-long funding of climate denial when their internal documents prove the company knew of the dangers and preferred to ignore them in the interests of short-term profits. Some cities are now joining this front, suing fossil fuel companies for the damages done to the urban environment.[120]

And notably there are several suits brought by groups of young people who are suing for the damage done to their futures.[121]

Legal challenges are not limited to the United States court system. There are many international legal efforts as well.[122]

The "Elections Don't Matter" Meme

Notable in ultra-left attempts to present a strategy, is the absence of any proposal to utilize electoral struggles. Hiding behind a radical-sounding rejection of both major political parties, many ultra-left groups are positively proud of granting the opponents of real change a free hand to monopolize electoral campaigns. These critics prefer a purity that ends up separating the movement from natural allies in the peace, labor, women's, and civil rights movements who are still involved in progressive electoral campaigns.

Of course, elections and electoral struggles are not "the" answer—they are but one field of struggle, a political space where we can reach those not yet involved, those still uncertain, those who have questions, those who don't yet see a way out. Elections by themselves won't fix everything, any more than any other kind of struggle. Elections can lead to illusions about the ability of the divided political elite to actual solve problems, and we should guard against such illusions. But to abandon this field to the deniers and the obstructionists, to let them run free to spread lies without challenge in the electoral arena or any other arena, would be a basic mistake.

The rapidly growing anti-gun violence movement, following the Parkland shooting, is not making that mistake. At every school walkout and mass demonstration, they are registering young voters, warning politicians of the danger to their political future if they continue to slavishly follow the dictates of the National Rifle Association (NRA).

How can any revolutionary movement hope to succeed by cutting itself off from the largest, most organized groups engaged in mass struggles? How can we hope to win fundamental change if we can't compromise enough to join with others who want to participate in the struggle on their own terms? How can we have a vision of struggle that separates us from working class organization? How can we win big victories if we don't even try to win smaller ones? How can we convince the millions to a more radical program if we give the proponents of the current system a free ride to use election campaign demagogy to confuse and delay? How can we overpower the coercive power of the state if we limit ourselves to revolutionary sloganeering? How can we claim to be for greater democracy in our economic system if we don't fight to utilize, protect, and extend political democracy?

Mainstream Liberal Politicians

The only realistic path to defeat the ultra-right and its stranglehold on way too much of our political system at the present moment, at the national and state levels, is to support Democrats. To defeat the vicious, anti-human, retrograde politics of the ultra-right, which is increasingly nasty, openly racist, and trending sharply towards fascism, to defeat obstructionist approaches of the Republicans in Congress, the Presidency, and in state houses and governor's mansions, we are forced to campaign for Democrats.

At the same time, many (though not all) Democrats seek to limit mass resistance, support many pro-corporate policies, and support a slightly more "humane" version of U.S. imperialist foreign policy. Most, though not all, Democrats in national office limit themselves to legislative struggles, ignoring the need for mass movements to back up more progressive policies. Many have cooperated for decades with Republicans to maintain the two-party lock on our electoral system.

Especially at the local level, there are new openings for the potential of a new kind of politics: for socialist candidates and labor candidates, for alternative political formations such as the Vermont Progressive Party, the Working Families Party in New York State and several New England states, and the Green Party, combined with the massive growth of independent voters. The spontaneous response to the 2016 presidential candidacy of Vermont Senator Bernie Sanders showed the hunger among millions for real alternatives to business-as-usual, for real progressive policies. His spearheading of the group "Our Revolution" to continue fighting on the issues that galvanized his supporters is a new aspect of U.S. politics, continuing the movement past the election. In the 2018 mid-term elections, record numbers of women are running for office, an attempt to partially address the chronic under-representation of women and other oppressed groups.

However, none of these signs of shifts in the political culture of the U.S. have as of yet been significant enough to change the basic electoral two-party calculus at national and state levels. Our options have in some ways become even more restricted, due to the polarization and ultra-right radicalization of the

Republican Party, the bizarre growth in free market fundamentalism, and the rejection by much of the political right of any role for government beyond military, police, and prison functions. Leftists have a longstanding quandary when it comes to electoral politics. Yet despite of the claims of some on the ultra-left, it is possible to support Democrats, even middle-of-the-road Democrats, without seeing them as consistent and dependable allies, without signing on to the limits of liberal democracy, and without being shackled by the lesser-of-two-evils choices the system offers.

Some of the attacks from the left on Democrats pretend that all Democrats are the same, are all sell-outs beholden to the slightly more liberal sections of the capitalist class. But some Democrats are progressive, determined fighters for the rights of the vast majority. They choose the Democratic Party because as of yet there is not a realistic alternative in most places, not if they seek to be elected to national or state office and to have a real impact on actual policies. For the Left to offer a real alternative to progressives who are in office, we must build a mass base for a breakaway from the mainstream two-party gridlock, while we function in the real world of electoral politics that requires us to support Democrats for many offices.

To defeat the fascist elements of the Republican Party—the Trumps, the Bannons, the Cruzs, we can't hold ourselves back from the dirty details of current politics. It is a reality that too many Democrats are beholden to the capitalist class, but we won't change the basic calculus of U.S. politics by being pure and standing apart from where the majority of our people participate, even if much of that participation is limited to voting.

Environmental issues are not separate from issues of basic democracy—voter registration, same-day registration, early and extended voting, access to the polls, fighting gerrymandering, preventing voter-roll purges based on specious evidence and phony reasoning, and so much more. If we want the majority to have a say in determining the policies governing us on environmental issues, we have to be allied with the broad fight to protect and extend democracy. Not because more democracy will automatically mean better environmental decisions, but because in the long run, the only hope for better decisions is for there to be the political space for protest, debate, voter pressure, and creating change in the halls of Congress and in the states.

It is not a matter of personal or political preference or purity, it is a matter of practicality. The real obstacles to significant progress for the people of our country come from the ultra-right, and our main fire must be directed at that side of the political spectrum. We need to endeavor to do that without encouraging illusions about the Democrats as a solution—an admittedly difficult line to walk.

Promoting Division

The political forces against progressive movements find ways to use division as a conscious weapon. They promote racism, sexism, anti-Communism, ultra-nationalism, xenophobia, not just to grow their own base but to help them split the progressive forces. They seek to blame one generation for the problems of another, telling seniors that youth are the cause of the problems they face, and telling youth that seniors are the obstacle to a better life by grabbing all the benefits for themselves.

When ultra-right politicians feel their political support slipping away, their first response is to kick up the divisive rhetoric, to escalate efforts to divide the resistance, to reach back into their grab bag of wedge-issue tricks to at least turn the public conversation back to fighting on their terms, over division, racism, sexism, and anti-communism. Trump has done this all through his career, and continues to revert to type whenever the narrative escapes his domination.

As the capitalist system becomes more threatened by a growing, radicalized environmental movement, we can expect much more of this, searching for scapegoats that at least their base will believe are responsible for the problems and crises we face.

Ruling Classes Use Violence, Agent Provocateurs and Spies

Police forces and secret police in many countries try to use violence, the expression of their power through military and violent means, to split, divide, instill fear, and raise the costs of resistance to the established system. Progressive strategies must concern themselves with self-defense against such attacks, but not be seduced into thinking that responding with violence is necessarily the way to fight the system.

In fact, at times the police forces of a country find it necessary to create excuses for their violent repression. They plant agent provocateurs in the ranks of movements, in addition to spies who report what is happening,[123] people whose job it is to instigate violence, to provide the system with justification to attack the left,[124] to set traps for militants, and to coordinate with police forces to ambush those they have fooled into thinking they are fighting the system.[125]

There have been times in history when violence is the only possible avenue for protest. In the countries occupied by fascist Germany during WWII all avenues of public protest, of peaceful demonstrations, of electoral change were cut off, yet there was a mass movement to resist the fascists, and the Resistance used military means, even actions that today might be thought of as terrorism, to fight back—blowing up bridges and munitions plants, mounting armed attacks on German installations, and others. With a growing danger of fascism in many countries, progressives and radicals may be faced with such difficult choices again.

But we shouldn't confuse the danger of fascism with the actuality of fascism in power. Why? Because when avenues of popular, democratic protest are still open, still available to change the balance of forces, violence is almost always counter-productive. Violence by those allied or seemingly allied with the Left is seized on by the system as an excuse for repression—and the system will always have more weapons, more military forces at its disposal, than a movement which has not yet reached a majority.

Sound strategy has to protect the movement against these provocations, against letting agents derail a movement, against giving the system an easy excuse for repression. We should also guard against agents planted in the middle of struggle organizations who report on activities.[126]

The Military/Intelligence Services and Climate Change

The military and intelligence services must wrestle with reality. They are not constrained by the rhetoric of the ultra-right, the need to attack science for political reasons. They seek to study trends to be able to predict future conflicts, flashpoints, and dangers. For institutions mired in conservatism and imperialist adventurism by their very nature, the military and intelligence services have been remarkably forthright about the dangers posed by climate change, predicting massive refugee populations, wars over increasingly scarce resources, and devastation caused by water and food stress resulting from a blisteringly hot world. A *Wired* article recounted that:

> ... defense and intelligence agencies have concluded that climate change—and its ensuant upheaval— could be a more immediate threat. A Council on Foreign Relations paper in 2007 offered specific recommendations on how to mitigate risk. Another report in 2008, commissioned by the CIA, attempted to predict climate change's impact on national security by the year 2030. By 2014, the Department of Defense had adopted the term "threat multiplier" to describe climate change ... [127]

The solutions proposed by the military and intelligence services are profoundly anti-democratic. They actually propose few if any solutions, instead using the dangers of climate change to bolster their arguments for more funding, larger contingents, and even more militarization.

That the military and intelligence organizations are aware of the reality of climate change should not blind us to the reality that the U.S. military is also one of the worst environmental actors in the world. It pollutes vast swaths of the globe with destruction, contamination, and totally useless production. The testing grounds for weaponry are a scar on the earth wherever they are set up. The use of weapons in neo-con military adventurism results in vast wastelands wherever they operate, for example in large swaths of the Mid-East.

Much of the pollution from air travel comes from the traffic which maintains a world-wide scourge of military bases, and the subsequent travel back and forth of the military personnel to staff those bases.

But their reports on the real dangers humanity faces are at least based on reality, and give the lie to conservative voices denying climate change and science. We can reject their militarized vision for the future while still using their reality-based predictions as ammunition in the public war over science and reality.

The Ultra-Right Challenge

The ultra-right, with a growing ascendency in the U.S. Republican Party for several decades now, is the main obstacle to finding solutions to many problems facing our country, from environmental regulation to issues of basic democratic rights.

The election of Trump has encouraged the emergence into full public view of the worst elements of our citizenry—racist, fascist, xenophobic, militaristic, bombastic forces and other vicious actors. The rise in hate crimes of many kinds can be directly traced to the success of Trump, to his encouragement of these worst elements, to his election in effect granting permission for them to engage in physical attacks, verbal assaults, extreme political language demonizing opponents, and working to destroy democracy.

The election of Trump wasn't a result of any massive shift in the nationwide electorate, but it did result in a shift of the political initiative, placing liberals, progressives, and radicals on the defensive, requiring defensive struggles against the depredations of ultra-right politics. It was also the result of the Electoral College, a Constitutional compromise with the slave-owning Southern states, an anti-democratic remnant of our racist history.

Trump's Electoral College victory was also the result of smart strategic steps by his campaign. They understood how to game the system. They focused on several key Midwest states where the campaign managed to "flip" the winner-take-all Electoral College votes by a tiny winning margin, due to a combination of demagogy, economic stress and voter suppression. This was coupled with the Trump campaign's social media targeting and appeals to racism and to anti-immigrant hysteria.

Unless the environmental movement understands that the environmental policies of Trump and his Congressional allies and enablers must be fought as part of the broader democratic struggle, we cut ourselves off from our own potential allies who are necessary for us to be able to win any victories, defensive or positive. Until other movements understand that environmental struggles are part of that broader struggle and that they need the environmental movement as a key ally, all these democratic struggles will suffer.

The ultra-right attacks on environmental regulation, on the EPA, on climate science, on governmental action, on our parks, national forests, and wilderness areas didn't start with Trump—they have been part of the framework of Republican and ultra-right political action for decades now. McConnell, Ryan, and the Republican caucuses in both houses of Congress are not proceeding on some new path, they are using the election of Trump as a way to accomplish their long-time policy objectives, though not very successfully as far as law-making is concerned. Trump's anti-environmental accomplishments have been in the fields of destroying regulation, eliminating enforcement, changing rules about mining on public lands, and eviscerating the EPA from within.

Right-wing parties in many countries are experiencing a resurgence, especially their proto-fascist elements. The rise of the ultra-right in U.S. politics is not separate and apart from political developments in Europe and other industrially-developed countries. Anti-immigrant parties are gaining publicity and votes in Germany, in Denmark, in Finland, and in Austria, to mention just a few. These ultra-right, semi-fascist parties are winning more seats in national parliaments and, in France with Marie Le Pen, becoming a major contender in the national election run-off in 2017—though she lost to Macron, she garnered many millions of votes. And millions voted for Macron only because he was the last alternative to Le Pen, not because they supported the phony populism which covered his moderately right-wing policy proposals.

While the climate science denialism of the Republicans is pretty unique, the anti-democratic, anti-immigrant, anti-human rights agendas of all the right-wing parties line up with each other. Victories in each country encourage the ultra-right in other countries. And even when right-wing politicians in Europe don't attack climate science itself, they too rely on conservative faux-faith-based, ultra-nationalist, free-market fundamentalism as a supposed solution for all problems, giving capitalists total freedom from restrictions, regulations, and limitations.

Ultra-right strategists understand, sometimes better than some on the political left, that environmental realities require steps that will restrict the ability of large corporations to make excess profits. Environmental realities require governmental action, regulation, restrictions on private property prerogatives, and socialized decision-making. These realities require making decisions on the basis of human need rather than on the basis of private profit and greed. Environmental crises challenge the very basis of the capitalist system.

While their opposition to any positive steps to protect our environment isn't central to the international right-wing appeals to masses of people (that is more rooted in anti-immigrant hysteria and ultra-nationalism), it is a common feature of the programs of all these proto-fascist parties. These parties hide their pro-big-business policies behind faux-populist rhetoric, but pro-big-business policies including anti-environmental policies are the whole point of what they seek to implement.

Behind their super-heated, xenophobic, militarist, nationalist rhetoric, the actual policies of the right-wing promise a dystopian hell of rampant gangster capitalism, chipping away at and eventually ending democratic rights to protest and resist, allowing unrestricted dumping of toxic waste, and of attempts to end to all efforts to protect the public from poisoning by air, water, and chemical pollution. This vision is not the dream they promise, it is the nightmare they will deliver unless stopped by the united action of millions of active citizens.

Chapter 10

Case Study: The People's Climate March

Strategy, Tactics, and Not Confusing Them

As I participated in the People's Climate March on September 21st, 2014 in New York City, and attended the leftist Climate Convergence Conference during the two days before the march (sponsored by System Change Not Climate Change and the International Socialist Organization [ISO] but attended by about 2,500 left-wingers of many stripes), I was struck by echoes of past struggles. The history of those movements provides important lessons which the growing and developing climate movement needs to learn.

The importance of such mass demonstrations goes beyond the experiences of those directly participating—it echoes through the body politic, it inspires millions, it causes others to start asking essential questions. And it offers an entry point into the more sustained aspects of the struggle.

I also had surreal experiences, like attending a panel at which the panelists argued that the Climate March was a waste of time, a sell-out, and useless to the real needs of the struggle. I asked myself, "Then why are they here?" They were in effect acting as parasites on the body of the mass movement, seeking to disrupt and disarm it using super-heated rhetorical excess and specious arguments.

None of the mass movements in the U.S. over the past century was monolithic, though they are often talked about as if they were. Negotiating the internal conflicts, bridging differences across class, racial, and gender lines, across many different kinds of organizations each with their own particular focus and strategy, was a constant challenge.

Movements can radicalize a generation. Both the Civil Rights and the Anti-Vietnam War movements brought millions into the arena of political struggle and experienced conflicts over strategy and tactics. Both had difficulty navigating the complex balance of maintaining broad unity between center and progressive forces, and a super-radical fringe that fed on the understandable frustration of many with the slow pace of change and the limitations of the struggle at various points.

These movements also spoke in moral, political, economic, religious, and ideological terms. There wasn't one single argument, nor any simplistic strategy that lasted decades, but a constantly flowing movement, impure, filled with temporary allies, compromises, divergent strategies and tactics, and many experiments in struggle. The history of these movements, of their ebb and flow, of their successes and failures, of their grand goals and mistakes, are a rich territory for the new activists of today.

A New Pathway to Radicalism

These echoes and many more were present in the 2014 Climate Convergence Conference and even more importantly in the 400,000-strong People's Climate March along with about 200,000 people in support marches around the world.

As during the anti-Vietnam War peace movement, we have a new generation being radicalized by an issue and movement, a wave of new activists who are passionate and who are not constrained by the limitations of the past, who express fervent moral indignation about business as usual. Some of them have little or no previous practical experience of struggle or organization.

Again, we have a mass movement which is growing and developing rapidly. People and organizations are building ties and forming coalitions and in the process experiencing varied tugs and pulls over strategy and tactics.

Again, we have a need to project a program which can unify the broad forces necessary to create change with the forces of radicalism which correctly explain the basic, root causes of the problems we face, alongside fringe groups which seem to make a point of advocating self-defeating tactics.

Again, we have a movement in which a crucial question is how to deepen alliances with the labor movement. Parts of the labor movement are already involved, others see themselves and their members as enemies of the environmental movement. Many rank-and-file union members are confused about what path to take. We have environmentalists who want to condemn the entire labor movement and the whole membership since it and they are not unified around a progressive position on all environmental issues. We have labor leaders who are hesitant to get too far out in front of where their membership sees the issues, as well as labor leaders who actively oppose environmental progress. Unity requires a persistent and protracted effort to build unity and overcome divisions, and ultimately this is crucial for the success of both movements.

On Confusing Strategy and Tactics

Many problems arise from confusion between strategy and tactics. Some critics cite, disdainfully, the fact that the People's Climate March organizers applied for a police permit for the march, as if refusing to talk to the police in every single instance is a principle that should never be compromised. As we learned during the Anti-Vietnam War struggle, marches, especially massive ones of hundreds of thousands, can't be run like demonstrations of twenty or thirty people. When it is possible to get the police to do their job, to grant a permit, to negotiate a march route, to stop and reroute traffic so those not involved in the march don't end up hating the demonstrators, that is not a betrayal of basic principles, that is a recognition of practical reality.

Undoubtedly, there are times, as in many of the civil rights marches in the south, when it is not feasible to get police cooperation, and that should not stop the struggle from proceeding. Only those for whom the point is to get other people into a losing pitched battle with the armed forces of the state seek to cause unnecessary difficulties.

The police shouldn't determine the course of our movements, but neither should we make it a point of pride to be obstructionist just for the sake of a fictional radical political purity.

Criticism Infused with Rhetorical Excess

There were limitations of the People's Climate March. The march organizers used corporate sponsorships to fund their work; they intentionally offered no specific demands at all, but rather relied on advertising to generate a bigger turnout. They offered the march as a blank slate on which any supposed "green" claim could be written. Some forces, including some of the major backers of the demonstration, were eager to limit the struggle to pressuring for minor reforms within the current political and economic paradigms, and still remain determined to fight any effort to challenge the capitalist system as a cause of the environmental calamities we face.

On the basis of these weaknesses, some critics try to ratchet up anger and rage in order to get around their sect-like isolation.

Chris Hedges, in an article before the March[128] claimed that, due to the limitations of the broad coalition sponsoring the march, the lack of specific demands, and the dire necessities of quick change dictated by the science, the March was the "last gasp of climate liberalism." He went on to say that "our only hope" for the movement rested with those who were planning civil disobedience. In his talk to a panel before the march, he at least had the honesty to acknowledge that his analysis comes close to that of the anarchists, though he made too much of a few minor differences.

Hedges stated that, "All attempts to work within this decayed system and this class of power brokers will prove useless." So how are we to organize those who are not yet as "advanced" as Hedges? Lectures? Shouting? Shaming? Talking to ourselves? Self-righteousness? None of those offer any realistic hope of organizing millions.

Hedges offers the bleak prospect that we will not see change in our lifetimes, but says that even so we should resist because otherwise we face spiritual and intellectual death. So he suggests that we should engage in impractical and symbolic acts of resistance and give up any real hope of change in the near term. How does he expect to organize anyone with this grim perspective? Or maybe the point is that he doesn't expect to organize very many, and that is the root of his near hopelessness.

Other sharp critics of the People's Climate March condemned the March before the fact in excoriating terms. For example, Arun Gupta, in *Counterpunch*, claimed, based on his personal experience toiling in the advertising industry, that the only purpose of the march was to generate good PR. He said, "But when the overriding demand is for numbers, which is about visuals, which is about P.R. and marketing, everything becomes lowest common denominator." He went on, "So we have a corporate-designed protest march to support a corporate-dominated world body to implement a corporate policy to counter climate change caused by the corporations of the world, which are located just a few miles away but which will never feel the wrath of the People's Climate March." He posits a fictitious alternate reality, in which if the March was just two days later, had not gotten a police permit, and routed itself past the UN Building or Wall Street, then much more amazing and radical things would have happened, if only we kept ourselves pure and untainted by any hint of corporate involvement or the "betrayal" of getting the police to do their job appropriately.

Gupta may look at the issue of numbers only through his advertising industry lens, and in that context numbers may be all about P.R., but the rest of us don't need to stick to such a limited view. Mass marches and massive numbers are also about proving that the movement has the strength and organizational muscle to pull off such an event—proving it to the ruling class, to the media, to the movement itself, and also to those who are considering joining the movement. It is an exhibition of power, of the ability to mobilize, of potential political clout, of mass attention to the issue, and yes, also about P.R. Demonstrating the ability to turn out 400,000 people and solve the innumerable challenges in doing so proves certain facts about the movement, about the organizations involved, about the unity it shows to the world.

Gupta also links to several other critics, like Quincy Saul, of Ecosocialist Horizons, who in advance damned the March as a "farce." Saul claimed that the March had no target, no timing, no demands, no unity, no history, and no integrity.[129] Saul said, "To invite people to change the world and corral them into cattle pens on a police-escorted parade through the heart of consumer society is astoundingly dishonest." He continued: "Climate justice requires nothing less than a global revolution in politics and production; it requires a historic transition to a new model of civilization, which will demand great sacrifice and creativity from everyone." But how is it not "lying to the people" to proclaim this but offer no realistic path to get there? Isn't it "astoundingly dishonest" to invite people to change the world and then corral them into pointless, strictly symbolic "resistance" that is unable to organize the very millions who will determine the success or failure of the movement?

He assumes that any reform movement that tries to apply mass pressure on politicians is wasting its time because, "The powers that be are deaf, dumb and deadly, and we will waste no further time trying to pressure or persuade them." But what if the point is not to persuade them at all, but to mobilize and organize more people into the struggle, people who do not as yet have any kind of revolutionary outlook? Is that too a waste of time?

He claims it is an insult to all the people coming for the March that the organizers got a permit. Did he think to ask any of these hundreds of thousands if they felt insulted? Or does he just assume, from his Olympian perch, that what he feels is what everybody else "ought" to feel?

Saul offers, as a shortcut to organizing millions, this simple path: "The only thing that we can do to meet the deadline for climate justice is to engage in a massive and permanent campaign to shut down the fossil fuel economy. But we have to do this strategically, not in the symbolic cuff-and-stuffs that are a perversion and prostitution of the noble ideals of civil disobedience and revolutionary nonviolence. So we are going to shut down coal plants; we are going to block ports, distribution centers and railway hubs where fossil fuels are transported; whatever it takes to keep the oil in the soil. We're going to put our bodies between the soil and the sky." This is either a path to irrelevance, to time in prison, to some version of revolutionary suicide, or to all of the above. Especially when completely divorced from the mass movement, this is a Weatherman-style re-run. And in the years since the March, we have not heard of any such successful actions by Saul and his cohort.

In a workshop at the Climate Convergence Conference, Saul called for people being ready to "throw themselves on the gears of the system," as if that was a path to change. It won't stop the coal industry, not unless Saul has some hidden cache of many tens of thousands of activists eager to throw away their lives in a fit of revolutionary romanticism. Such action doesn't change the system; it gives the system an excuse for intensifying repression.

There is nothing wrong with enthusiasm per se, but enthusiasm is no substitute for organization nor for winning the majority of workers. Instead of seeing marchers as allies, Saul compares them to the enemies of the movement: "The spectacle of thousands of First World citizens marching for climate justice, while they continue to generate the vast majority of carbon emissions, brings to mind the spectacle of George W. Bush visiting New Orleans in the aftermath of Hurricane Katrina." In his mind, it is the fault of the people who are trying to do the right thing. It is the fault of those who are entering the struggle that they aren't radical enough yet! Is it really true that the marchers themselves are responsible for the majority of emissions, or did Saul just get lost in his own overheated rhetoric? A few questions for Saul: How many First World citizens participated in deciding to build coal-fired plants? How many First World citizens own industrial plants, or fleets of trucks, or decided to deforest old growth timber? He is blaming the victims, brushing us all with the brush he should reserve for the capitalist class.

Even More Critiques of the March

All these critiques of the People's Climate March are just more sophisticated versions of the Revolutionary Communist Party's endless chanting of "Revolution—Nothing Less," as if the slogan itself could magically bring forth a mass revolutionary movement. As if cranking the volume on their bullhorn up to the highest level could convince anyone.

Anne Peterman, in an online article, said in the headline that "direct action is the antidote to despair" and that "the UN is worse than useless." Driven to that conclusion by the failure of the UN to negotiate a serious, binding treaty to tackle climate change, she was ready to desert an entire arena of struggle, leaving it to the liberals and the obstructionists. Instead of her readiness to abandon this arena of struggle, radicals could leverage their participation in aspects of the UN process to rivet and unite the international community of activists. At the very least, it is another arena of contending ideas which the environmental movement should not abandon to the opponents of real change.

We should not have illusions about the UN as the savior of the world from climate change, any more than we should have illusions about capitalism being the solution. But by ceding participation in the UN process, Ms. Peterman unintentionally gives away weapons to the opponents of action.

Direct action is indeed one tactic that can be usefully employed by the movement in particular battles, but it is not a one-size-fits-all strategy for success in the longer war against greenhouse gas emissions, and is no substitute for a mass movement that has the actual power to create fundamental change. In Ms. Peterman's thinking, because the UN has "cracked down on dissent" at previous climate summits, it is obviously the enemy and we should stop trying to work for an international treaty. She wants the whole movement to follow her example, be proud of getting banned from future summits and congratulate ourselves about how much purer we are than those who still try to pressure the UN. This approach divides the movement, the opposite of the broad unity necessary to enable it to succeed.

A False Hierarchy of Militancy

Intentionally or not, the strategy that ultra-left critics advocate either states or implies that only the most militant, confrontational struggles should be engaged in, because these are the highest form of struggle possible, or even that they are the only worthwhile form of struggle. Intentionally or not, they set up a hierarchy of types of struggle, discounting mass marches as less militant and/or less effective.

This artificial hierarchy is a false ranking of kinds of struggle. It posits mass mobilizations as less valuable than direct action, which is not as good as civil disobedience and getting arrested, which is less valuable than direct and immediate revolutionary struggle, presumably armed struggle. This gets around the need for real, in-depth analysis of the actual political situation; all you have to do is climb up the ladder of escalating militant struggle, dragging a few people with you. No need for an actual strategy, no need to actually try and win millions to the cause.

Naomi Klein, in her otherwise excellent book *This Changes Everything*, almost mythologizes what she calls "Blockadia." She reports on struggles around the world, many led by indigenous groups, that physically stop mining, pipeline construction, and other destructive corporate efforts to develop access to more fossil fuels. Many of these actions are admirable, inspiring, and sometimes victorious. But that doesn't make them *the* blueprint for change under all circumstances. (I should note that Naomi Klein serves on the board of 350.org, one of the main sponsors of the Peoples Climate March—so she certainly doesn't advocate limiting struggles to blockades and civil disobedience. See my review of her groundbreaking book in the *People's World*.[130])

Civil disobedience can be a very effective tactic, and in certain situations may be the only path of struggle available, especially to disenfranchised groups. But by itself it is not a strategy for all circumstances, nor is it effective unless harnessed to a mass movement as one part of a suite of tactics, utilized only where appropriate. It is an important tactic when seen as part of a much broader tactical toolbox.

Substituting more militant-sounding tactics for a long-term, coherent strategy appeals to some who understand the depth of the challenge of climate change and are appalled by the way the system resists change, especially change that threatens super-profits, but don't see any realistic way out—so they fall for unrealistic approaches.

What a Mass March Can and Can't Accomplish

There is often a misunderstanding of the role, potential, and limitations of mass marches and other more mainstream tactics. A march, even a gigantic one like the People's Climate March, cannot by itself directly accomplish much in the way of immediate basic change. The results of such a march are measured in changes in public opinion, in more people getting inspired to join the ongoing movement, and in marking an important way-station on the path to much more grassroots organizing. It is a test and demonstration of the movement's strength, a way to make the media and the political and financial elite pay attention, a boost to the visibility of the ongoing work the environmental movement is doing. It inspires, it excites, it offers a deadline to work towards, a handle for those looking to get involved. By itself, a march does not change laws, change policies, nor can it fundamentally transform a society by itself, but it can play an important role.

A march can, however, be the important beginning of a new phase of struggle. Historically, mass marches have been a major point of entry into full engagement in struggle.

Critiques such as those of the Peoples Climate March are based in part on inflating the expectations of what a march "ought" to accomplish and then knocking down that straw man. They take some justifiable criticisms of the limitations of the March and inflate them into an utter condemnation of the value of mass mobilizations.

The overarching need at this political moment is to get millions of people in our country, and billions around the world, into motion, into the streets, into action, into organizations. For that goal, a mass march is an excellent tool.

Masses learn from their own political experience, from running up against the system themselves, from trying everything short of revolution and seeing that reforms by themselves are not enough.

Masses don't become revolutionary because someone chants louder or has a bigger red flag or gets arrested more often, or makes a principle out of never asking for a police permit.

But with many of the hundreds of thousands who joined the Peoples Climate March, the Left has an open door, an open door with a welcome mat, to offer a program that actually addresses the environmental crises. As Naomi Klein noted in her closing plenary speech to the Climate Convergence Conference, the March represented the current state of the movement. It does not, and we should not expect it to, represent some idealized manifestation of the fevered dreams of the most radical participants, who wish to substitute revolutionary romanticism for a hard look at what is actually required of us. That kind of diversion is a way to focus on the favored tactics of the few rather than the long-range strategy of the main movement.

Another echo from past struggles is the 1999 Battle in Seattle, organized by a broad coalition opposed to the World Trade Organization (WTO) meeting there. A catchy slogan from that day worked to bridge the gap between movements: "Turtles and Teamsters Unite" exemplified the broad unity of the march that day. The main march of over 45,000 received virtually no media attention.

Instead, the media seemed mesmerized by the tactics of about 600 anarchists. Their window-smashing and trash-burning was a diversion from the real politics. The main march united many from both the environmental movement and the labor movement, setting the stage for the tasks of unity-building we have today.

The idea that real revolutionary struggle is all about being politically pure, never compromising with the system, never uniting with disdained liberals, is a dead-end, a way to avoid the difficult work of unity. Most ultra-leftists act as if political purity is more important than actually having real-world impact, more important than bringing millions into the struggle. We *do* need to talk about the system as the root of the problem. When it is the best or only available avenue of struggle open, we *do* need to use confrontational tactics. Getting arrested as part of the struggle *is* necessary more often than it should be. Civil disobedience *is* a worthwhile tool, if the target is chosen carefully and the participants thoroughly prepared.

But the movement must guard against illusions—both the illusion promoted by liberals that the capitalist system can ultimately solve our numerous environmental challenges, and the illusions of the ultra-left that radical demands and the most confrontational tactics by themselves are the only answers. Some tiny left sects act as if we would just shout their slogans louder or preach with more self-righteousness, that would make all the difference.

The illusion that a movement can be built, radicalized, and become effective without actually working with organized groups of workers and allies who are not yet ready to break with the system is responsible for the sect-like activity of many ultra-left grouplets. They swirl around major mobilizations, trying to pick off any who are ready to listen to their apocalyptic rhetoric. They condemn big demonstrations, but go to them anyway—but why, if they are so certain that such demonstrations will have no impact, are a waste of time? They offer only the false hope of changing the system in the short term though some fictional direct action by a small handful of activists, and that is poor gruel instead of the rich and varied strategic meal the movement needs.

Constructive Criticism

In an article in *The Nation*, September 30, 2014, Jonathan Smucker and Michael Premo note that the Climate Justice Alliance, sponsor of the Flood Wall Street demonstration, worked to link the big March with their direct action the following day.[131] They addressed the ultra-radical critics directly. They pointed out that there are positive ways to link mass marches with civil disobedience, which was done the day following the big march by the "Flood Wall Street" action at which there were dozens of arrests, disruption of normal traffic in the financial district, and direct confrontations with at least some bankers and other financial operators. Smucker and Premo point out that there is great unifying value to the entire movement for radicals to be at the table, to work in broad movements from the inside and not separate themselves as outside armchair critics.

Smucker and Premo also noted that "outside" actions involving much smaller numbers can be easily ignored by the political system and the media. They go on to say, "Having the most radical-sounding solutions in the world is all for naught if those solutions are only believed by a relatively small number of self-identifying radicals. We have to engage broader social bases by meeting new participants at the on-ramps by which they initially enter into collective action. The Peoples Climate March provided such an on-ramp to many thousands of newcomers. Those of us who identify with the left end of the progressive spectrum need to be honest with ourselves about our current lack of capacity for building such on-ramps on our own. If we want to move more people in a radical direction—to fundamentally reengineer the roots of a broken system—it behooves us to build and maintain good relationships with organizations that have more resources and a greater reach, even if they do not share all of our politics. The left of the left spectrum has to muster the courage and savvy to enter into alignments that are too big for us to be able to control." They asserted that, "Such an alignment will, of course, be full of challenges. But these are good challenges to have." Often, the ultra-left makes it a point of principle to not be savvy enough to enter into such alignments.

The authors pointed out that some of these intentional outsiders are, "just engaging in self-righteous sideline critique." For some of these splinter groups, making any progress short of ultimate revolution is condemned on principle, and this approach is a prime feature of their political philosophy, not a bug.

There are plenty of constructive criticisms of the March, of the organizing that went into creating it, and of various outlooks for the future path of struggle. The March had basically no demands beyond "taking action on the climate crisis." Previous efforts have been hampered by too long a list of demands, in effect requiring endorsement of a more comprehensive program before groups and individuals become involved. The admirable and fairly successful approach by the organizers of the People's Climate March aimed to broaden participation and gain sponsorships from a great variety of organizations. Part of the way they accomplished this was to get away entirely from any specific demands. In my opinion, this let the pendulum swing too far. Having no specific demands at all meant the March had less impact than it otherwise could have, on the mid-term elections that fall, on the debate over solutions, and on future organizing.

Not requiring that everyone condemn, for example, the Keystone XL pipeline project was a concession that enabled some unions (though not many construction unions) to endorse and participate. That was, in my opinion, a net positive. Some compromises on program were necessary to make the March as broad and large as possible. That doesn't mean giving up the fight against the pipeline. It just means that a tactical move sideways to not force every important environmental issue into the list of required demands was, on balance, a good thing.

As well, not insisting that everyone who participated be somehow environmentally pure opened the door to some major contributors. And those contributions enabled hiring experienced (and inexperienced) organizers to provide the muscle necessary without having all the organizational structure usually needed to pull off such a large gathering. But by opening the door as wide as they did, the main sponsors of the March ended up opening the door to "greenwashers"—to corporations that wanted to burnish their public image without actually taking any positive actions. It is not a matter of being pure, but of balancing the essential need for major funders with a wary eye to those just interested in self-promotion and in hiding their actual environmental policies.

Unfortunately, the success of the March was not backed up with enough ongoing organizational effort. The March relied on the "no demands" policy and the relatively spontaneous response of people to substitute for the difficulties and challenges of building permanent struggle organizations.

No Shortcuts

Learning from the process of the movement means learning how to translate public sentiment into organization, organization into action, action into victories small and large, victories (and defeats) into fundamental conclusions about the changes society needs to make.

The main weaknesses of the March were the same as the main weaknesses of the movement. The main initiator of the march, 350.org, is a web-based movement focused on inspiring and initiating actions. It relies on spontaneous responses as opposed to building ongoing structure and institutions capable of organizing consistent, on-going mass action. It has been successful at getting a worldwide response to various demonstrative actions, but lacks the permanent institutional structure to connect all those who respond.

The compromises to gain financial sponsorships for the March, which in my opinion went too far, were an effort to take a shortcut around real organization. One main contributor to the organization of the March was Avaaz, a somewhat amorphous "online activism" entity with an agenda that seems to coincide with not confronting corporate power directly, with the "no demands" strategy. As well, their over-use of paid staff for the March, many often with little actual previous organizing experience, was not geared to movement capacity-building but to demanding super-human individual efforts to substitute for the limited existing coalition efforts.

Refusing to have any specific demands at all will not build unity on the basis of a common vision or program, nor will we be successful at uniting around a common program by demanding purity and revolutionary fervor from all involved. Broad agreement, though not unanimity, is needed on a basic set of demands, with each group able to promote their own programmatic proposals.

A positive feature of the March and its preparation was the aggressive activity to engage participation from civil rights groups and to address the racism that has kept those movements from fully entering into alliance with the environmental movement. The March was led by a large contingent of indigenous peoples from all over the globe. Outreach to communities of color and to groups trying to bridge the difficulties between the environmental movement and many types of civil rights struggles and organizations was important in making this March, in addition to being the largest, also the most diverse of national environmental marches. Much more effort is necessary to reach all those who can be involved, and it won't happen without actual organization on the ground in many places. It won't happen without more actual engagement in civil rights movements. But there were positive steps to encourage diversity to change the face of the movement.

This movement must of necessity be committed to the struggle for the long haul. Success requires massive changes in how we produce and distribute goods and food, fundamental changes in the production process for almost everything made by human labor, a basic shift in how we decide on priorities for public policy and investment, and much more. These issues will be with us for many decades to come, and will only play a greater and greater role in public consciousness and become even more important parts of public debate and struggle. The climate crisis is not a short-term problem that will go away by the time the next election cycle comes around. Making progress requires on-going organization, requires building lasting coalitions, requires serious rethinking of public priorities, and requires efforts to win a large majority to back a radical program.

The necessary on-going work doesn't happen as a result of one march no matter how large. While the People's Climate March was a watershed event in this long struggle, much more outreach and trust-building is demanded of the environmental movement and of other progressive movements as well.

The Beginning of Strategy, not the End

Many leftist critics correctly understand that capitalism is a major part of the environmental problems we face. They correctly understand that time is running short to make changes that will avert the worst climate catastrophes. They correctly advocate for socialism as the goal, namely the reorganization of society in ways that will involve millions in the process of finding solutions.

However, they treat these conclusions as if they have come to the *end* of developing strategy. That is a denial of process, a rejection of dialectics, a willful ignoring of the complexity of reality. Those conclusions, while valid, are only the *beginning* of the process of developing a strategy that can guide the movement through many ebbs and flows.

The myopia of the Climate March's "radical critics" is based on a confusion of ultimate goals with immediate tasks. It is the problem of having a firm hold of one piece of the truth and convincing yourself that you have the whole truth. That allows you to think that if you only say that piece of the truth louder, or more sharply, or more often, or with a bigger sign or more leaflets, others will see it exactly the way you do. This is an idealist (in the philosophical sense) approach to creating change. It is placing theory above practice, instead of understanding their dialectical unity.

Any tactic, however useful in specific situations, that masquerades as a strategy which should be applied to all circumstances, ends up creating defeats and despair. Such disillusionment can send people down dead ends that separate them from the main movement.

There are real, difficult issues to work through in building the broad-based, working class-led, multi-racial, multi-issue, multi-generational, multi-gender, environmentally-focused, struggle-oriented international movement necessary to implement fundamental change. The goal of Left activists must be to be active participants in solving these challenges, in bringing movements together, in linking issues and organizations, in taking advantage of every field of struggle, and in taking advantage of any and all splits in the ruling class.

The struggle is joined; millions are moving into motion. We have difficult times ahead, from natural disasters happening with increased frequency to political issues that are complex and entwined with, and complicated by, economic worries and survival fears.

A crucial part of strategy is to identify the goal to aim for, but that is only the first step. The harder part comes from figuring out where we actually are, and how we can get from where we are to where we need to be.

This requires a dialectical process of engaging in the actual struggles of today, with all their strengths and limitations, and figuring out the issues, demands, coalitions, and connections which will lead to the next higher level of struggle. This means identifying the partners necessary for victory, building ties with those forces, understanding their particular reasons for fighting, and successfully making links between those forces and other issues, movements, organizations, social groups, and local conditions. It is learning how to fight on many fronts at once, and not conceding important territory to the opposition without a battle.

Compromises, coalitions, and utilizing tactics in ways that match the political moment—these make up the path that millions still have to tread. Our job is first of all to help those millions get started, then to inspire and energize them, and finally to help them to draw deeper conclusions. In the process we must provide coherent organization, structure, and strategy.

There are no shortcuts to winning fundamental change. Such thoroughgoing change can only happen with the organized power of the majority of the multi-racial, multi-national, multi-gender, multi-generational working class along with many, many allies such as indigenous peoples, women's groups, civil rights organizations, and many others. We have a bumpy, difficult road ahead, but we must persevere, for ourselves, for our children and grandchildren, for the future of developed human existence on this planet.

Chapter 11

What's Strategy Good For, Anyway?

Strategy is important for many practical political reasons. Having a worked-out, long-range vision:

- Helps avoid attempts at shortcuts that end up being self-defeating.
- Helps us prioritize what issues are most important to work on.
- Helps us recognize new developments and enables us to adjust our vision to accommodate those developments.
- Helps us to prioritize alliance-building, and to see opportunities for cross-issue coalitions.
- Enables us to place today's struggles into a context of how they can fit into and lead to future struggles.
- Offers a tool to help us judge the balance of forces.
- Can help us identify the gaps and missing pieces of our plans, the key elements we need to work on.
- Can help us identify a realistic path forward, a way to navigate through the complexities of struggle, politics, and organization-building.
- Enables us to offer a path of struggle that is realistic enough to convince others to join with us.
- Helps us create a shared vision of the future we are working to bring into being.

These are worthwhile and necessary aspects of strategy, reasons which are enough on their own to spend the time and energy to work on developing a strategic vision. Without such a process, organizations can be isolated from natural allies, can end up working very hard at dead-end projects and veer off on unnecessary tangents. Without a long-range vision, the struggles of the present moment can overwhelm us; the lack of basic purpose can make us feel like we are floundering in a never-ending process which is ultimately unsatisfying since it doesn't feel like we are addressing the underlying causes of the problems we face. Good strategy helps inspire with the confidence that our struggles are leading somewhere positive.

Developed strategy also helps us pick tactics that match our long-range vision, helps us decide which of a variety of tactics will meet not only the needs of the moment but also set us up for long-range success. While tactics are about the immediate present, they also lay the basis for where we will be once the current moment has passed, once the current struggle has been either lost or won.

A developed strategy can help us convince our allies, and ourselves, that once a victory is won, that can lay the basis for a deeper unity.

But there are also more personal reasons why strategy is important.

A long-term strategy provides the basis for realistic hope, for seeing past the ebbs and flows of struggle and politics to the potential of the future. People need hope, need to be able to see a reason for taking the risks of struggle, which can be considerable. Hope and confidence are necessary ingredients for building the commitment of individuals and groups to the long haul that faces us.

Long-term strategy helps avoid disillusionment and depression when a particular battle is lost, when it seems that the struggle leads to endless work that is never resolved. It helps us persevere through periods of loss and retreat, helps us to understand that setbacks are only that, not permanent defeats. It provides a perspective that places our immediate issues into the long struggles ahead, so we can understand the need for continuing to fight even when the situation looks dire. This is especially important for current environmental struggles, since damage to the environment is ongoing, since the potential consequences of the damage already done are so disastrous, so potentially cataclysmic, that it is sometimes tempting to give up hope and abandon the very work needed to avoid the worst consequences of what is to come.

Developing a strategy for alliance, coalition, and progress that is shared by many is part of creating the trust and understanding necessary—and that is as true of individuals as of organizations.

We also must recognize the limitations of any strategy. It is a moving target, both because any human endeavor is embedded with flaws, gaps, and misunderstandings, and also because the terrain of struggle keeps changing around us. Any worthwhile strategy requires regular development and revision. To the degree that it is static, like a finished document, to that same degree it will fall short of the understanding we need.

The process of developing strategy is a crucial process for any serious movement or organization to engage in. But developing strategy is not a substitute for doing the work, for organizing, engaging in struggle, building alliances, winning victories. In reality, doing the hard work of movement-building is the only way to test the validity of a strategic outlook. Doing the work is the way to improve and refine the details, to correct the mistakes, to discover the missing elements. Strategy is identifying the path we need to walk, but we have to actually walk the path ourselves.

A developed strategy is not a blueprint, an exact plan for how to proceed no matter what. Rather, it is more like a flexible map to an ever-changing terrain, shifting as the balance of power shifts, adjusting as we learn from the struggle. The goal is certain, but also ever-changing as circumstances change, as we proceed on the path and learn as we go. It is the process of developing strategy that is most important, because circumstances are always changing and hence we need to know how to adapt. We need the skills we learn in the process of developing strategy, because those skills are essential for all aspects of our struggles.

Strategy is important for political, organizational, and personal reasons. A strategy is not a simple "elevator pitch" to sell an immediate task. Successful strategy takes a collective process to develop, and in that process trust, confidence, hope, and vision are created, and we all need all of that.

Part 4:
The Next Steps

In order to stave off the worst effects of climate change, in order to rebalance the relationship between humanity and nature, the world needs many kinds of fundamental trans- formations. We need technological fixes and transitions, with new ones being invented every day.[132] We need major changes to the production of energy. We need to shift to a new political and economic paradigm.

This section discusses some possible changes, mainly some places to start followed by some longer-range possibilities, from technological improvements to major cultural shifts. These solutions are all linked by helping us make contribu- tions to a better world. This section also discusses the problems embedded in our current production processes (much more deeply rooted than just how we produce energy) and proposes looking for the intersections of problems as the places where the effects of concerted action can be amplified.

We don't need to construct a fictional and impossible utopia. Real life is first of all rooted in our material existence, in facts. As the discussion of philosophy pointed out, there are and always will be contradictions, difficulties, and problems. There will always be conflict between different groups of humans— we should not succumb to the ahistorical claims some make about human nature being inherently evil, but there will never be a world with total, complete, and everlasting harmony. For geographical, cultural, political, historical, linguistic, and social reasons, all humanity will never be totally united as one. As well, there will always be contradictions between humanity and other parts of nature.

Another reason there will be no utopia is that climate change is already baked into our future; there is so much accumulated greenhouse gas in the atmosphere that we do not have the option of preventing all human-induced climate change. We do, however, have the option of preventing catastrophe for humankind. That may not be utopia or paradise, but it is much better than the alternative of environmental degradation, con- stant extreme weather disasters, and runaway climate change.

Chapter *12*

The Range of Solutions

While I argue that partial solutions presented as total solutions are counter-productive, the reality is that all solutions are partial. There is no magic bullet to fix any of the environmental problems that are at risk of tipping into crisis. We must work on *all* these linked issues step by step, in a methodical, comprehensive way that recognizes how they are interlinked, how actions taken in one part of the environment affect all other parts of the environment.

In the 1970s in the U.S., many early environmental efforts attempted to, in effect, place a filter on the top of smokestacks— to limit the amount of pollution emitted into the atmosphere or the water we use to drink. This resulted in some significant immediate improvements—just look at comparison photos of Los Angeles in the 1970s and today. The smog level is so obviously better, this real-world experience proves that the opponents of regulation are lying when they claim that all regulation is bad or useless.

However, dealing with pollution after it has been created is a strategy with limited success. Much better is to redesign processes and equipment from the ground up, using the most current level of knowledge and technology, to prevent pollution from being created in the first place.

This approach, so obviously better in the long run, requires a significant investment first in the engineering and design of such processes and equipment, and also in the production of new machinery. So it conflicts with the economics of the massive amounts of installed capacity already in existence. This means that in many cases it is not profitable to approach fundamental redesign in this way. Even in those cases where it is profitable in the long run, it is hard to convince owners and managers of the need for the upfront investments required.

There is a related design issue, well-argued by Michael Braungart and William McDonough in their book *Cradle to Cradle*. While it is a positive step to introduce recycling in as many places and ways as possible, even better is to redesign things from the start so that they can be reused. Otherwise, recycling is an example of the dead hands of the past weighing on us; it was often more profitable and convenient to design things for mass production when it was assumed we would just dispose of and replace all goods rapidly. Goods were designed to have a short functional life—what is called planned obsolescence. In part, that was due to ignoring the costs for society of waste disposal, pollution, contamination, and other negative impacts which never appeared on the balance sheets of the original manufacturers.

But if we need to maximize the ability to reuse things, to prevent the need for recycling in the first place just as we need to reduce the production of pollution in the first place, then redesigning things from the start is necessary. Toasters, for example, could be designed to make them easy to take apart and the component elements reused again. We would not have to just throw old toasters away, adding to the waste stream, and buy new ones constantly. Multiply that by all the tools, machinery, equipment, and appliances we use for modern life and over time this kind of redesign will contribute greatly to both the quality of life and to reducing unnecessary pollution and waste.

As a society-wide project, redesigning both the machinery and processes we use to create products and redesigning the products themselves would result in a much healthier way for all humanity to live. It would enable us to create more goods and living-wage jobs for more people without creating more environmental problems.

There are many modern conveniences which could be available more widely, such as toasters, dishwashers, washing machines, dryers, and other consumer goods. However, some appliances we in the U.S. think of as essential are not needed or used by many people in the world, and we should not measure the quality of life simply by the number of appliances someone has on the kitchen counter. As well, if we make them as throw-away items, they end up just being added to our already massive waste stream.

People all over the world do need refrigerators, stoves, and ovens. But if we create them using current machinery and current design, we make our environmental challenges worse. The goal is not to force people to endure hardship; it is to provide a better life for individuals and families in the short run while also guaranteeing a better world for humanity in the long run.

The Precautionary Principle

It is harder and more expensive to solve health problems after they are created than to prevent their creation in the first place. It is harder and more expensive to solve environmental problems after they are created.

A much-needed change in how we impose technology on nature is to institute the precautionary principle wherever possible. This is the idea that when we are not sure about the effects of an action such as introducing a new chemical compound into the workplace, we should err on the side of caution; we should not allow the introduction of untested chemicals or industrial processes or genetically-modified seeds into the world. Only when there is scientific certainty should such steps be taken. This puts the burden of proof on those who seek to impose uncertain results on the rest of us, to prove that their actions will not cause harm.

We don't know, for example, the exact synergistic effects of the hundreds of inorganic compounds introduced into the workplace in the U.S. each year. It is a safe (or rather unsafe) bet that many of them have at least some carcinogenic or endocrine-disrupting effects on the workers using them. Taking sensible precautions even before we know exactly which compounds produce which negative effects is just common sense, including much more testing before exposing workers to unknown health risks.

The precautionary principle should apply to the natural world as well. We know that the presence of certain amounts of chemicals and particulate matter in the atmosphere leads to more respiratory problems, responsible in part for the huge increase in asthma and asthma-related illnesses. Prudence dictates that we err on the side of caution, to reduce such chemicals and their use and reduce particulates even before we can prove a direct connection between a specific factory's emissions and specific people's specific health problems. Instead, now we act as reckless bulls in a china shop, randomly breaking things around us before we know how our actions can be connected or how harmful our actions can be.

In all human interactions with nature, there can be unintended consequences. For example, in August 2017 in the Pacific Northwest, a net constraining several hundred thousand Atlantic farmed salmon broke, releasing farmed salmon into the wild to mate with native stocks. The industry claimed this was due to high tides, which were a factor, but further investigation implicated a massive failure to adequately maintain the pens. As a result, the state legislature passed legislation outlawing all farmed salmon in the state and its waters.

The nuclear industry is fond of issuing assurances that they have implemented every available safety measure. Yet an unexpectedly high storm surge resulting from a tsunami swamped the Fukushima Nuclear Reactor in Japan. They had safety measures and fail-safe processes in place, but they had not anticipated the fury and size of the extreme weather that happened.

Acting on untested assumptions and hoping for the best is the opposite of the precautionary principle. When significant harm to the public is a possibility, caution is the appropriate stance to take. Planning for weather beyond the old normal is not sufficient; we need to adjust for the new normal, to expect impacts from the environment that are more severe than in the past.

The precautionary principle should apply to the workplace, to agriculture, to plant design and construction. It is one step to help keep our environment from getting worse.

Green Synchronicity

When we look for solutions at the intersections of systems, we can make concerted efforts that will ripple throughout many systems. This helps us work with nature in the way that nature itself works, through networks of interconnections. Just as harm can ripple throughout the natural world, so can progress and positive efforts.

For example, planting trees can be an important part of carbon capture, but it can also help with erosion problems, species diversity, wildlife habitat, rainwater retention, shade to deal with increased heat, creating renewable raw materials for construction, and, by planting fruit trees, creating food for our growing population. By working at the intersection of soil, water, carbon, and food, we can create a more beautiful, resplendent world for our senses. Such synchronicity makes our efforts more effective. Efforts to improve one aspect of the environment can create improvements for many other aspects of the environment.

Just as all of life is connected in a web, our solutions can be constructed in such a way that improvements can ripple across that web, and impact many areas of life. For example, in Minnesota a law helped encourage firms constructing solar arrays to cooperate with commercial bee-keepers, planting bee-friendly seeds underneath solar panels, helping to address the massive loss of bee habitat.[133]

Redundancy Can Build Resilience

Nature teaches us that while efficiency is a necessary goal in many cases, redundancy can create more resilience. Maple trees, for example, propagate by growing an over-abundance of seedlings, most of which will never take root, never reproduce. But some will. The trees guarantee enough reproduction by scattering mass quantities of potential new trees. This can be seen as wasteful, and it is certainly not the answer in all cases, but building in redundancy to our human-created systems can help prevent catastrophic failure due to an over-reliance on a single approach and in the process facilitate long-term sustainability.

You can be efficient at doing the wrong things as well. Just like any kind of technology or equipment, what matters is the use to which it is put. What is most efficient is not always most effective. Systems which are designed to be totally optimal can cause great damage when they break down. This is one of the lessons from the history of the electrical grid—when not bolstered by redundancy and multiple pathways to deliver electricity, theoretical efficiency can contribute to massive blackouts, with little hope to get electricity to homes until the exact problem is diagnosed and fixed. With built-in redundancy, there can be multiple ways to work around the outage until the problem can be solved, with less pain and discomfort to millions of consumers.

A similar example of the need for redundancy is the history of the cultivation of bananas. A single strain was cultivated, that strain was almost wiped out by disease, another single variant was substituted, and now that type of banana is also threatened by disease. The world could be without bananas very soon, all due to an over-reliance on short-term profit being the basis on which we make decisions. As well, within the next fifty years, world stocks of both coffee and chocolate will be threatened with either extinction or with massive relocation with undetermined consequences.

The natural world provides a wealth of variety, and such variety is more resilient, more sustainable, than the monoculture preferred by food corporations which decide based on what is easiest to produce and creates the most profits in the present moment.

Understanding Interconnections

Some kinds of progress require more than one kind of change to be most effective. Understanding the interconnections can help us maximize our impact on environmental challenges.

For example, it helps the environment when more people buy hybrid cars, which create less greenhouse gas pollution, especially when only the pollution directly caused by the automobile's functioning is measured.

All-electric cars make even more of a contribution. But for a variety of reasons, they are still a minor part of the car market.

They cost way too much, they are often hard to charge away from home, their range per charge is much more limited than the range that people have come to expect from gas-powered autos, there is uncertainty about their reliability, and so on.

All-electric cars will make much more of a contribution to our climate change and pollution problems when charging stations have been constructed in many more places, making it easy to recharge. If that is combined with tax credits to encourage the purchase of more all-electric vehicles, that will help too. If technological improvements and economies of scale as production ramps up are added to the mix, even more positive synchronicity is created.

However, if the electricity to charge all-electric cars comes from coal-fired plants, that limits the progress made from all these combined steps.

In other words, a real program of addressing the ways that transportation adds to pollution of all kinds including greenhouse gas pollution would involve many pieces:

- More goods shipped by rail on an improved high-speed rail system
- Having more food locally sourced, cutting the need for some transportation
- Reducing and eventually eliminating all overseas military bases, cutting the demand for more air travel
- Providing tax credits for the purchase of hybrid and all-electric cars
- Utilizing technological progress to develop the cheapest, most efficient vehicles
- Improving the technology of batteries, to extend the range of all-electric vehicles, and to speed up recharging
- Using the government to guarantee a market for more all-electric vehicles, in effect subsidizing economies of scale in the manufacture of these vehicles
- Rapidly changing our mix of energy towards much more renewables, so the sources of electricity for vehicles are as environmentally-friendly as possible
- Building a widespread network of charging stations, combined with phone apps that enable people to find them

- Improving bus service to small communities, so that cars are not the only method of realistic travel
- Subsidizing mass transit in cities, to lessen the need for car commuting

All these steps together need to be part of a comprehensive plan to transition our transportation systems. And taken together, they will also have additional positive impacts on people's health, use of time, stress, debt, as well as the satisfaction that comes from contributing to a solution to global warming.

Chapter 13

Some Incorrect Tangents

Under-Projecting

One issue with the projections of the impacts of climate change is that the Intergovernmental Panel on Climate Change (IPCC) uses a consensus model, seeking the broadest and best-supported data on the impacts of climate change, as they should. However, in cases where enough data or knowledge don't yet exist, some aspects are not included in the projections. As a result some likely contributors to future climate change are ignored or discounted, as if they were unknowable.

For example, the rate and scale of warming in the Arctic is leading to melting permafrost, which releases massive amounts of additional greenhouse gases. But since we don't know how much or how quickly, this release of greenhouse gases is not included as part of the basis for predicting future climate change. For another example, while more research on the warming and acidification of oceans has happened, we still don't know at what point or at what rate the capacity of the oceans to absorb extra carbon dioxide will slow down.

As well, the disastrous potential of extreme tipping points is not factored in, in part because we don't have the data on which to base accurate projections. We can be certain that the projections made by the IPCC are not accurate, because they are based only partial information. In each report from the IPCC, seven years apart, the worst-case scenario from the previous report becomes the most-likely scenario. As more data is collected, we develop more understanding of climate change and its challenges, of how bad the trends are will which affect our shared future. Change in the real world will certainly be worse than the projections.

This "undercounting" problem is built into the consensus approach of the IPCC, and is only a criticism in the sense that the IPCC projections are given too much weight, as if they were the final word, in a way they were never intended to be used.

The reality is that there is still considerable scientific uncertainty about climate change, but unlike the fantasies of the climate deniers, the uncertainty is almost all on the down side—in other words, in underestimating how much and how quickly climate change will affect major systems around the world.

The "Sunk Investments" Curse

An underappreciated obstacle we face is the amount of inertia built into the constructed systems which surround us: the installed capacity of machinery and industry, the deeply-rooted practices in how we produce food, the transportation networks for goods, food, and people. Millions of people have based their lives and decisions on the way things are. To replace any part of these systems is not an easy matter, not a simple exchange, but involves rooting out the deeper realities of each system. Each change we make brings along a new and different set of challenges.

For example, it would contribute greatly to reducing greenhouse gas emissions if we replaced most of the traffic in goods and food currently moved by truck and instead expanded our rail system and utilized it much more intensively. This doesn't necessarily involve any new technology or untried methods of machinery. Formerly, much transport of goods was done by trucking firms, but over the past four decades truck transportation has been decentralized, with truck ownership devolving to individual contractors. If we make significant changes to transportation, what will happen to the tens of thousands of trucks that individuals and families have purchased based on the assumption that old methods will continue? In many cases, those contractors, many of whom had been formerly employed by trucking firms, have invested their life savings to buy the trucks and set up personal businesses. Are we to abandon them? Ignore their problems, which are mostly not their own fault? Or should we plan for a just transition, compensating for the loss of work and investment as we shift to rail transport?

While millions of family farms have disappeared over the last century and much of that land has been converted into corporate industrial monoculture, there are still millions of people reliant on their own relatively small farms for survival. What about the farmers who have invested in mechanized agriculture? They often owe money to banks for their equipment and rely on purchasing fertilizer to maintain yields. Whole families and communities rely on our current assumptions about the economics of farming.

Moving to labor-intensive organic resilient farming would be much better for the planet in many ways, and over time the yields could be maintained and increased, though this can take years. For example, a family wheat farm that converts to "no till" methods will likely have to wait at least three years to see positive results from leaving the wheat chaff on the ground rather than plowing it under. Is it only on those families to last out that period using their own finances? Should we force these farmers to stay in debt to the banks for machinery that they can no longer use? Can we just outlaw the use of massive amounts of petroleum-based fertilizer and the gas that gets used in mechanized agriculture? Or should we plan the deliberate path of just transition that takes the reality facing family farmers into account?

These are just several small examples of the challenges we face in making the transitions necessary for a healthier relationship between humanity and the rest of nature. The loss of jobs for coal miners, the loss of jobs at plants that manufacture drilling equipment for the oil and gas industries, the replacement of comparatively high-wage employment by lower-wage hand agriculture—all these will cause large-scale dislocations in the job market. We cannot just discard those people or ignore their difficulties.

The inertia of installed capacity, the inertia of sunk investments in machinery, the habits of how we do things—these are all obstacles we need to plan how to overcome. A movement that hopes to succeed in creating fundamental transformations in many aspects of human life must be able to win people who face these difficulties, or they will become opponents.

We are faced with the dead hands of old technology and old social and economic assumptions.

We often look at machinery and see an abstract piece of equipment, a tool that by itself does not have morality but which derives morality or lack thereof due to its use by humans. However, when tools, processes, machinery are invented, they are invented using the realities of the time—the level of technology, the level of social organization, the ways in which raw materials are acquired, and expectations of how waste will be disposed of. As well, new developments build on previous ones, so the assumptions of previous levels of society and technology are "baked into" how new designs happen.

As a result, many features of the complex life around us contain hidden elements, built-in limitations based on old technology and history.

Technological Change Helps, But is Not a Total Solution

In some sense, all solutions are partial. But some proposals are mere shams, like "green business solutions" presented as "the" answer for our environmental challenges. Various market solutions are often touted as all we need to solve environmental problems, such as cap-and-trade carbon credits. These are sometimes no more than an excuse to legally allow industries to continue polluting.

We should acknowledge that capitalism can and is making progress on some fronts. Many capitalist economies, through a combination of governmental support, technological improvements, mass-production economies of scale, and increased public and private investment, have begun to make the transition to utilizing more renewable energy. There are capitalists who are making bucks manufacturing solar cells, installing solar and wind technology, and creating new energy to feed the grid. The problem is not that capitalism can't make *any* progress, the problem comes when a little progress is sold as a complete solution, as the only way to go, as *enough by itself*.

Technological improvements and innovations are essential parts of creating the future we need, with industry redesigned from the ground up. Much of the progress we are making requires new technology. New ways of creating energy, packaging, transportation, and improvements in many other fields are constantly being invented. We need that to happen, even to accelerate. But hoping or waiting for technological solutions to solve the entirety of humanity's imbalance with nature would condemn us to always playing catch-up, always waiting for a technological solution even when the solutions lie in the realms of politics, culture, and economic organization.

Some "Solutions" Make Things Worse

Another series of solutions that turn out to be false rely on making "us" safe in "our" locality, region, or nation. We can't solve problems in one area in isolation, because all our natural systems are connected to all other natural systems. The world is a global system, and environmental problems have been globalized even more than industrial production and distribution. Atmospheric pollution is present and increasing over the Antarctic, where there is no industrial production. This is because winds and weather patterns are no respecters of borders. Pollution of the oceans affects people in every country touched by the oceans, no matter where the pollution originates. No one is safe unless all of us are safe.

The opposite problem is that some environmentalists turn themselves into crisis utopians and devise abstract and unrealistic ways of totally reorganizing the world, as if borders and nations were going to disappear instantaneously because bioregions cross most if not all borders. Their view of the scope of problems and the scope of necessary solutions is sometimes correct (we do need to resolve some issues on a bioregional basis[134]), but the idea that we can devise governmental forms that will somehow develop automatically (without class struggle) leads down blind alleys and wastes time. Some "expect bioregionalism to remake society without encountering opposition from the powerful economic forces that now largely govern it. This would be a remarkable conjuring trick, for there is no way to reorganize society along ecologically sound lines without challenging head-on the powerful, politically conservative forces—more plainly speaking, the corporations—that now control the system of production."[135]

Another set of dangerous "solutions" come from those who see the dangers to the earth and humanity, but see no way to organize people to create fundamental transformation. So they seek solutions in various untested, untried, and potentially extremely hazardous geoengineering schemes.[136] These include proposals to seed the atmosphere with chemicals which might delay warming by some years, or to place giant screens in space to deflect the sun's rays, or various other sci-fi unrealistic and likely harmful scenarios with a high potential for unintended consequences. Untested, untried geoengineering proposals might very well be as bad or worse than the problems they try to solve.[137]

Geoengineering proposals are dangerous, not because those who propose them have bad motives, but because they seek untested and risky solutions to avoid the tough choices we have to make right now, right here on earth. A related danger is that one country or another might try to implement such experiments on their own, placing the entire world's population at risk. We must first stop making the problems worse; we have to make a break with business-as-usual. Otherwise, any theoretical benefits from geoengineering will only serve to postpone the inevitable catastrophic failures.

The Ecological Footprint Approach

International environmental problems are often explained using gross averages, which end up concealing more than they reveal. When figures for "average per capita energy consumption" are used to compare the "energy footprint" or "carbon footprint" of people in different parts of the world, those averages conceal the gross differentials in energy usage *within* countries. They conceal who has decision-making authority over industrial production, energy production, distribution systems, and national environmental policy. The average person in the U.S. has no more of a role in deciding whether or not to build another coal-fired electricity generating plant than the average person in Indonesia plays in deciding how much of the rainforest to cut down. The average North American plays no more of a role in setting up the systems that require constant car use by individuals (suburbs, lack of public transportation, long commutes) than the average sub-Saharan African plays in setting up the systems (or lack thereof) that result in cutting down precious trees to make charcoal.

Averaging my personal energy footprint with that of Bill Gates or Donald Trump doesn't provide much useful information, but it can be used to blame everyone who lives here for causing problems that only the capitalists are responsible for. No one voted to build coal-fired electricity plants; those were private property decisions, or in some cases decisions by public utilities acting as if they were private companies.

Energy consumption and water consumption are driven by more than individual choice. Individual consumer choice has little to do with irrigation systems that draw down water tables faster than rainfall replenishes aquifers, little to do with power plant construction, little to do with the financial decisions that result in massive loans for energy industry projects, and little to do with whether or not governments decide to subsidize nuclear energy plants or coal-fired plants. Individual choice has even less to do with foreign policy towards oil-producing countries (or else the 70-80% of U.S. individuals who wanted an end to the Iraq War would have ended it many years before Obama's almost complete draw-down of U.S. military forces).

Chapter *14*

Some Common Sense First Steps

Contrary to the accusations of some skeptics, many of those worried about environmental crises are not pessimistic. Rather, we are profoundly optimistic about the ability of humanity to be proactive, to take positive steps to change our circumstances and to avoid environmental catastrophe. We are optimistic about the positive effects of combining personal decisions that individuals make (like recycling), social action (organizing a union or local environmental struggle), political action (demanding that politicians act on environmental problems), and global action (the Paris Accords), with the best and most current scientific knowledge. Scientific knowledge by itself isn't enough; personal change, social struggle, and political action are necessary; no one without the others will get us where we need to go.

We need to learn the First Law of Holes—if you are in a ditch you don't want to be in, the first thing is to stop digging. This means that we need to take *immediate* steps to stop making the problems worse. What follows is not a comprehensive program, but does offer some ideas about what to aim for and which directions to go.

People debate whether adaptation or prevention is the way to go. Clearly, serious efforts at conservation would provide both functions, both adaptive and preventative. Clearly, efforts of all kinds are needed—scientific, technological, political, economic, social, diplomatic. We have to do it all, to a significant degree.

Change Transportation

One contributor to the release of excess carbon is plane travel. While it would be impractical to stop all plane travel, we need to stop building bigger airports, building more planes to carry more people more often, and paving over significant swatches of photosynthetic surface as we go.

Much of air passenger travel is business travel, and much of that is due to corporate meetings and sales and advertising efforts that are not socially necessary. Much air travel is military, so if we reduced the number of U.S. military bases around the world that would cut down the need for air travel considerably. Another factor driving the increase in air traffic is the shrinking amount of free time that workers have, resulting in shortened vacations, and shrinking or eliminating time off to take care of family matters.

Air travel is the least energy-efficient and most polluting form of travel, and we need to find ways to reduce air travel. Make it more efficient, eliminate most military and non-essential business air travel, and provide alternate fast means of travel like fast railroads. More time off, longer vacations, and using tax subsidies for mass transit and railroad construction and repair (rather than for more highway construction and additional air travel capacity) would be better allocations of scarce resources, without greatly lessening the ability of people to travel.

As well, we need to slow down the rush to find the cheapest labor possible based on our ability to transport everything over huge distances using non-renewable resources in the process, whether by air, ship, and/or truck. Just because we can ship many things for long distances doesn't mean we should.

We need to move away from fossil-fuel powered vehicles. As parts of the world such as China and India improve standards of living for millions, they are also increasing the number of automobiles and paving over more of the earth's surface for roads and highways. Improving fuel-efficiency standards is one measure that will help. Improving mass transit to lessen the need for driving long distance for commutes would also help. Hybrid cars will help more as they become more affordable for more people—tax credits can help speed up the process—and there are important experiments with all-electric and compressed-air cars which may in the future give us even better alternatives.

The transformation of our transportation systems is an example where personal changes (such a buying and driving electric cars) must be combined with large-scale spending (on charging systems, road improvements, an updated rail system) that only the government can tackle. Taxing the rich can not only help address income inequality, it is also essential to provide the funding for such massive system reconfiguration and construction.

More Science

Technological development is too often seen in a linear fashion rather than dialectically. For example, we see that too often pesticides increase pests, hospitals become the foci of infection, fertilizers deplete the soil they are supposed to enrich, the Army Corps of Engineers builds levees but increases flood damage.

One crucial step is to significantly increase our scientific research into all aspects of climatology. Some of the warnings about horrific consequences from global warming are peppered with "maybe," possibly," "it seems likely," "we don't know yet, but," and so on. The solution is not to throw up our hands and say we don't know enough, so there's nothing we can do. We can learn more; humans have been doing that for many thousands of years. Knowing more can lead us to better decisions, lead us to improve the solutions we've already started, and keep us from "solving" one problem while making others worse. The actions of the Trump administration move in exactly the wrong direction—to less information, less knowledge and understanding, less accuracy, less progress.[138]

Some global warming skeptics tell us we don't need to worry so much, technology will come along and help us solve the problems before they overwhelm us. This will only be right if government and engineering research actively pursues helpful technologies that can be part of the solution. The solution is not to sit around waiting for technology or the market to solve the problems for us as if by magic. Currently, how research is directed is based on the priorities of government funding which are affected by corporate lobbying, by corporations looking for near-term bottom line improvements. Changing funding priorities based on the needs of society as a whole can help find more solutions than the piecemeal approach now prevalent.

We need to utilize technology, science, and development to increase unity with natural systems rather than to increase futile attempts to control nature or to focus on making fast, short-term profit. We have to build in our own feedback loops, to measure and monitor how our predictions and solutions are working in the real world, and so we can constantly adjust them if and when we are mistaken.

In Japan, for example, they have found that certain kinds of moss act as a bioindicator of pollution levels, reacting to the environment in ways that scientists can read. No expensive equipment required, but lots of essential information acquired. Similarly, a natural way to create fire breaks to protect towns against fire is to use goats.[139]

Planting beans mixed with tomatoes protects the tomatoes from late blight, but it doesn't sell tractors. It lessens the need for the commodities of the chemical fertilizer and pesticide industries, so this common-sense, simple additional planting technique is often ignored. We can introduce horses into orchards to eat the weeds, and leave straw in the fields to encourage hunting insects and spiders that kill pests. These too are ideas that can't be sold and resold by Monsanto, so they are not important enough to promote widely when profit is the measure rather than need and sustainability.

Instead, chemical companies are marketing genetically-altered terminator seeds designed to be incapable of natural reproduction, so farmers have to buy them anew each year from the manufacturer—which harms the long-term economic viability of small-scale farming. They also claim that these seeds are more pest-resistant, but this hasn't proven to be true in the real world. Such short-sighted nature-altering processes may be profitable for corporations in the short run, but they do not help agriculture, farmers, consumers, the earth, nor the broader economy in the long run—another example of a way that capitalism is unnecessarily destructive of natural systems.

Renewable Energy

One set of solutions is the need for large-scale development of wind, biomass, and solar energy to replace our dependence on fossil fuels. If the U.S. government had guaranteed decades ago that it would buy solar energy cells on a large scale, it would have become economically feasible much earlier to mass produce them in a way that would bring the unit costs down to an affordable level for many more people. Government purchases could still be used to shift government buildings to solar power, saving public funds within a few years. A guaranteed government market would bring down prices for everyone. If the U.S. government had taken this approach when solar cells first became available, as some scientists and environmentalists advocated, we would be much further along in our transition to renewable energy.

Also in development are coverings for windows which would act as solar collectors. Thus far, their efficiency is low, so right now they are not economically feasible as a major source of power. But that is already changing, as the cost and efficiency of all solar is rapidly improving.[140] Roof tiles which are solar collectors are soon to be available on a mass scale, another step forward to energy transformation, to decentralizing the electricity grid, and to lower long-term costs to consumers. There is a Swiss firm experimenting with embedding solar cells in a concrete rooftop, skipping the step of having to add solar panels on top of a roof.

Ultimately, solar, wind, and biomass energy all come from the sun, and this will be available for millennia to come. We need large-scale public investment to help create economies of scale in the functionality, production, distribution, and installation of these systems. We also need more research into wave, tidal, and geothermal generation of energy—none of these offer a quick way out, but if we want to have options in the future, we'd better study and experiment more now.

Another way to generate electricity, in the beginning stages of development, is to use evaporation from lakes and reservoirs. A plastic strip is coated with spores which expand and contract in response to evaporation and to changes in humidity. This movement can be turned into electrical energy. It has the advantage that evaporation is not intermittent like wind and solar but rather relatively constant day and night. It is still years away from real-world application and might have negative consequences from covering large parts of a body of water, but holds promise for another path to renewable energy to replace fossil fuel-based energy production.

Also in development are water-run turbines that can be situated in rivers, in water mains, and in sewer systems, tapping the potential power from these already-existing resources. A diversified smart grid which integrates power from a great variety of sources will be more resilient and more resistant to outages and breakdowns and can avoid the problems associated with over-reliance on one single source of energy.

Experiment with Carbon Capture and Sequestration

When conservatives and the fossil fuel industry talk about "clean coal," they are throwing up an unrealistic smokescreen. They talk as if it was currently possible to run coal-fired electricity plants in a way that captured most carbon dioxide emissions, injected those emissions into rock or abandoned mines without allowing it to escape, and do so in a cost-effective manner. All experiments thus far have been too expensive for wide adoption, and the danger of leaks or releases of carbon dioxide is serious. Research may develop better processes that are more economically feasible, but right now there is no such thing as "clean coal." It is a fictional spin to promote short-term political gains and continued carbon dioxide emissions from burning coal.

However, there are several experiments going on that offer some hope, and the research and experimentation should continue. One experiment in Switzerland uses excess heat from a nearby plant to provide power and heat to a greenhouse, which captures carbon from the air and uses it to help grow plants. Another Swiss plant turns carbon from the air into rock.[141] Another, in Iceland, extracts carbon from the air and turns it into rock using a process called "enhanced weathering." Neither of these is yet economically feasible on a large scale, but they do offer the promise that one piece of a climate change solution could be lowering the carbon dioxide in the atmosphere by extraction and sustainable sequestration.

Plant More Trees, Stop Paving the World

We need to stop paving over the world; more of the ground needs to be porous. Unrestrained highway building, more and more massive parking lots, increasing numbers of runways, urban and suburban sprawl, all contribute to pollution, water problems, erosion, and flooding. Private golf courses for the rich eat up productive land and huge amounts of water.

There is a worldwide crisis of housing; a growing population needs much more housing, and part of the solution to homelessness is getting more people into more affordable housing. We need to:

- make sensible choices about what kinds of housing construction to use,
- make sensible decisions about where to build to minimize water usage,
- build houses for masses of people rather than mega-mansions for the super-rich,
- use the most up-to-date methods of insulation,
- use the most environmentally-sound forms of heating and cooling,
- and use planning and design standards to limit urban and suburban sprawl.

We need to create synergistic, resilient communities that provide more of the necessities of life from local areas wherever possible. This requires new kinds and levels of public planning and design for whole communities, not just for single buildings. It requires integrating rooftop gardens, public parks, and tree plantings, all the way up to creating eco-cities and agro-towns, which are being experimented with in both China and Cuba.

Other solutions we should start on right away include those that require a long time to mature—reforestation being a prime candidate. Forests take many decades to mature to the point where they will have a serious positive impact on screening carbon dioxide out of the atmosphere. So we'd better get to planting. Replanting areas that have been recently devastated by forest fires are a good place to start reforestation efforts. We need to stop cutting down the remaining forested areas of the world—in the Amazon,[142] Siberia, Canada, and Indonesia. However, reforestation by itself will not approach the threshold needed to seriously reduce carbon dioxide in the atmosphere—this is only one aspect of the comprehensive program we need, one important way to stop making our climate change problems worse.

Reforestation can, however, help with several problems at once—it can contribute to soil formation and limit erosion in addition to absorbing carbon dioxide and emitting oxygen, plus provide habitat for great varieties of wildlife species. As well, in forests such as the Amazon, the tree canopy is an essential aspect of recirculating water.

Open lands without hard surfaces or impermeable paving or structures can act as carbon sinks. If we build more mass transit, that will cut the pressure to constantly build more highways, parking lots, and other impervious surfaces. We need more passive open space in our urban areas, in addition to protecting and expanding our parks and national forests. Parks and wildlands also fulfill a crucial need in human psychology—the developing movement for classrooms without walls for young children is showing that humans, especially small children, need an intimate connection with nature, need to experience the complexity and wonder of the natural world in order to feel complete as human beings. The movement to connect people to the farms where their food is grown is another aspect of rebuilding such connection.

More Reflective Surfaces

Much of the existing stock of housing, buildings, and roads is made up of surfaces which increase the absorption of heat—a contributor to the urban "heat island" effect. We can paint roof-tops with reflective paint and coat our roads and highways with more reflective material. This would result in improvements using standard, easily-applied materials and make a noticeable difference in heat retention, as well as lessening the energy requirements to heat and cool buildings.

Cut Methane

Even though carbon dioxide in the atmosphere is the most significant and longest-lasting cause of global climate change, we may gain time by focusing first on decreasing the production and release of methane. While methane stays in the atmosphere for about ten years as opposed to over 100 years for carbon dioxide, methane has a much greater capacity to absorb heat, intensifying the greenhouse effect—methane is about 80 times more potent than carbon dioxide. Limiting methane won't solve our longer-term problem, but it can help delay the tipping points that threaten to destroy the ability of the planet's natural systems to recover.

We need to reduce the amount of material going into landfills which create and emit methane, capture and reuse methane produced by existing landfills, and change our production, distribution, and packaging processes and habits so that so much waste is not produced in the first place. Significant amounts of methane are released in the fracking process, as well as greenhouse gas emissions from burning the oil extracted by fracking.

Cut Beef

If we start to shift away from so much meat in our diet, that reduces the market for more cattle, which produce a huge amount of methane. The production of beef not only creates methane emissions from the cattle farts and burps (one of the top four or five major contributors to greenhouse gas emissions, alongside transportation, home heating and cooling, burning of fossil fuels, and melting permafrost), it also rests on top of a pyramid of significant land and grains to feed the cattle, all based on massive water consumption for the land, the grain, and the cattle. Cutting back on beef production will cut back on pressure for the overuse of water systems and slow the depletion of aquifers, and reduce pressure to cut the rainforests of the Amazon and Central America for grazing land. The costs of refrigeration and transportation of beef would be reduced. It doesn't require everyone to become a vegetarian or a vegan, just people scaling back on beef consumption.

It turns out that adding a certain type of seaweed to cattle fodder can cut methane emissions from cow farts by almost 90%. As with much else, this is not a solution, but combining this discovery with cutting beef consumption, restricting or ending rainforest destruction for grazing land, and finding other substitutes for beef, all can be small pieces of moving in the right direction.

However, just cutting cow-based methane emissions doesn't "solve" the tremendous impact of cattle on the environment. A massive use of water and energy results from transforming agricultural land to grow feed for cattle instead of for direct human consumption. The transportation of beef around the world, the energy used for refrigeration, and the toxic waste generated by factory farming of animals are other issues to be addressed. All this on top of the negative health impacts of excessive beef consumption.

The reality is that not everyone is going to become an instant vegetarian or vegan, no matter how vociferous the advocates of those are—and some are quite shrill. But more people becoming vegan and vegetarian is one part of the solution to stopping the seemingly endless increase in beef consumption worldwide, currently most noticeable in developing economies.

Less Plastic

We should use plastic which is made from petroleum when it is a necessary component of an essential product such as keeping medical equipment and supplies sterile. Plastic bags at the grocery store don't meet that standard. Plastic egg cartons rather than cardboard ones don't meet that standard.

Pop bottles don't meet that standard. Double and triple layers of packaging don't meet that standard, no matter how shiny and brightly-colored they are. The plastic rings used to hold bottles that end up in the ocean and can strangle oceanic animals don't meet this standard. Micro-beads used for liquid hand soaps are also destructive in streams, rivers, lakes, and oceans.[143]

Plastic trash in the world's oceans is a growing problem. Every year "at least 8 million tons of plastics leak into the ocean—which is equivalent to dumping the contents of one garbage truck into the ocean every minute," a report finds. "If no action is taken, this is expected to increase to two per minute by 2030 and four per minute by 2050. In a business-as-usual scenario, the ocean is expected to contain one ton of plastic for every three tons of fish by 2025, and by 2050, more plastics than fish (by weight)."[144] That accumulated plastic harms fish and the tiny creatures at the bottom of the ocean food chain, plankton and protozoans. There are currently several promising experiments underway to develop technology and machinery to begin to remove some of the massive amounts of plastic waste that have accumulated in the world's oceans, but not letting non-biodegradable plastics be discarded into the oceans is the most important piece of solving this problem.

Biodegradable replacements for oil-based plastics can be made from hemp and cassava—a partial solution, but a significant improvement over petroleum products since they can degrade in landfill and water relatively quickly. Not all plastics can be replaced this way, but many can, and that would be an improvement.

Minimize Military Exports

Decreasing the export of military goods will cut environmental destruction from the use of those weapons, will cut pollution from their production, and will cut the amount of waste material left after weapons are used. We can start by immediately ending all taxpayer subsidies to military manufacturers which are disguised as "foreign aid." Right now, the U.S. is the world's largest producer and exporter of military goods and weapons,[145] the world's largest arms dealer. These range from guns and tanks to extremely expensive and sophisticated airplanes and missile defense systems. Reducing and eliminating military weapons exports would be a contribution to world environmental progress as well as to world peace.

Serious environmental solutions require peace and international cooperation on a new level. Preemptive war, invasion and occupation, research on developing "bunker-busting" nuclear weapons, and the unilateral militarization of space, are the opposite of what humanity needs.

Enforce and Improve Existing Laws & Regulations

We should fully fund the EPA and similar state agencies to enable them to hire and train enough personnel to do the jobs they are mandated to do. The EPA can also be refocused on ways to stop pollution from being created in the first place, rather than only on regulating it after it is already in existence. "There is a basic flaw embedded in the U.S. environmental laws: they activate the regulatory system only after a pollutant has contaminated the environment—when it is too late."[146]

We can renegotiate international trade agreements so that labor rights and environmental restrictions can't be overruled by supra-national committees of trade organizations, heavily weighted with corporate representatives. Penalties have to actually penalize, otherwise many companies will just treat even major fines as simply a cost of doing business.

Restrain Population Increases

One of the common-sense measures we should take right away is to work much harder at population control—funding birth control around the world, improving the economic and social lives of women (the single most effective method of restraining population growth), guaranteeing abortion rights and information, and providing incentives for having fewer children.

We are headed for serious adjustments, either planned or involuntary or both, which are necessary to recalibrate the balance between humans and the nature on which we depend. If we take steps to lessen the number of people at the same time as we take steps to change our energy, agricultural, industrial, and distribution processes, that can provide positive synchronicity, reinforcing the benefits. If we wait until nature does it to us, the negative synchronicity will impose horrendous impacts on human life.

Educating women, providing for easy accessibility of family planning, legal equality for women, all have been shown to reduce family sizes, to lessen inequality, and to make all of society more fair and more just—which will benefit the males of the species as well.

Shorten the Workweek

We need to take advantage of the exponential increase in productivity that we are in the middle of to improve the lives of all people. Right now, with computerization and automation, with the use of robots in manufacturing and elsewhere in the economy, it is both possible and necessary to cut the workweek for all workers. Right now, the benefits from these shifts are all going into the pockets of the super-rich, and have been for the past three or four decades. Capitalist economists keep telling us that productivity increases are necessary if workers' wages are to increase, but productivity has gone up considerably while workers' wages have remained stagnant at best in the U.S. since the 1970s.

A shorter workweek would help eliminate unemployment, would stop the hemorrhaging of jobs from the major developed economies, would spread the benefits of increased engineering knowledge, computerization, and robotization to the entire working class. This would be part of the shift to increasing the quality of life rather than just increasing the quantity of commodities, offering opportunities for more fulfilling lives for many millions. It also could mean that the shift from industrial work to service work could be accomplished without eliminating high-wage jobs, only to replace them with low-paid service jobs—wages could begin to be equalized and increased, one step towards lessening the inequality that plaques developed capitalist countries.

Experiments are underway in several places in the world with a guaranteed basic income program, freeing at least some people from the need for paid employment. If adopted widely, such programs could spread the benefits of productivity increases much more widely, move away from income inequality, solve the unemployment problem which has become endemic in many developed capitalist countries, and shift human activity more toward cultural and educational endeavors. We should note that this is a complex issues where the details matter—a Guaranteed Basic Income (GBI) is not a sufficient substitute by itself for living wages, for major changes in the tax code to reduce income inequality, nor for an adequate social safety net.

Tax the Rich

Progressive taxation that goes after the rich, after the people who have profited from business-as-usual, is the way to pay for new and improved public programs, job retraining, and a much more robust safety net for all. During the 1950s, during the Republican Eisenhower administration, the tax rate on the top incomes was 92%. Simultaneously, the U.S. economy was booming. Part of that boom had to do with extra business for U.S. corporations due to the destruction of the industrial capacity of European countries and Japan that occured during World War II, but having a high tax rate by itself does not contraindicate economic growth, nor sufficient profits. Instead of placing the burden of adapting and mitigating climate change and other environmental problems on workers, we need to go where the money is. Not only will this provide funds to accelerate economic transformation, it will also help reduce income inequality.

Chapter 15

More Advanced Steps

The proposals and observations above are just a start. More fundamental transformations in most aspects of how humanity interacts with the natural world are needed. Paradigm shifts in culture and society towards more fulfilling lives should be based on an expansive understanding of human fulfillment, not on accumulating more and more commodities.

Redefine Progress

Improving quality of life for all is not the same as continual expansion of quantities of commodities being sold world-wide. We must shift the paradigm of what constitutes a rising standard of living to focus more on increasing the quality, creativity, and health of life rather than on the constant consumption of more goods and more energy resources. This is another reason why capitalism is incapable of making the changes needed, since capitalism is all about continually expanding markets for commodities, expanding production of commodities, expanding sales of commodities, and expanding the profit made from selling commodities.

This provides additional reasons to redesign industrial processes and work:

- to make production more efficient,
- to eliminate pollution that particularly harms people with respiratory problems, many of whom are older,

- to create more jobs that aren't physically draining,
- to end speed-up and extend vacations, shorten the work-week, and
- to create flexible working conditions, universal health benefits, and income guarantees that allow a broader range of people of all ages and abilities to live longer productive and creative lives.

If we succeed in restraining the birth rate and our health systems continue to extend human longevity, we will have an older world population. In many developed countries, most increases in population necessary to sustain the workforce and care for the elderly can come from immigration.

Industrial Redesign

We need to redesign many industrial processes from the ground up, to prevent the creation of pollution in the first place, to reduce waste of all kinds, to use resources more wisely, and to produce for human needs rather than profit. " . . . we have been relying on production technologies that despite their initial profitability, are limited in their ability to support long-term economic development largely because of their harmful impact on the environment. They represent investments that, guided by the principles of free enterprise, promised to yield the greatest return in the shortest time."[147]

There are examples already of basic redesign, some of them economically feasible under capitalism. A project to redesign a textile factory from the ground up, including re-engineering equipment and reconfiguring the dyes used in order to eliminate toxic material and harmful waste, as described in *Cradle to Cradle*,[148] ended up saving money and increasing profitability.

Such redesign would mean massive long-term investment. The goals of such redesign include reducing and eliminating all toxic chemicals; eliminating pollution; reducing and recycling waste products; capturing and reusing lost heat and other energy and creating synergies where the waste products of one industry provide the raw materials for another nearby industry. For example, there is a clothing designer who makes designer clothes and accessories using only scraps and cut-tings from other firms.

Since the ways in which we organize industrial production are at the root of many of the environmental crises we face, making basic changes to these systems is a key element of creating a sustainable balance between humanity and nature. The environmental movement must be in favor of finding new methods to provide necessary goods to the world's growing population. In the process we can correct a key mismatch, "between the cyclical, conservative, and self-consistent pro-cesses of the ecosphere and the linear, innovative but ecologi-cally disharmonious processes of the technosphere."[149]

Agricultural Redesign

We also need to redesign many of our agricultural practices. Land is becoming poisoned with salt; erosion is increasing, especially in delta areas which have been deprived of their natural silt and water flows by dams and irrigation projects. Desertification is accelerating in many areas at an alarming rate. We are wasting water to grow crops in places that require altering the natural flows and cycles of water and rivers, or for places like Las Vegas and Phoenix which have little or no natural fresh water themselves, and face not only increasingly blistering heat waves but also water crises.

We need to reverse the increasing dependence on chemical fertilizers, the production of which drains energy and oil in addition to the long-term harm it causes to the soil. We need to restore the soil, decrease the use of chemicals, pesticides, herbicides, and fertilizer, decrease erosion rates, and in the process rebuild soil that absorbs more carbon, helping to buy time to solve global warming. We need to increase the use of local agriculture. These changes will in turn decrease fuel costs from mechanical plowing and shipping, helping farmers achieve financial stability in the long run.

To accomplish this, we can:

- adopt intensive organic farming methods,
- adopt no-till and conservation tilling methods,

- respect the contours of the land,
- increase crop rotation and crop diversity,
- institute large-scale composting,
- plant continuous ground cover,
- engage in more experimentation with small-scale intensive farming, and
- encourage more urban agriculture such as rooftop and community gardens.

Agricultural yields have been decreasing around the world for years now, which will cause serious problems in feeding a growing world population. Reversing the long-term depletion of the soil requires developing a deeper understanding of the microbial world. This is necessary for "a solution to one of the oldest problems plaguing humanity—how to grow food without depleting or destroying the soil . . . The solution depends on understanding the microbial world, the unseen reality of soil teeming with tiny creatures and microbes . . . by nurturing the microbial life below ground, we can reverse much of the damage caused by the ancient practices of plowing and the modern overuse of pesticides and fertilizers."[150] This will improve human health as well by increasing the nutritional value of the food we eat.

An additional benefit will be avoiding a treadmill of pesticides to kill pests, which develop resistance to the chemicals, requiring ever-greater applications of more destructive pesticides. Reviving the soil includes reviving the resistance of the soil to pests, and planting a variety of crops avoids the danger of massive crop loss from a single type of pest infestation. Improving the soil leads to "catalytic effects of restoring life to the soil."[151] Fixing the soil illustrates dialectical principles of seeing the big picture, understanding the history of a process, learning the details but also putting the details back together to understand the whole: "Learning to work with our ancient microbial friends [to improve soil] means using long-term thinking to guide short-term practices—something easy enough in theory, but much harder to do."[152]

There are interesting experiments with hydroponics and vertical farming, using the latest in agricultural science to design and construct optimal growing environments. These are almost the opposite of organic farming, but could be useful adjuncts to help address the limits of land available for agriculture—as Mark Twain said, "Invest in land, they aren't making it anymore." However, pursued in a capitalist environment, these experiments could develop to have all the drawbacks of industrial monoculture. Similarly, experiments with algae as food, as fuel, or as soil enhancer are not magic bullets, not one-shot solutions. No one method will fit all plants or all places, but testing and experimentation can give us a broader range of alternatives.

Transportation Redesign

Redesigning our support systems, especially transportation and distribution, would minimize the creation of pollution of all kinds and reduce the drain on non-renewable resources. This means large, long-term investment in a renewed railroad system for the long-haul transport of goods and people. It means not letting temporary, profitable cost-efficiencies drive us ever farther down the road of globalized excess transport of food and commodities. It means not letting U.S. auto companies get away with continuing to produce vehicles with lower standards of fuel efficiency than European, Chinese, and Japanese automakers. We need these steps rather than the continuous shrinking of our rail and bus systems which we've experienced over the past decades. The U.S. can join China, France, and the U.K. in committing to ban sale of new fossil-fuel vehicles by 2040 or 2050. Scotland has plans to ban the sale of gas and diesel vehicles by 2032. Paris is considering banning all fossil-fuel vehicles in the city by 2030, another example of cities leading the way to fight climate change.

Currently, long distance bus transportation wastes considerable fuel navigating within cities, battling slow traffic, old streets, and awkward intersections to reach downtown bus stations. If we design bus hubs on the edges of cities which connect to urban transit systems such as subways and light rail, time and energy will be saved by avoiding long-distance buses having to negotiate downtown traffic. We could have bus lines stop in many more small communities the way they used to, providing a realistic transportation alternative to cars.

Eliminate International Debt

Forgive the debt of poorer countries. Right now, the need of many countries for hard currency to repay the interest on massive international debt is driving the transformation from agriculture for local consumption into production of agricultural goods for the export market. Countries that used to be self-sufficient are now forced to import food. The banks which lent the money in the first place have mostly been paid back many times over, but because all the payments have been primarily interest instead of principle payments, the debt remains long after a reasonable profit has been made. This is a modern form of usury, stealing from the poor to overcompensate the already obscenely wealthy. There is a religious-based movement called Jubilee, which tried to eliminate international debt by 2000, and continues to push for serious debt relief.[153] This is an example of a policy which could exhibit synchronicity, by easing the pressure on underdeveloped countries' budgets, lessen income inequality internationally, lessen the power of the banks to dominate foreign policy, and provide funds for ameliorating the effects of climate change.

Drastically Reduce Military Production

We should reduce and where possible eliminate military production, which is completely wasteful of resources we desperately need for survival. War is not only viciously destructive of people, it is destructive to the environment and to economies. Eliminating military production and transforming our research systems to focus on human needs rather than military research will direct much needed scientific, technological, and research resources to the problems we most need to address.

Nuclear weapons are the most destructive military production of all, so we should eliminate them step-by-step. Instead, currently the military is trying to design "battlefield nukes" which would be small enough that armies could actually use them. But once used, what stops the use at small bombs? This is the wrong kind of research for the wrong kind of solution to the wrong problem—a total waste. In the research, the manufacture, and especially the use, military production is currently the very definition of a lose-lose-lose proposition.

Spread Health and Education

Invasion, occupation, and militarization don't bring democratic results. World Bank/IMF Structural Adjustment Programs (cutting public services for health, water, sewage, and education, and privatizing everything) don't result in democracy (nor in lasting economic improvements for the poor). Neither does the neo-liberal prescription of "the market" as the supposed solution for all problems.

The way to spread democracy is first to spread public education, access to potable water, adequate sewage systems, especially in slum and "informal housing" areas, and health care. Decreasing the infant mortality rate is not just the right, humane thing to do, it is an effective population control measure.

Creating a world where people have time to be active citizens, a world where improving the quality of life is more important than increasing the quantity of goods, where immediate survival needs don't trump everything else for billions of people, will be a world where people can take the time to learn, think about, and act on the long-term survival needs of their neighbors and all humanity.

Giving people more educational and cultural opportunities, including as life-long participants, is a part of shifting away from consumerism and endless consumption. Everyone ends up with richer lives, filled with humanist values, and has good reasons to stop accumulation for the sake of accumulation.

The World Can't Afford the Rich

The burden on the entire world of the super-rich and of international finance capital is too great—we need that money and value (which workers create in the first place) to implement systems that benefit all and work for the survival of humanity. In order to pay for the changes that humankind needs to make, we need to get money from the people and institutions that have it—the super-rich, the international banks, the major multinational corporations, the financial speculators.

A start would be a basic shift in tax policy to tax capital gains at the same rate as other income. Even a modest tax on international financial speculation would bring in significant amounts of money to help us tackle climate change and income inequality.

A world of equality and justice is necessary to address climate change. If we ask only the majority (workers and poor people) to make sacrifices, while the rich and super-rich continue to abscond with the fruits of our labors, we will never win enough people to tackle fundamental change and we will never have enough money to finance that fundamental change. Those who have gotten the most benefit out of the economic system that led to the climate crisis need to pay the greatest share of the costs of change.

This leads us directly to the next section: The Vision

Part Five:
The Vision

Chapter *16*

Environmental Socialism

The environmental problems we face are fundamental, therefore the solutions need to be fundamental. Solutions to our collective problems must be collective solutions. "Solving the environmental crisis—as distinct from somewhat diminishing its effect—is fundamentally a political problem because it calls for the establishment of a new, social form of governance over decisions that are now exclusively in private, corporate hands."[154] As well, without such fundamental transformations to our economic system, capitalism will destroy the material basis for socialism, leaving a world depleted and devastated with little capacity to support a positive, developed life for all.

Socialism as a Complex Adaptive System

Socialism, the collective ownership of and authority over the major means of production, distribution, and finance, is necessary to mobilize the resources of whole societies and of the whole world. We need social control of those resources in order to fund and accomplish the massive changes we need to make, to change the tools we use to measure progress and development, to put people and nature before profits.

A starting point is to work to transform the political and economic system that is ruled by a tiny class of people, one that privately expropriates maximum profit from socially-produced goods and services. We need to move to a system led by the vast majority, motivated by the collective survival and sustainability needs of humanity as a whole. As with fundamental solutions to other problems such as racism, inequality, and economic exploitation, socialism is a necessary precondition for the survival of the human race, for the kind of fundamental solutions humanity needs. Otherwise, the economic and political power of the capitalist ruling class will be used to chip away at and destroy any gains. This is evidenced by the continuing attacks by mainly Republicans on Social Security, unemployment insurance, and welfare programs, on all the advances won during the New Deal.

Socialism is a better choice, with democratic, social decision-making about actions to solve our collective survival needs. We need cooperative politics, expanded public debate, expanded public power to implement change, economic democracy to make economic decisions in the interests of the majority, much more public knowledge about environmental problems and potential solutions, and an end to the tyranny of private profit and private industrial and large-scale agricultural property.

Many of these goals are goals not just of the socialist movement. To create such fundamental change requires alliances of many kinds of people from many different political viewpoints. This future will not be built by socialists alone. The unity we will build will be a multi-layered unity, a unity of many groups and people working to make a better world.

Often, people seek a simple definition for socialism, one that covers all eventualities. That kind of definition doesn't work in the real world, in the complexity of modern life, given the worldwide division of labor and the interconnectedness of all things.

Socialism won't be one exact thing the world over—it will morph and adjust to the differing geographical, economic, historical, cultural, social, and ecological circumstances in each country. Each socialist country will be different, just as the political systems in all the Western democracies are each significantly different, such as the difference between the U.S. winner-take-all style of elections and the parliamentary form in most European countries.

Socialism is, and must be, a complex adaptive system, one that changes and innovates constantly, one that harnesses the latest in science, technology, and social organization to benefit all.

It will of necessity adjust and adapt as circumstances change. Isolated socialist countries in a world dominated by imperialist powers, first of all the by U.S., have had, of necessity, to focus on defense and protection in a way that can be discarded once imperialism is no longer the dominant international force. Thus far, most attempts to build socialism have been mounted in poor countries, not in advanced industrial ones, and that has shaped the view of what socialism is, what it has accomplished, and its limitations to this point.

Often people have been sold a myth, that socialists and communists want to and plan to overthrow political democracy, meaning the U.S. Constitution. The Constitution is a flawed document, for example with the designation of slaves as only worth 3/5ths of a human being, and the Electoral College subverting direct democratic election of the President and Vice-president. Nonetheless, the Constitution includes the provision for amendments, for adapting our political structure to changing times. Socialism would not require the elimination of the U. S. Constitution but rather changes to democratize U.S. elections and decrease and eliminate the power of money in our political processes. Socialism would require filling the form of U.S. political democracy with a more human-centered content, with real economic democracy, with placing human rights above private business property rights.

Socialism is not about nationalizing everything including personal private property. The aim is to fundamentally shift the control of the major economic levers of society, not to impinge on the personal, individual property of everyone. Houses could still be privately owned, also clothes, cars, boats, computers, TVs, art, music, and much more. Business property, above a threshold determined by the democratic process, would be subordinated to social control, to the rule of law, to the priorities of society as a whole rather than run in the private interests of the super-rich.

Another benefit of socialism would be to eliminate many kinds of wasteful economic activity. A universal health care system would eliminate the massive amounts of paperwork, forms, and conflicting restrictions inherent in our current private health care insurance system, which often account for

20% or more of health care costs. Advertising for harmful and wasteful products could be done away with, as could much business litigation. Rather than the convoluted attempts to regulate private business, government could make decisions in the public interest without challenge and subversion by money-hungry owners and managers. The relentless pressure to privatize everything from prisons to school systems would vanish. All this would save considerable money now wasted on unnecessary spending. Even more significant would be the decrease in the need for military spending. Socialism has been hampered by the necessity of wasting resources and human capital on armaments to protect itself against imperialist attacks, by attempts to take short-cuts to development by adopting technology designed for capitalist economies, and by an unnecessary preference for large-scale projects with large-scale impacts even when those impacts are largely unknown and potentially negative.

Once multi-national corporations no longer corrupt and infiltrate, the threat of military invasion by imperialism (witness invasions or attempted invasions of Russia, Nicaragua, Grenada, Cuba, Vietnam, Cambodia, Laos) is not the foremost threat to socialism. The financing of fascist regimes and efforts to overthrow progressive governments (as has happened in Chile, Brazil, Iran, Guatemala, Greece, and many more) will recede and then disappear.

With developing socialism, humanity will finally be able to breathe more freely and develop with fewer anti-human constraints. Humanity will be able to achieve many cherished, long-held goals: freedom, justice, equality, peace, and a richer life for our children, grandchildren and for many generations to come.

Revolutionary Conundrum

However, we can't wait for socialism to preserve our existence on this planet. We need to stop making things worse now. Socialists and Communists must support changes to make things better while capitalism still rules. Major changes in how things are produced need to happen now, and in the process, some capitalists will make serious money. We must be part of movements to create change now, even ally ourselves with some capitalists who will make money, all while we fight against illusions that capitalism can solve our environmental problems. We have to be advocates of making things as good as possible under capitalism, while simultaneously working to end capitalism. This seeming paradox can put us in uncomfortable positions, as if we advocated two opposite strategies. This is one aspect of the revolutionary conundrum.

As well, confronting environmental problems and their social and economic causes are a crucial aspect of convincing millions that the fundamental change we need is socialism. The reality is that large majorities of people in capitalist countries are not yet ready to fight for socialism. That is a practical and political reality independent of our wishes, independent of the objective need for fundamental transformation now.

Part of our political reality is that we must work with people who are trying to reform capitalism. Participating in the trenches of environmental struggles right now, limited though they often are, is the only way to win activists to understand the need to go much farther than those current struggles can take us. The path to revolutionary change is through struggles for reforms, in part. The path to winning a majority to the need for fundamental transformation is by working for partial reforms now. This is the other side of the revolutionary conundrum—not only must we work for changes possible under capitalism, but also working for those changes now and winning some victories in the process is the only way to win a majority. And winning a majority is the only way to create revolutionary change that sticks, that has lasting power.

We must wrestle with this contradiction in the course of practical daily work to create change. The only way to get past the revolutionary conundrum is to go through the revolutionary conundrum, a dialectical thought-challenge.

Command Economies

"Wait just a minute," you cry, "haven't socialist command economies failed? The failure of the Soviet Union proves that socialism won't work!"

There are several problems with this argument. First, capitalist enterprises are the very definition of top-down command economies, so if command economies were so fatally flawed, this would condemn capitalism too. This is even more the case since the development of so many large transnational corporations, for example Walmart, which uses extensive and detailed computerization to organize, monitor, and control their worldwide supply chain.

Second, the restoration of capitalism in the former socialist countries of the Soviet Union and Eastern Europe has been an unmitigated economic and environmental disaster for the vast majority of people, so the replacement of socialism by capitalism is a proven failure. That makes it all the more imperative to build democratic, ecologically informed, sustainable socialism.

Third, we now understand better some of the objective limits on top-down command approaches to solving all economic challenges—the "butterfly's wings" aspect of Chaos Theory. This explains that the more complex the system, the more that small changes at the beginning of a process can cause large-scale disruption as they ripple through the system. The larger and more complex the system, the more that total top-down management becomes counter-productive.

Some of the large-scale changes we must create require centralized financing and decision-making. But the answer is not a top-down command approach for each and every problem but only when that is an essential requirement. We need more centralism and planning, *and* we need more decentralization and individual initiative; we need more production geared to sustainable human need rather than to capitalist profit. The developing structures of rural community councils in Venezuela are an example of how to combine national decisions with increasing local input, control, and democratic activity.

If, instead of basing ourselves on projections of the way things are done currently, we redefine growth away from gross numbers of production units and profits and towards measures of quality and human satisfaction, including education, culture, and public health, we can imagine a world of constant growth of a different kind, one based on satisfying a wide range of human needs beyond just the physical.

If we further imagine socialism, with the democratic majority making decisions in the interest of the whole society, we can conceive of a society where growth consists of a better life and fewer working hours for all, rather than more production of commodities to create excess profit. We can conceive of a society that uses profit to fund programs to address human needs, instead of buying luxuries for the obscenely wealthy.

As automation and improved technology are implemented, the benefits can be for society as a whole—fewer working hours, more vacation time, more social benefits, more support for mass culture and mass athletics, more education.

We can conceive of a society that is not "no-growth" but which promotes managed growth including the growth of non-economic improvements and more socially-funded services. We can conceive of a society where humanity works in concert with nature, rather than exploiting and degrading natural resources, alongside exploiting and oppressing poor and working people.

We Need Socialism, But that's Not Enough

Socialism is an essential aspect of the changes we need to make to protect the survival of our species, but it is not a sufficient condition by itself. Socialism is crucial to the environmental, industrial, agricultural, and distribution changes we need to make, but by itself socialism won't be enough. We need to integrate socialist economics with environmental science. We need to integrate class consciousness with environmental consciousness.

Socialism includes democratic collective ownership and collective authority over the means of production. This is a necessary, essential aspect of the changes we need to make to protect the survival of our species. But it is not a sufficient condition by itself. Socialism is necessary to mobilize the resources of whole societies to fund the massive changes we need to make, to change the measures of progress and development, to put people and nature before profits, to create a more peaceful world.

But just because socialism *can* do all that doesn't mean it *will*. Real existing socialism has had both environmental successes and failures.

While the history of socialist countries contains positive environmental steps such as Cuba's recycling, organic agriculture, and reforestation programs, such as Lenin's leadership creating massive parks in early Soviet Russia, it also has produced some very negative examples, such as the Aral Sea and Beijing's smog.

Our definition of the "greatest good" must not be the greatest amount of material goods. Instead, we must focus on improving the living and health standards of all humanity while facilitating the continual reproduction and restoration of the natural conditions which we need to survive. We can't have a healthy humanity without a healthy natural world.

Economics and development must be based on the ability of nature to reproduce itself, must be based on maintaining a healthy balance between human needs and the needs of the natural systems humanity depends on. If economics and development don't work to maintain that balance, they work to the detriment of humanity, and that is as true of socialist development as any other kind. Ultimately, any environmental failures and problems of socialism represent a failure to think, research, plan, and implement dialectically.

One problem of reaching the right balance between development and sustainability is that benefits from development can occur rapidly, while the negative consequences can sometimes take much longer to manifest. It takes time for toxic chemicals to accumulate and concentrate in water and soil, time for them to concentrate up through the food chain, time for the negative effects to show up in the health of people, and more time to correctly diagnose and address the underlying causes of the problem. During that time, toxic chemicals continue to accumulate and impact the health of more people, making remediation more difficult. So socialist planning has to include the precautionary principle, and take a long-range view of the environmental costs and impacts of some kinds of industrial development.

In the Soviet Union, a notable environmental success was the eventual clean-up of Lake Baikal in Siberia. Polluted by several paper-making plants, a struggle by scientists and citizen-activists resulted in returning the lake closer to its pristine condition. That illustrates what is possible by making changes in production, in the placement of factories, in the redirection of waste disposal, and in the social control of natural and industrial systems to create harmony and progress. Since capitalist restoration, there have been continuing struggles to keep new development away from the lake, which is the largest freshwater lake by volume in the world.

The Soviets also used urban design to promote much greater use of mass transit, to implement "green zones" around cities, and to separate industrial zones from housing in many places.

There is much justified criticism about pollution in the former socialist countries of Eastern Europe and the Soviet Union. This is used to argue that socialism itself is an environmental failure. There are several major things wrong with this argument.

First, some of the problems were the result of a rush to industrialization caused in large part by imperialist economic and military pressures and threats, which distorted development and resource allocation. They were not caused by defects inherent in socialism.

Secondly, an often-unnoticed side effect that capitalism has on socialist countries is that in the rush to industrialization socialist countries adopt technology and machinery directly from capitalist countries. In doing so, they unintentionally import built-in capitalist economic and environmental assumptions made by engineers and designers. Those include assumptions about labor, waste disposal, natural resource use, and the costs associated with those factors.

Third, the environment (as well as the living conditions for the vast majority of people) has gotten significantly worse since capitalist restoration in Russia and Eastern Europe. So even though there were serious problems in those socialist countries, bringing back capitalism is going in the wrong direction to solve them. For example, Siberian forests are now being cut at a much-accelerated rate by Western timber companies, and this is nearly as destructive to the world's ecosystem as defor-estation in the Amazon.

Fourth, the effects of driving millions of people down into subsistence survival makes solving environmental problems more difficult, stressing both human and other natural sys-tems to the breaking point. When people live in grinding pov-erty, of course their focus is on immediate survival issues, not on how to do what is best for the planet in the long run.

Fifth, those who embrace socialism and social justice need to understand that if capitalism does a thorough job of ruining the environment, then the material basis for social justice and socialism will be harmed or destroyed.

We should also note that in virtually every country where capitalism has been restored, the result has been sharper and more destructive assaults on the environment and on the living and health standards of the vast majority of people. Since the transition back to capitalism began in 1989-90, the number of people in those countries living in extreme poverty went from around 14 million to over 168 million in the space of a few years, all while creating a handful of multibillionaires, the oli-garchs. As Mike Davis notes in *Planet of Slums*, this constituted "an almost instantaneous pauperization without precedent in history." It has also proven to be tremendously environmen-tally destructive.

There are many contradictions and tensions between humans and nature, and socialism doesn't make those dis-appear—those contradictions will still drive struggle and change. Contradictions are not just between exploiters and exploited, they also appear between humanity and nature. As well, uneven development is a reality of all change, and that by itself can result in contradiction and conflict. Neither socialism nor communism are immune from these contradic-tions and conflicts.

In addition to socialist ownership of the commanding heights of the economy, we also need education, democratic inputs from popular struggles, independent environmental organizations, much more scientific knowledge on which to base sensible decisions, and a deeper understanding of the interrelationships between land, water, weather, agriculture, industry, and society. Planned economies need to include nature's requirements in their plans.

Marxist economists pay great attention to the necessary balance between production of consumer goods and the production of the means of production. These concepts have to be expanded to include the restrictions of limited natural resources (the finite amounts of coal, oil, natural gas, precious metals, etc.), the requirements of nature to not be so overloaded that it can't absorb waste products, and the necessary balance of planetary climate systems.

While we can find in Marx and Engels many references to the necessity of basing ourselves on the imperatives of the natural world, most socialist planners subordinated these to the imperatives of increased production and increased industry. Where these came into conflict with nature, industrialization won out in many cases. The history of the early Soviet Union contains many important environmental laws and attempts to maintain a healthy balance between nature and industry.[155] But many environmental actions were victims of the Soviet leadership's drive towards rapid and large-scale industrialization, driven in large part by capitalist invasion, encirclement, and embargo, and by the looming fascist threat throughout the 1930s. Objective needs and objective pressures contributed to over-centralization, which buttressed Stalin's personal power, leading to other mistakes and crimes against people, nature, collective leadership, and against socialist legality.

Unlike some so-called "deep ecologists" who argue for ignoring human needs to let nature triumph, and unlike limited socialist thinking based on fallacious assumptions of "man's triumph over nature," we need a rounded, all-sided, in-depth understanding of the interrelationships between human and natural systems.

Our ecological crises will be solved not only by direct environmental struggles, but also by uniting them with all struggles against capitalism's exploitation of nature and labor.

Uneven development is a reality of all change, and this is not only true of the changes from primitive societies to slave societies to feudalism to capitalism, it is true of the transition to socialism. The basic truth is that all development and change is driven by contradiction. Neither socialism nor communism will alter this fundamental reality—contradictions of many kinds will continue to challenge humanity.

Serious environmental solutions require a socialism based on a scientific understanding of the need to correct the current imbalance between human activity and production and the natural systems essential for human survival.

Why We Need to Build on Some Strengths of Capitalism

Socialism will be built on the base created by capitalism, and needs to learn from the development of capitalism. One of the great strengths of capitalism is the built-in drive to constantly revolutionize production, the restless and relentless process of never-ending incremental change to industry and production. Socialism needs to find a way to incorporate some of that drive, without the subsequent anarchy of production that results. A planned economy doesn't have to be organized down to the smallest screw, down to every Mom and Pop store on the corner. Nationalizing the commanding heights of the economy is not identical to nationalizing everything and trying to manage all of it centrally.

Capitalism has resulted in the past in an increased standard of living in some parts of the globe, though often at the expense of poor people living elsewhere. The net flow of capital from "Third World" countries in the form of interest on their international debt is astonishing, and over the decades far outstrips the amount lent in the first place, a form of modern usury. That is just one way in which capitalists in the "First World" rip off the rest of the world—poor countries, poor people, and working people including those in "First World" countries.

We must reject the exploitation and oppression which results in super-profits for the very few and which results in escalating income inequality at the same time that workers' incomes have stagnated for over three decades in the U.S., even as productivity has grown exponentially. But innovation and some kinds of entrepreneurship are worth promoting. Finding ways to build in incentives within a socialist economic paradigm is a challenge to socialist economic theory—Marxists from Marx onward have discussed ways that socialism will be built on the advances and progress of capitalism. But one major advance of capitalism is its built-in impetus to constantly revolutionize production, and socialist economic theory has not paid sufficient attention to this aspect.

China: Things Change

To condemn China by ignoring the positive is as counter-productive as praising the positive while ignoring the negative impacts China is already engaged in or planning. Both contradictory aspects are part of reality. We need to understand all of reality in order to make the best decisions, and in order to make the best and most persuasive case for serious, decisive action to transform humanity's relationship with nature.

Ten years ago, the relationship between China's drive to industrialize and the environmental needs of the planet looked very different than they do today. China's approach at that time to international climate negotiations was that since the industrialized West had created most of the carbon pollution already in the atmosphere, China should have no restrictions while it industrialized or only limited ones on how much greenhouse gas emissions they created in the process.

China's plans at the time included building new coal-driven electricity plants at the rate of one a week for the foreseeable future—which would have been catastrophic for efforts to limit carbon pollution. At the time, more than a few Western politicians claimed that the West also should never agree to carbon limits, since no matter what, China's plans would swamp those efforts. For a time, during the Bush administration, it looked like the West and China provided each other with a handy double-sided excuse to avoid any binding international agreement.

In the last decade, China has begun to reverse many of their destructive policies. They have become advocates of binding international agreements on climate change. They have not only abandoned plans for many of their new coal-fired plants, they have begun the process of closing old ones. China has become the world's powerhouse of producing solar panels and wind turbines, shifting over to renewables faster than anyone contemplated.

There are many Chinese scientists and political activists including within the Chinese Communist Party who argue for a more realistic approach to development, one that takes the environment into account much more decisively. This has become a much higher priority for the country's leadership as well.

China is now working on the development of a conscious, comprehensive strategy for an ecologically sustainable development path, for a new socialist relationship with nature's need to reproduce itself (and humanity's need to let nature replenish the natural systems we depend on). This approach has not yet reached the maturity needed, is not yet comprehensive enough, but an impressive start has been made. As Chinese President Xi Jinping said in opening the 2017 19th Chinese Communist Party Congress: "No country alone can address the many challenges facing mankind. No country can afford to retreat into self-isolation. Only by observing the laws of nature can mankind avoid costly blunders in its exploitation. Any harm we inflict on nature will eventually return to haunt us. This is a reality we have to face."[156]

The quality of the environment in China illustrates the dangers when socialist planning downplays the natural consequences of development. China also illustrates the potential when socialist control of the economy is marshalled to address the problems of a massive country with an even more massive population. China has become the world leader in producing the equipment and supplies necessary for renewable energy.

China's development plans include massive irrigation projects which threaten large ecological systems, and large-scale construction of very polluting coal-burning electricity-generating plants (though they have already cancelled many of these plants and are moth-balling older ones). Pollution from coal-fired plants, dust blown from eroding agricultural land and rapidly increasing desertification, and increasing automotive transport work together to pollute the air in Beijing so much that an almost permanent haze covers the greater urban area, worse than smog in Los Angeles ever was. That is part of the truth, one that the China "officially" didn't fully understand as having significant negative long-term consequences for the health of the millions of Chinese people who daily breathe that polluted air.

Pollution in China, especially air quality in Beijing and in heavily-industrialized cities around the country continues to be an immediate health hazard to millions, with some of the worst air quality measures ever.

Most U.S. environmentalists viewed China as a big part of the problem, and condemned China's meager environmental efforts as virtually worthless. But this ignores a key component of China's industrial development, that it is inextricably linked to exports to the U.S. The two economies are tied fairly closely, and much of the industrial pollution in China comes from the manufacture of products for the U.S. market. This is another weakness of the ecological footprint approach—we could just as well allot a significant portion of China's carbon dioxide output to the U.S., including that of U.S owned factories in China.

An example of the link between the two economies is exhibited by the fact that as China increases restrictions on the kinds of recycling waste that can be imported, improving their environmental standards, that is starting to cause a problem for recyclers on the U.S. West Coast, which have been shipping mixed waste to China for at least three decades. As China tightens down on such U.S. export of toxic and harmful material, U.S. companies and cities will have to find alternatives. When people in the U.S. demand that China work harder to improve its environmental practices, we should recognize that the corollary is that the U.S must also improve, that it will no longer be possible to export our waste problems to China or elsewhere.

Beijing's air quality remains terrible, resisting clean-up efforts. Particulate pollution is a stubborn problem, made worse by the rapid expansion of car production, ownership, and the resultant pollution. Massive cities don't turn on a dime—air quality is not a simple matter to change. The clean-up of air quality in Los Angeles took many years and is still a problem, though significantly improved.

China is engaging in experiments with building green cities, where new construction is designed with rooftop

gardens, balconies filled with greenery, fast public transportation, sustainable industries, housing construction
that is highly insulated and takes advantage of natural
wind, sunlight, and shade to lessen the need for heating
and cooling buildings, and smart placement of amenities
to encourage biking and walking to shops. Heating and
cooling buildings is responsible for close to 40% of greenhouse gas emissions in many countries, so this by itself
will be a major step forward.

Another action the Chinese government is taking relates to
the fact that, with global warming heating the atmosphere,
there is more evaporation and more water in the air, hence
there is more rainfall in some places. Add to that the rapid
industrialization and urbanization China has experienced
and the result is more problems with flooding in urban areas
with inadequate infrastructure. In response, China launched
a "sponge city" program in 2015, investing several hundred
million dollars in retrofitting urban infrastructure to help
absorb water, using wetlands and rooftop gardens. They are
also experimenting with sidewalks and other paving that
is permeable, letting water soak through to the soil below,
instead of impermeable surfaces which increase run-off, erosion, and flooding.

China is learning to take advantage of the power of social
control over banking and investment to accelerate the development of renewable energy, leapfrogging most Western
countries which offer meager tax credits and subsidies in the
hope that the mythical free market will solve the problems of
transitioning to sustainable energy production. While some
Western countries have made significant progress, such as
Germany and the Netherlands, most are moving in a much
slower fashion than China.

Still rapidly growing, China looks to become the world's
biggest economy within another decade or two, and to do so
with development and energy policies much more beneficial
to the environment than happened in Europe, the U.S., and
Australia. By creating mass production of renewables, they
have driven down the price of solar cells and wind turbines
to the point where these renewables are cheaper than coal and

other fossil fuel-based forms of energy production. China has positioned itself to be the main producer and supplier of wind turbines and solar cells for much of the world.

While China still suffers from an inadequate regulatory infrastructure unable to enforce all labor and environmental laws, those laws are, on the whole, more comprehensive than in the U.S. China leads the U.S. in requiring lower emission standards for new automobiles. The rapid pace of industrialization in China is proving that development in poorer countries doesn't have to be based on heightened exploitation of fossil fuels. This offers another path to developing countries, one that will greatly benefit the whole world.

However, there are still massive amounts of pollution in China, from old factories built long before current environmental policies, from unfettered capitalist development based on foreign investment and its profit-based decision-making, from corruption, and from ignoring the long-range costs of cheap short-term development practices.

But the lessons of the changes thus far in China over the last decade should warn us that negative projections and assumptions based on current trajectories are subject to significant change. Mathematical calculations of how much carbon dioxide will be emitted can't account for the ways the underlying assumptions on which those calculations are based can change as reality changes. As well, "carbon footprint" calculations about China ignore that much of the goods manufactured there are made for export, to the U.S. and Europe, and therefore are not emissions created by the Chinese for the Chinese alone—some of China's emissions need to be "credited" to the U.S., the single biggest importer of Chinese goods, through corporations like Walmart.

These shifts in Chinese policy also show that centralized decision-making and social ownership and control have strengths that a strictly capitalist society is incapable of. Capitalist corporations are command economies, which only take into account the needs and goals of the owners, major stockholders, and managers, not of society as a whole nor the needs of the earth to replenish itself. As it became clear to the Chinese leadership that their current path was unsustainable, they were able to make major and massive shifts in a way that an economy mired in private profit decision-making can't.

Changes in China will also affect the coal industry in the U.S. Claims that the coal industry could be brought back to the old standards of mass employment in mining were based, in part, on the idea that China and India were going to continue building coal-fired electric plants and would need to import large quantities of coal. Plans were made to expand rail lines and ports on the West Coast to ship coal to China and India. But now that both China and, to a lesser extent, India are cutting back on coal plant construction, the economics of coal export have shifted so much that previous plans are no longer economically feasible.

What we don't always see in the U.S. are the struggles going on within China, nor the positive efforts they are making, such as large-scale reforestation programs, innovations such as green rooftops, planting tree barriers to decrease the amount of wind-blown particulate matter reaching Beijing, and efforts to at least slow the desertification of agricultural land.

We also don't see, behind the massive projects like the Three Gorges Dam, that there are many smaller-scale positive projects, such as investment in mass transit and experiments with new "green" cities. If nations adopt the Chinese-developed "green GDP," that will help make clear the real costs of environmental problems.

In another positive step, China banned production of CFCs, which harm the ozone layer, phasing them out by 2010—while this was late, it was the right step to take and we should applaud it. In 2014, the World Bank reported that, "In the past two decades, the World Bank worked with China to phase out Ozone Depleting Substances (ODS). The Fourth Phase-out Project (1997-2013) helped China to completely phase out production (more than 100,000 tons) and consumption (110,000 tons) of ozone-harming gases and substances, ensuring fulfilment of its obligations under the Montreal Protocol ahead of schedule and contributing greatly to climate change mitigation."

We also don't always see that even though China is producing many more automobiles, Chinese auto manufacturers are already adhering to much stricter, higher emission standards than U.S. automakers.

However, more automobiles mean more highways, roads, and parking lots, taking land away from food production, stressing energy resources even more intensely, creating more pollution, causing water run-off and erosion problems, and diverting resources from other kinds of construction and production. This results in the creation of more problems, and more extensive problems, rather than real solutions. China has announced that it will join France and the U.K. in banning the sale of fossil-fuel vehicles in the 2040s or 2050s, a positive step, though sooner would be better than later.

China's economic planning enables China to marshal the resources of the entire society to tackle social and economic environmental problems on a scale unimaginable in the capitalist U.S. If China finds ways to enforce their reasonably good environmental laws instead of letting both state-owned companies and capitalist enterprises run roughshod over these laws, that would benefit both the Chinese people and the world. If they use their power to tackle global climate change challenges, China has the potential to lead the way, rather than excusing their way to making the problems worse; in some fields, China is already leading the way.

Cuba

Cuba is engaged in innovative scientific research into the environment and health, has transformed much agriculture to organic and urban farming, has created more small-scale integrated farming and moved away from monoculture farming, and has mass popular education about the ecology of their island nation. Begun on a large scale due to necessity in the early 1990s, Cuba now has arguably the world's most advanced and comprehensive recycling system. Cuba has earned the right to play an important role in the world debate about the nature, scope, and depth of the environmental crises we face.

Cuba offers many examples of how to transform a society and economy. From radical recycling to a massive boost in organic agriculture, to providing education and health care for all, to making the decision to change all the lightbulbs in the country to more energy efficient ones, Cuba has paved the way for the rest of the world. They planned a shift to mass use of bicycles in large cities, a model for the world in making such transitions. Some of the changes in Cuba were forced on them by circumstances (the Special Period of retrenchment and reevaluation following the demise of the Soviet Union, Eastern European socialist countries, and all the economic ties Cuba had with those countries). That led to many kinds of changes—a massive shift to bicycle transport including redesigns of streets, highways, and laws, the recycling of almost everything it is possible to recycle down to and including toothbrushes, efforts to move people back to the countryside to engage in intensive agriculture, urban gardens, and an international posture supporting serious and binding action on climate change by all countries.

Cuba has also, over several decades, increased the amount of the country which is forested from 15% at the time of the Revolution to 30% today. Cuba is currently one of the few countries in the world with a net increase in forested area. Cuba's planned response to natural disasters, such as the hurricanes which regularly hit the island, is a model for the world. Successful experiments with urban agriculture, with community health, with local democratic organization, and with international solidarity are all world pacesetters.

Though some scoff because the Cubans started getting serious about the environment on a large scale only when their economic situation forced them to, this is no different from the situation facing the entire world now—climate change costs and impacts are increasingly forcing us to confront and learn to solve environmental problems. Even some capitalist corporations, like insurance companies, are feeling the pain of climate changes and increased storm intensities.[157] We are reaching a point where the whole world will be forced to make adjustments, so we face the same issues as the Cubans, who have the virtue of having already begun to make changes that are now necessary for the whole world to make. Cuba is as well an example in many ways of grassroots democracy, contrary to U.S. propaganda.

While still a relatively poor country, Cuba has health standards and outcomes that rival and surpass many much more developed countries. Cuba far outstrips other Central, Latin American, Caribbean, and tropical countries that shared similar levels of development before the Cuban Revolution in 1959. Following the relaxation of a few aspects of the U.S. blockade and restoration of diplomatic relations between the two countries in 2015, for the first time, Cuban medical innovations are becoming available in the U.S., including a vaccine for lung cancer. Now, the Trump administration is working to reverse even these minor steps towards progress in relations between the U.S. and Cuba.

Compared to other Caribbean countries and all of Latin America, Cuba has a higher percentage of its population working in scientific and medical fields, and devotes a higher percentage of its budget to education. Since science is strongly supported by the socialist government, the results of research are seen as public information, allowing the sharing of discoveries and research across institutional boundaries, since there are no proprietary concerns about who will make the most money from discoveries and medical advances. This avoids the "silo" problem endemic in U.S. universities, research institutions, and corporate research facilities of not sharing data and discoveries.

Cuban science, according to Richard Levins, has a style that emphasizes "historicity, social determination of science, wholeness, connectedness, integrated levels of phenomena, and prioritizing of processes over things." He notes that, "As in other fields, Cubans take a very broad view of the environment. The conception of an ecological pathway of development is emerging from the perspectives of conservation of natural areas, agriculture, public health, urban planning, alternative energy, clean production and waste disposal, community participation, environmental education, and issues involving different sectors of society, particularly vulnerable habitats. Workplace and neighborhood pollution problems are included within the same framework."[158]

Cuban agriculture shows that high agricultural yields are possible with organic methods. Cuban public policy shows that well-designed systems of responding to hurricanes can protect the populace and save lives, Not only has Cuba provided an example of resistance, it has provided many health-care professionals and services to many poor countries around the world, and trains doctors, including students from the U.S.

Levins reports that, "agriculture is evolving in the direction of agronomically and socially sustainable diverse production that emphasizes combining rural, suburban and urban farming; diversification; and biological and natural pest control." He goes on, "There are no externalities—environmental harm that can be thrust upon the society as a whole and responsibility denied."

However, Cuba is still a poor country. The people still face many serious challenges. It is not a mythical "workers' paradise" nor have the Cubans solved all the serious problems which face a small country with limited natural resources under an economic blockade. All socialist countries and countries with a socialist orientation thus far have faced unrelenting attacks, some from direct military intervention, some from economic blockades, some from exclusion from international organizations, some from all of these and more.

But Cuba shows what is possible with a socialist government. They have government policies aimed at health care for the entire population,[159] combined with a spirit of scientific innovation and experimentation, with universal literacy and education, and with an holistic approach which includes environmental concerns.

Part Six:
Putting it All Together

Chapter 17

In Conclusion

Humanity depends for survival on the natural world, on the systems of air, water and soil, as well as the natural resources from which we draw all raw material which we use to produce all food and goods. Humanity needs to develop a new, balanced, sustainable relationship with the natural world. A healthy humanity requires a healthy natural world capable of regenerating itself.

The environmental challenges facing humanity are not limited to climate change but are rather wide-ranging problems and difficulties across the entirety of our relationship with nature. These problems are embedded in how we grow, transport, and distribute food, how we produce, manufacture, distribute, and promote material goods of all kinds. These difficulties affect the ways in which we work to create health and well-being, the ways we produce energy, the ways we design our social, cultural, and political systems.

The System We Confront

We confront an economic system that has tremendous economic, political, and social power. This profit-driven system has distorted our public dialogue, our politics and governance, our culture, our health, our entertainment, our sports, our media, our home lives, our ways to acquire the necessities of life, our working lives, our educational institutions, and the ideas we debate and consider.

269

We confront a system steeped in racism, based on the super-exploitation of oppressed peoples, based on continuing racial inequality. Challenging racism is certainly about changing people's attitudes and prejudices, but it is more about the institutional racism which daily benefits from paying African Americans and workers of other oppressed nationalities and ethnicities at a much lower rate, benefits from disenfranchising and suppressing the votes of large groups of those who would mostly vote in a progressive, even radical way, benefits from preventing large sections of the populace from participating fully in the political life of our country. Many right wing politicians and the super-rich benefit from spreading racist demagogy, from appealing to the worst in many white Americans, from spreading division, hysteria, and prejudice. The capitalist class as a whole benefits from keeping the working class from uniting, from working together to demand that the political and economic systems respond to their needs and rights. Racism is both a financial boon to the capitalist class as a whole and a prime weapon in its arsenal to divide workers.

Similarly, the capitalist class gains immense financial benefits from the wage discrimination against all women. It is hard to change the systemic discrimination against women when those who dominate the halls of political and economic power gain financially and politically from maintaining and exacerbating the divisions in society, from racism, from sexism, from discrimination against immigrants. Some in the capitalist class work hard (or hire people to work hard) to regenerate these divisions and tensions.

Seeking to unite the working class along with building unity of many movements and struggles and allies around the working class, requires tackling these divisions head on, requires that all progressive movements include attacking racism and sexism as an integral part of their programs.

To face this system is not just a political problem or a social problem or an economic problem, it is a problem which challenges all of our assumptions, all of our standard practices. It requires flexibility, compromise, sticking to principles, making temporary alliances, tacking and weaving through the daily shifts of public discourse. Humanity needs fundamental transformation across all of our intersections with nature, across all of the ways humans interact with each other, across the entire globe. We need a dialectical approach to solving the interconnected problems and issues that face humankind all over the world. All the ways in which humanity and nature connect and intersect and mutually interact must reach a sustainable balance, and that requires actions and changes by humanity.

Dialectical Environmental Philosophy Summary

Changing environmental policy and practice requires economic, political, and social change. We need an understanding of philosophy so that we don't get stuck in static, mechanical ways of thinking about either the world or social change. We need to have ways of looking at many movements and organizations to seek out the points of unity, the ways to build trust and alliances. We need to integrate a knowledge of the history of those movements with where they are currently focused, with what their strengths and weaknesses are. We need to understand the trajectory of these struggles, the ways in which they fit into the changes in society and the economy as a whole. And we need to understand the importance of these movements in order to address the needs of humanity as a whole. All that requires a consistent philosophical outlook.

All life is matter in motion. All life consists of systems of interlinked processes, which affect each other and affect the whole web of life. Within each multidirectional process there are contradictions which drive struggle, change, and motion. Processes go through small, quantitative changes, and also through qualitative leaps to a new state of existence. Change is the only constant. The tension and unity between form and content matters, internal and external forces interact, and time, place, and circumstance can impact the rate, scale, and even the nature of change.

Humanity is approaching several crucial tipping points, beyond which recovery and acceptable human life become much more difficult. The whole world is one interconnected web of human and natural processes; human activity interacts with the rest of the natural world. The processes of nature go through small, quantitative changes, and also through qualitative, non-linear leaps which lead to fundamental transformation. We have to act in advance of complete and total understanding of all processes involved, because to wait has unacceptable risks of fundamentally transforming the natural world upon which we depend in ways that will harm or end humanity.

Just changing one bad practice or production method is not enough; we need a series of connected, world-wide assaults on emissions of methane and carbon dioxide to address climate change. These changes need to mesh with improved water usage and agricultural solutions, and with ending other forms of pollution, especially of persistent organic pollutants which impact human and animal reproductive systems. We shouldn't use up nonrenewable resources, and we can't act as if the waste-absorbing capacity of the natural world is infinite. Environmental changes are an essential part of the fundamental social, economic, and political changes we need to make.

Capitalism has proven incapable of the comprehensive planning, social investment, and human decency required to solve global climate change. Capitalism operates on deadly assumptions: that nature is "free," that natural resources are limitless, that the waste-absorbing capacity of nature is infinite, and that progress equals more commodities, markets, sales, and profits. Environmental problems, like social problems, will not be solved without changing the economic system which generates and exacerbates those problems.

General Conclusions

Karl Marx famously said, in the 11th of his *Theses on Feuerbach*, "Philosophers have hitherto tried to understand the world, the point however is to change it." We *do* need to understand the world, we *do* need a philosophy which helps us understand the real challenges that face humanity. But we *also* need a strategy of how to create fundamental change.

The collective problems of humanity require the collective thinking and action of humanity. That is part of what democracy is about, including real economic democracy: the mobilization of our collective intelligence, ability, and activity to solve our shared problems and fulfill our shared needs. We need to frame our strategy as part of the fight for more complete democracy—in politics, economics, and the rest of society.

The key necessity for making these changes happen is a worldwide environmental movement with a broad strategy with the ultimate aim of creating fundamental transformations—in the economy, in agriculture, in society, in culture, in politics. A mass movement that allies itself with other progressive movements of workers, women, youth, immigrants, progressive politicians, scientists, and others. Building such a movement, much broader than what we've seen thus far, will help reach a tipping point. Only such a movement will defeat the deniers and reactionaries, who are only interested in protecting their short-term profits, and the right-wing politicians who serve them. That defeat will open the way to creating solutions, winning victories, and setting the stage for even more fundamental transformation.

Human life matters, and the natural world required by human life matters. Significant shifts in what and how we produce and in how we package and distribute goods are necessary for our survival as a species. We have to redesign our industrial processes to eliminate the creation of pollution, and take other steps to decrease the negative impacts of human activity on the natural world. We have to restore and rebalance our relationships with nature, including altering many of our agricultural practices.

Fredrick Engels postulated that "Freedom is the recognition of necessity." Only by recognizing the restraint required of us by natural systems can we become truly conscious actors in improving the world for ourselves and our descendants. Only by recognizing environmental imperatives and limitations will we be free to make the right choices for humanity's survival.

We need an economic system whose foundation includes the collective ownership of the commanding heights of the economy and which bases decision-making on human need, not capitalist greed. Transforming our economic system to socialism is a crucial part of the environmental, industrial, agricultural, and distribution changes we need to make, but by itself this won't be enough. We need to integrate socialist economics with environmental science, understanding the limits that the natural world places on industrial development and production. In order to do this, we have to change the ways in which knowledge is created, owned, financed, disseminated, and utilized. Human knowledge, and human and plant genes, need to belong to all of us, not to transnational corporations or to university departments funded by them.

Workers of city and country, of hand and brain—the vast majority of the world's people—will benefit from such a program of fundamental change in many ways, including the improved prospects for human survival. That survival requires that we change our economic and social relationships with each other as well as with the natural world.

Since the environmental crises which we currently confront are so fundamental, we need to understand the kind of movement necessary to create the power to fundamentally transform human life—our production, our distribution, our flawed, unequal, and unjust economic system, our very understanding of the way humanity interacts with the world on which we depend.

The tipping point to creating real solutions to our environmental challenges includes many elements, including public sentiment and opinion, making personal changes for millions of people, technological fixes, scientific research, international treaties, but the crucial element is the environmental movement tipping point. The active involvement of billions of people worldwide in creating the political power to institute change against the resistance of the capitalist class and the inertia of the system is the hope of humankind, the possibility of a better world, a better future for ourselves, our children, our grandchildren.

We must reach an environmental movement tipping point, one that mobilizes changing public opinion, that promotes public campaigns for changes in personal habits, that utilizes every available field of struggle from online petitions to mass marches to legislative and legal struggles to mass civil disobedience to campaigns to shame corporations and harm their public image to divestment campaigns to international treaties to technological fixes to transforming our energy and industrial and agricultural practices—all that and more is needed. Reaching this transformation of public consciousness through agitation, education, and mobilization, combined with institution and organization building—that is what will lead to the essential environmental movement tipping point.

Reaching that tipping point requires a comprehensive strategy, requires the unity of many movements. It also starts with each of us. While I have argued against the frame of making change mainly about individual purity, the action of millions and billions does require the decision to act by each of those people as individuals. We each of us can get involved in the struggle and learn about the struggle in the process, and learn about ourselves and our abilities to create change in the process.

There is no one perfect place to start—to start is the important thing. It might be in your union, your church, your community organization. It might be running for local office on an environmental and social justice platform. It might be going to school to study environmental science. It might be collecting samples from a local stream. It might be attending an environmental demonstration near you. It might be all of those things, or a combination. Each of us has a role to play. All these levels and kinds of activism must be linked into a broad strategy for fundamental transformation.

Strategic Conclusions

Unity in struggle is the path, the only real way forward; unity in struggle is the solution.

We can see the general outlines of a winning strategy for the environmental movement. We need a movement:

- that welcomes all who are ready to take action, even if each action by itself is not enough. Participation in a movement that moves masses into motion brings people to more fundamental conclusions about the kinds of change humanity needs.

- that unites individual action with campaigns to enroll billions of people to take both individual and collective action, multiplying the impact of those individual changes.
- that helps impel people into motion in defensive struggles against the retrograde actions of conservative governments and against the destruction inherent in much corporate behavior, and then helps transform those defensive struggles into campaigns for positive and permanent solutions.
- that sees itself uniting with many other progressive movements. One that seeks unity and coalition with civil rights movements of many kinds, with struggles for decent jobs and living wages and union organization, with women's rights and women's health campaigns, with the struggles of youth for an affordable education and a world with a future for them, with immigrant rights movements, with the peace movements in many countries.
- that can offer hope and potential in times of setbacks and temporary defeats, a movement that understands that environmental victories can only be won by engaging in other struggles for peace, justice and equality as well. We need a movement that recognizes that while we need revolutionary technology, technology by itself will never create enough change to meet the challenges we face.
- that understands the connection between reformist struggles capable of partial victories and winning partial solutions with the longer-range necessity of the fundamental transformation of our politics, economics, and industrial and agricultural systems.
- that understands the need to connect the best and most current science and technology with political organizations building the power to impose change on a resistant system.
- that recognizes that there are no shortcuts around building a mass movement based on the workers of the world—the only force with the potential power capable, in alliance with many others, of transforming virtually every aspect of human existence.

- that is broad and massive, reaches to all corners of the inhabited earth, and unites many diverse currents into one massive river of protest, resistance, organization, and change.

Environmentally-Conscious Socialism

Our movement must see the links between immediate struggles and long-term goals, between the limitations of the temporary victories which must be won in hard-fought battles and the ultimate transformations required for permanent solutions. In order to win some intermediate victories, we need to have an idea of what positive steps are possible right now.

In order to solve basic environmental problems, an environmentally conscious socialism is a necessary long-term goal. An environmental movement linked to the many movements for social progress and justice will help to lay the basis for the fundamental transformation of our economic and political systems.

People and Nature Before Profits, the CPUSA Environmental Program, says: "The inclusion of environmental concerns in the working-class struggle today ensures that they will become foundations in the building of a socialist economy that will operate in ways that protect the environment as a matter of course."

Some of the benefits of an environmentally conscious socialism would be:

- real economic democracy,
- elimination of the waste of profit for the already super-rich,
- elimination of profit as the only worthwhile economic measurement,
- new forms of industrial development with less impact on natural systems,
- improved health, job security, democracy, education;
- integrating people-centered economics with the latest in environmental science, and
- more social justice.

The collective problems of humanity require the collective thinking and action of humanity. That is part of what socialist economic democracy must be about, the mobilization of our collective intelligence, ability, and activity to solve our shared problems. The collective democratic organization of society, the collective power to make decisions affecting society including economic decisions, and collective participation in the carrying out of those decisions are all socialist principles we need to enable us to tackle today's environmental problems.

Socialism is crucial to the environmental, industrial, agricultural, and distribution changes we need to make, but by itself that won't be enough. We need to integrate socialist economics with environmental science. When Marx and Engels were developing their theories, they paid great attention to the latest in scientific discoveries and research, but science has developed extensively since then, and human impact on the environment has worsened significantly. Our new reality must be integrated with our understanding of social and economic processes.

In order to achieve the changes that we need in the world, we need a comprehensive, long-range strategy for building a movement capable of creating those changes. I invite you to join me on this path, the path of developing the strategy we need, and then together organizing the broad, working-class based movement for social, political, and environmental transformation.

A better world is not only possible, a better world is necessary.

Epilogue

A Tale of Five Marches   October, 2014

1965 in Washington DC
The first national demonstration against the War in Vietnam
25,000 people, more than I had ever seen
when I was 13

the second, that Moratorium March in 1969
chanting my throat raw through the hilly streets of San Francisco
cresting a hill, looking down on block after block of people
the traffic helicopter reporter said
"Oh my God, there must be 350,000 or 400,000"
the canned national news on the same station
five minutes later, said 120,000
the Portland *Oregonian*, bought on the way back to Seattle,
reported 80,000

the third, again to Washington DC
sent by Local 1488 to Solidarity Day 1981
500,000 workers, their power not a theoretical construct
when we chanted, the buildings shook

the fourth, the Battle in Seattle
marching like it was 1999, and it was
all attention diverted
to the window-smashing trash-burning anarchist rampage
instead of the Turtles and Teamsters together
all 45,000 of us

the fifth, New York City 2014
the People's Climate March
400,000 aiming for a future
in the flat of Manhattan, no way to see the whole damn thing
just like the climate crisis
too big to hold in your brain or eyesight

all five filled with
chants, slogans, signs, banners
a cacophony of voices and ideas

the marchers, the watchers
the flow of thousands slowly edging forward
toward a future that requires us to create it

From many other times, many other places
these five stand out
each a signpost on the way to what could be
and what is becoming

signposts of my life
a rag-tag coalition
anti-war, anti-business as usual
pro-workers' rights, international economic justice
and for a planetary future
for my smiling granddaughter
and the generations of her future

Notes

1 https://www.dallasnews.com/news/weather/2017/08/29/
   refineries-chemical-plants-spewedtons-pollutants-harvey-
   forced-shut
2 Page 74, *Barry Commoner's Contribution to the Environmental
   Movement*, David Kreibel, Editor, speech by Barry Commoner
3 https://sustainabledevelopment.un.org/index.
   php?page=view&type=400&nr=670&menu=1515
4 https://www.cbsnews.com/news/salt-water-fish-extinction-
   seen-by-2048/
5 https://www.commondreams.org/views/2017/11/13/
   lets-just-admit-it-capitalism-doesnt-work?utm_
   campaign=shareaholic&utm_medium=facebook&utm_
   source=socialnetwork
6 Preface, *Eaarth* by Bill McKibben
7 https://www.theguardian.com/environment/2017/oct/26/sea-
   levels-to-rise-13m-unless-coal-power-ends-by-2050-report-says
8 https://earthjustice.org/features/everything-you-need-to-
   know-about-methane?gclid=CjwKCAjw4KvPBRBeEiwAIqCB-
   XiWonCcU7Gy9Hwq2cwH2b4eN12TL_9a4VBfWjThSli1ega9p
   HGzMBoCuecQAvD_BwE
9 *The Long Emergency: Surviving the End of Oil, Climate Change,
   and Other Converging Catastrophes of the Twenty-First Century*, by
   James Howard Kunstler
10 https://insideclimatenews.org/news/26102017/antarctica-
   sea-level-rise-ice-sheet-tipping-point-climate-change-study
11 https://insideclimatenews.org/news/02042018/antarctica-ice-
   sheet-shelf-glaciers-grounding-line-receding-worst-case-sea-
   level-rise-risk?utm_source=twitter&utm_medium=social

12   https://www.smithsonianmag.com/science-nature/
     ancient-earth-warmed-dramatically-after-one-two-carbon-
     punch-180953610/
13   https://www.scientificamerican.com/article/ocean-
     circulation-may-have-released-co2-at-end-of-ice-ages/
14   http://apps.seattletimes.com/reports/sea-change/2013/
     sep/11/oysters-hit-hard/
15   https://www.bizjournals.com/portland/news/2017/10/06/
     scientists-warn-of-hypoxia-season-threatening.html
16   https://www.nbcnews.com/science/environment/why-year-
     s-dead-zone-gulf-mexico-bigger-ever-n789636
17   http://www.kgw.com/news/local/central-coast/dead-zone-
     off-oregon-coast-is-one-of-the-worst-in-a-decade/482392480
18   https://www.lrb.co.uk/blog/2017/10/14/mike-davis/el-
     diablo-in-wine-country/
19   https://www.dailykos.com/stories/2012/11/28/1165340/-
     Doha-Day-2-McKibben-pens-letter-to-COP-Negotiators
20   https://www.theguardian.com/environment/2017/nov/11/
     us-groups-honouring-paris-climate-pledges-despite-trump
21   https://www.arb.ca.gov/fuels/lcfs/lcfs.htm
22   https://inhabitat.com/chicago-green-roof-program/
23   https://www.huffingtonpost.com/entry/
     exxon-climate-change-harvard-study_
     us_599e8708e4b05710aa59c615?section=us_business
24   https://www.theguardian.com/environment/2013/
     nov/20/90-companies-man-made-global-warming-emissions-
     climate-change
25   https://jobscleanenergywa.com/
26   https://www.washingtonpost.com/business/economy/
     this-miracle-weed-killer-was-supposed-to-save-farms-instead-
     its-devastating-them/2017/08/29/33a21a56-88e3-11e7-961d-
     2f373b3977ee_story.html?utm_term=.9189cd5c7bb9
27   https://www.lrb.co.uk/blog/2017/10/14/mike-davis/el-
     diablo-in-wine-country/
28   https://www.theguardian.com/environment/2017/oct/18/
     warning-of-ecological-armageddon-after-dramatic-plunge-in-
     insect-numbers?CMP=share_btn_tw
29   https://en.wikipedia.org/wiki/Planetary_boundaries
30   http://www.livescience.com/13032-earth-7-tipping-points-
     climate-change.html
31   https://www.pik-potsdam.de/services/infodesk/tipping-
     elements/kippelemente?set_language=en

32 http://ideas.ted.com/the-9-limits-of-our-planet-and-how-
    weve-raced-past-4-of-them/
33 http://en.wikipedia.org/wiki/Arctic_methane_release
34 https://www.huffingtonpost.com/entry/oceans-vital-
    gulf-stream-system-weakest-in-1600-years-scientists-find_
    us_5ad019b2e4b016a07e9ad2cb
35 http://www.pik-potsdam.de/~stefan/Publications/Book_
    chapters/rahmstorf_eqs_2006.pdf
36 https://en.wikipedia.org/wiki/2003_European_heat_wave
37 Page 75, *Eaarth* by Bill McKibben
38 https://thinkprogress.org/health-impacts-global-warming-
    ruin-economy-fe3a2d560860/
39 https://www.ecowatch.com/air-pollution-deaths-2498942499.
    html
40 *Too Many People* by Angus and Butler
41 https://www.ecowatch.com/pope-francis-climate-change-
    hunger-2497286479.html
42 https://www.ecowatch.com/global-water-access-
    quality-2549813548.html
43 https://www.nytimes.com/2017/08/23/climate/exxon-
    global-warming-science-study.html
44 https://decodingscience.missouri.edu/2017/10/16/
    mckibben-urges-climate-action-in-campus-lecture/
45 http://www.nytimes.com/1988/06/24/us/global-warming-
    has-begun-expert-tells-senate.html?pagewanted=all
46 http://www.peoplesworld.org/article/tipping-points-stop-
    trump-and-restrain-capitalism-to-save-the-world/
47 https://www.ecowatch.com/drill-arctic-artificial-
    island-2498548130.html
48 http://www.rollingstone.com/politics/news/kayactivists-try-
    to-block-shell-oil-rig-leaving-to-drill-in-arctic-20150615
49 https://www.theguardian.com/business/2015/jul/31/
    portland-bridge-shell-protest-kayaktivists-fennica-reaction
50 https://en.wikipedia.org/wiki/Gulf_Stream
51 https://www.washingtonpost.com/news/energy-
    environment/wp/2018/03/14/the-melting-arctic-is-already-
    messing-with-a-crucial-part-of-the-oceans-circulation-
    scientists-say/?utm_term=.e29c535170bd
52 http://grist.org/business-technology/none-of-the-worlds-top-
    industries-would-be-profitable-if-they-paid-for-the-natural-
    capital-they-use/
53 http://www.paulhawken.com/biography

54   http://www.nickhanauer.com/
55   https://www.theguardian.com/environment/2017/nov/05/
     the-cop23-climate-change-summit-in-bonn-and-why-it-matters
56   http://peoplesworld.org/review-this-changes-everything-
     capitalism-vs-the-climate/
57   https://www.theguardian.com/environment/2017/nov/02/
     climate-change-will-create-worlds-biggest-refugee-crisis
58   http://peoplesworld.org/the-pope-tackles-climate-change-in-
     new-encyclical/
59   http://www.nytimes.com/2015/12/02/business/economy/
     imagining-a-world-without-growth.html?_r=0
60   http://www.nytimes.com/2014/07/09/business/blueprints-
     for-taming-the-climate-crisis.html
61   https://www.researchgate.net/publication/232932129_A_
     Critique_of_Degrowth_and_its_Politics
62   https://medium.com/insurge-intelligence/100-renewables-
     wishful-thinking-or-an-imperative-goal-9879a8947d1b
63   https://thinkprogress.org/stunner-lowest-price-solar-power-
     f3b620d04010/
64   *The End of Growth*, by Richard Heinberg
65   Page 99, *Eaarth* by Bill McKibben
66   See extended discussions of these changes in *The Closing Circle*
     and *Making Peace with the Planet*, both by Barry Commoner
67   https://www.theguardian.com/environment/2015/dec/02/
     worlds-richest-10-produce-half-of-global-carbon-emissions-
     says-oxfam
68   http://ecowatch.com/2015/11/30/michael-pollan-time-to-
     choose/
69   https://www.ecowatch.com/food-water-crisis-puerto-
     rico-2498944175.html
70   *The Shock Doctrine: The Rise of Disaster Capitalism*, by Naomi
     Klein
71   http://www.rollingstone.com/politics/news/global-
     warmings-terrifying-new-math-20120719
72   https://www.newyorker.com/magazine/2015/04/13/
     weather-underground
73   Page 72, *The Hidden Half of Nature* by David Montgomery and
     Anne Bikle
74   *Thinking Along With Marx* by Michael Parenti, in *Political
     Affairs*, September 1983
75   https://monthlyreview.org/2016/10/01/marxism-and-the-
     dialectics-of-ecology/

76 https://www.santafe.edu/
77 Page 76, *The Hidden Half of Nature* by David Montgomery and Anne Bikle
78 https://en.wikipedia.org/wiki/Rosa_multiflora
79 https://www.researchgate.net/publication/8653423_The_hyperthermophilic_origin_of_life_revisited
80 https://www.khanacademy.org/science/biology/history-of-life-on-earth/history-life-on-earth/a/hypotheses-about-the-origins-of-life
81 https://www.mnn.com/earth-matters/climate-weather/stories/everything-you-need-to-know-about-earths-orbit-and-climate-cha
82 https://en.wikipedia.org/wiki/Hanford_Site
83 http://www.zerohedge.com/news/2016-10-02/fukushima-radiation-has-contaminated-entire-pacific-ocean-and-its-going-get-worse
84 https://www.nytimes.com/2015/04/13/us/mighty-rio-grande-now-a-trickle-under-siege.html
85 https://en.wikipedia.org/wiki/Albedo
86 https://en.wikipedia.org/wiki/Thermohaline_circulation
87 https://www.theguardian.com/environment/2017/feb/24/drastic-cooling-north-atlantic-beyond-worst-fears-scientists-warn
88 https://www.theguardian.com/environment/2017/jan/25/europe-faces-droughts-floods-storms-climate-change-accelerates
89 Page 46, *Eaarth* by Bill McKibben
90 https://en.wikipedia.org/wiki/Punctuated_equilibrium
91 https://en.wikipedia.org/wiki/Cambrian_explosion
92 https://www.nytimes.com/2017/10/21/opinion/sunday/how-protest-works.html?smid=fb-share
93 https://www.thenation.com/article/martin-luther-king-jr-50-years-later/
94 *The Third Reconstruction* by the Rev. William Barber
95 See the movie *Sir, No Sir* for an extended exploration of this movement by participants
96 https://en.wikipedia.org/wiki/Fort_Hood_Three
97 https://www.washingtonpost.com/news/posteverything/wp/2018/04/09/what-if-the-absence-of-strong-unions-is-at-the-heart-of-much-of-what-has-gone-wrong/?noredirect=on&utm_term=.9fe0abed5f01
98 https://en.wikipedia.org/wiki/Flint_sit-down_strike

99   https://www.thenation.com/article/labor-movement-must-learn/

100   http://www.epi.org/publication/how-todays-unions-help-working-people-giving-workers-the-power-to-improve-their-jobs-and-unrig-the-economy/

101   http://www.peoplesworld.org/article/if-theres-a-war-on-coal-coal-already-lost/

102   https://www.jacobinmag.com/2017/08/victory-over-the-sun

103   http://www.peoplesworld.org/article/bluegreen-alliance-seiu-hit-trumps-dump-of-clean-power-plan/

104   https://jacobinmag.com/2017/08/living-not-just-surviving

105   http://www.peoplesworld.org/article/no-jobs-on-a-dead-planet-a-just-transition-to-the-new-economy/

106   Page 83, *Barry Commoner's Contribution to the Environmental Movement*, David Kreibel, Editor, speech by Barry Commoner

107   https://www.nytimes.com/2017/11/20/opinion/climate-capitalism-crisis.html

108   http://nymag.com/daily/intelligencer/2017/07/climate-change-earth-too-hot-for-humans.html

109   http://inthesetimes.com/article/20337/climate-change-personal-consumption-capitalism-socialism-neoliberalism

110   http://www.npr.org/sections/thesalt/2017/10/26/559733837/monsanto-and-the-weed-scientists-not-a-love-story

111   Page 2, Introduction, *Barry Commoner's Contribution to the Environmental Movement*, David Kreibel, Editor

112   http://mashable.com/2017/11/08/arctic-satellites-going-dark-sea-ice-congress-destroyed/#FxuoR3NNLBqo

113   https://en.wikipedia.org/wiki/Program_evaluation_and_review_technique

114   https://www.theguardian.com/us/environment

115   http://www.fdrfourfreedomspark.org/fdr-the-four-freedoms/

116   *The Third Reconstruction* by the Rev. William Barber

117   https://www.huffingtonpost.com/entry/arizona-navajo-hopi-coal-plant_us_59e61e0fe4b02a215b3379d7?ncid=inblnkushpmg00000009

118   https://earthjustice.org/blog/2018-march/climate-change-forces-the-quinault-tribe-to-seek-higher-ground

119   http://fortune.com/2013/09/18/one-mans-quest-to-loosen-fossil-fuels-grip/

120   https://www.theverge.com/2018/2/20/17031676/climate-change-lawsuits-fossil-fuel-new-york-santa-cruz

121 https://www.washingtonpost.com/news/energy-
     environment/wp/2018/03/07/the-trump-administration-
     just-failed-to-stop-a-climate-lawsuit-brought-by-21-
     kids/?utm_term=.c32ba5fba062
122 http://www.dw.com/en/four-climate-change-lawsuits-to-
     watch-in-2018/a-42066735
123 http://apjjf.org/2017/20/Golden.html
124 https://www.telesurtv.net/english/news/JFK-Files-Expose-
     CIA-Plot-to-Stage-Miami-Bombings-and-Blame-Fidel-
     Castro-20171027-0013.html
125 http://www.peoplesworld.org/article/agents-provocateurs-
     and-the-manipulation-of-the-radical-left/
126 https://www.theguardian.com/world/2010/sep/14/
     photographer-ernest-withers-fbi-informer?CMP=share_btn_fb
127 https://www.wired.com/2015/10/how-climate-change-
     became-a-national-security-problem/
128 http://www.truthdig.com/report/item/the_last_gasp_of_
     climate_change_liberals_20140831
129 http://truth-out.org/opinion/item/26215-like-a-dull-knife-
     the-peoples-climate-farce
130 http://www.peoplesworld.org/review-this-changes-
     everything-capitalism-vs-the-climate/
131 http://www.thenation.com/article/181799/whats-wrong-
     radical-critique-peoples-climate-march
132 http://www.greenmatters.com/news/2017/10/13/AXki6/
     mit-researchers-air-breathing-battery
133 https://www.smithsonianmag.com/innovation/solar-power-
     and-honey-bees-180964743/
134 http://www.cbc.ca/news/canada/british-columbia/
     western-u-s-states-disregard-trump-to-form-united-front-
     with-b-c-in-fight-against-climate-change-1.4580727?utm_
     source=Sightline%20Institute&utm_medium=web-
     email&utm_campaign=Sightline%20News%20Selections
135 Page 172, *Making Peace with the Planet,* by Barry Commoner
136 https://www.theguardian.com/environment/true-
     north/2017/mar/27/trump-presidency-opens-door-to-
     planet-hacking-geoengineer-experiments
137 https://www.ecowatch.com/outlandish-ideas-to-cool-
     planet-2548497056.html
138 http://www.rollingstone.com/culture/features/trump-is-
     crippling-storm-forecasting-when-we-need-it-most-w510011
139 https://earther.com/firefighting-goats-devour-fuel-across-
     the-west-before-i-1819707513

140   http://www.newsweek.com/fossil-fuels-transparent-solar-panels-harvest-energy-windows-msu-691308
141   http://www.greenmatters.com/renewables/2017/10/16/XGR8U/negative-emissions-stone
142   http://www.peoplesworld.org/article/brazil-oligarchy-versus-the-amazon-rainforest/
143   https://www.huffingtonpost.com/entry/oceans-plastics-nurdles-pollution-wildlife_us_5a02def4e4b04e96f0c683c3?ncid=inblnkushpmg00000009
144   https://www.ecowatch.com/there-will-be-more-plastic-than-fish-in-the-ocean-by-2050-1882154887.html
145   https://www.usnews.com/news/articles/2016-12-27/americas-arms-exports-dominate-despite-global-competition
146   Page 59, *Making Peace with the Planet*, by Barry Commoner
147   Page 91, *Making Peace with the Planet*, by Barry Commoner
148   *Cradle to Cradle*, by Michael Braungart and William McDonough
149   Page 15, *Making Peace with the Planet*, by Barry Commoner
150   Page 2, *The Hidden Half of Nature* by David Montgomery and Anne Bikle
151   Page 88, *The Hidden Half of Nature* by David Montgomery and Anne Bikle
152   Page 251, *The Hidden Half of Nature* by David Montgomery and Anne Bikle
153   http://jubileedebt.org.uk/
154   Page 173, *Making Peace with the Planet*, by Barry Commoner
155   https://www.nytimes.com/2017/08/07/opinion/lenin-environment-siberia.html?action=click&contentCollection=opinion&module=NextInCollection&region=Footer&pgtype=article&version=column&rref=collection%2Fcolumn%2Fred-century
156   https://www.huffingtonpost.com/entry/trump-china-climate-change-xi-jinping-paris-agreement-air-pollution-greenpeace_us_59e762c6e4b00905bdadf416?ncid=inblnkushpmg00000009
157   https://www.ecowatch.com/losses-california-wildfires-2499087854.html
158   *How Cuba is Going Ecological*, by Richard Levins, article in *Capitalism Nature Socialism*, Volume 16, Number 3, September 2005.
159   http://www.yesmagazine.org/issues/just-transition/what-cuba-can-teach-us-about-health-care-20170919

Bibliographical Notes

There is a rapidly growing body of literature on environmental issues, and many of these address in detail the causes and realities of climate change in ways that this book doesn't try to do. Many books have explanations of the basic science behind climate change, projections of where it is taking the world, and actions you can take as an individual.

In my opinion, the single best book on environmental issues, though no longer up-to-date, is *Making Peace with the Planet* by Barry Commoner. His *The Closing Circle* was one of the first and best also, with extended discussion of the links between industrial production and environmental devastation.

The following books happened to be the ones I read before and during the writing of this book and the essays and articles on which it is based; they informed, inspired, and challenged me. None of the authors are responsible for any mistakes I've made nor for any of the analysis I present, nor does inclusion here imply an endorsement of each and every aspect of these books, nor that they would endorse my conclusions.

Collapse by Jared Diamond, about previous environmental destruction of civilizations
When Rivers Run Dry by Fred Pearce, about the water crisis
With Speed and Violence by Fred Pearce, about environmental tipping points
Field Notes from a Catastrophe and *The Sixth Extinction* by Elizabeth Kolbert, about global warming, species extinction, and loss of biodiversity

Planet of Slums by Mike Davis, about the problems of rapidly escalating urbanization

The Beak of the Finch by Jonathan Weiner, about evolution that we can see and measure

Red Roots, Green Shoots by Virginia Brodine, about Marxist environmentalism (edited and with an introduction by Marc Brodine)

Marx's Ecology by John Bellamy Foster, about returning to Marx's analysis of environmental and agricultural systems

Dirt by David Montgomery, about soil and agricultural crises

The Hidden Half of Nature by David Montgomery and Anne Bikle, about the microbial world, our agriculture, and our health

People and Nature Before Profits, the CPUSA Environmental Program 2nd Edition, by Dave Zink and Marc Brodine, about the nature and causes of environmental crises and the program needed to address them

The Road to Socialism USA, the Program of the CPUSA, about strategy from now till socialism

Cradle to Cradle by William McDonough and Michael Braungart, about the redesign of industrial processes

The Two-Mile Time Machine by Richard B. Alley, about ice ages, Greenland ice cores, and world climate

Complexity, Life at the Edge of Chaos by Roger Lewin, about attempts by scientists to discover and explain the patterns of the world's pervasive complexity

The Weather Makers by Tim Flannery, about climate change

Eearth by Bill McKibben, about the generalized crisis of the human balance with nature

This Changes Everything by Nami Klein, explaining how and why capitalism is the problem and why environmental crisis affects all other struggles

The Third Reconstruction: How a Moral Movement is Overcoming the Politics of Division and Fear by Rev. Doctor William J. Barber II, about the moral and practical need for coalition and struggle

Tropic of Chaos: Climate Change and the New Geography of Violence by Christian Parenti, how climate change will exacerbate tension, conflict, resource wars, and escalate the refugee crisis

What Every Environmentalist Needs to Know About Capitalism by Fred Magdoff, an explanation of the links between economics, the environment, and social change

How Cuba is Going Ecological, by Richard Levins, article in *Capitalism Nature Socialism*, Volume 16, Number 3, September 2005. Excellent article by a scientist integrally involved in helping Cuba redesign its agricultural systems

The Dialectical Biologist by Richard Levins and Richard Leowinton, about linking dialectical thinking with scientific research and understanding

Dialectics

Below are some books which deepened my knowledge and understanding of dialectical materialism.

Materialism and the Dialectical Method (three volumes) and *Philosophy for Socialists* by Maurice Cornforth, good introductions to Marxist philosophy

Dialectical Materialism by David Guest, a British philosopher who died fighting in the Civil War in Spain, another good introduction to Marxist philosophy

Elementary Principles of Philosophy by Georges Politzer, a French philosopher who died as a Resistance fighter, a series of lectures for workers

Marc Russell Brodine is a writer, guitar player, woodblock print artist, community activist, husband, and father. He lives in Roslyn, Washington in the Cascade Mountains, where he is Chair of the Roslyn Library Board and serves on the boards of the Roslyn Farmers Market and RTown Community.

Growing up in St. Louis, Missouri, he attended civil rights and peace demonstrations with his parents. After moving to the Pacific Northwest following high school, he became co-chair of the Seattle People's Coalition for Peace and Justice (PCPJ), one of the two main local anti-Vietnam War coalitions. He has attended many local, regional, and national demonstrations, conferences, and conventions over the years, from the first national anti-Vietnam War demonstration in 1965 to AFCSME conventions to the United Nations Annual NGO Conference in 2007 on Climate Change to the People's Climate March in New York City in 2014.

He is the author of the self-published mystery *Blood Pressure* which is set during several union campaigns at a fictional Seattle hospital, based in part on his 20 years working in several Seattle hospitals. He served on the Executive Board of AFSCME Local 1488 at the University of Washington and Harborview Hospitals, worked as an orderly and technician, and was nine-term treasurer of that local. He also worked as an office manager and system administrator at a Seattle-area immigration legal service non-profit. For over two years, he hosted a bi-monthly blues show on Ellensburg Community Radio.

He has been a member of the Communist Party USA since the age of 16, has been Washington State Chair since 2000, and is a member of the CPUSA National Committee and National Board. He has written on political and environmental issues for the *People's World*,

Political Affairs, and the Chinese journal *International Critical Thought.* He has presented papers and reports on environmental issues to the CPUSA National Committee, to several CPUSA Conventions, to a conference of the World Association for Political Economy in China in 2008, and to the Arctic Initiative Conference sponsored by the Finnish Communist Party and the Party of the European Left in Helsinki, Finland in 2016, as well as taught classes on strategy, fascism, dialectical materialism, and Marxism and the environment. He co-wrote the Second Edition of the CPUSA Environmental Program *People and Nature Before Profits* with Dave Zink, and chaired the committee which drafted the CPUSA Program *The Road to Socialism USA,* adopted at the 2005 Convention. He edited and wrote the introduction to *Red Roots, Green Shoots,* a compilation of his mother Virginia Bodine's environmental writings.